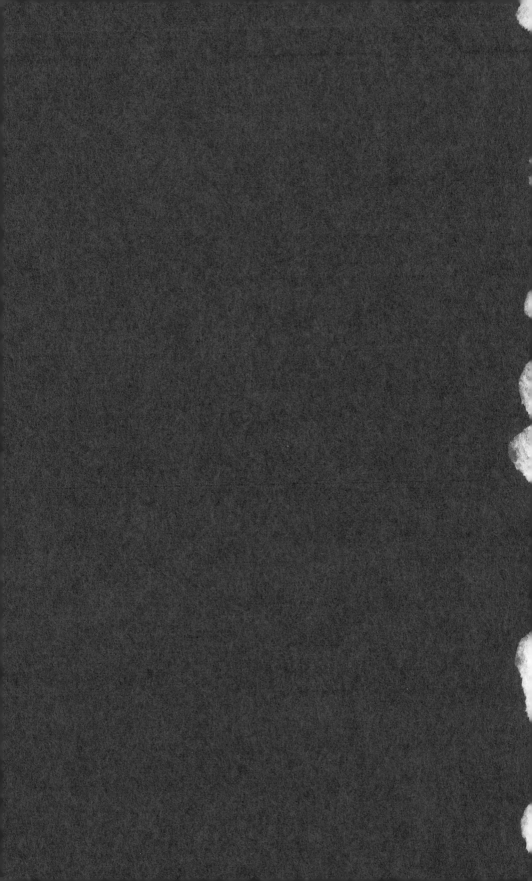

RICH
WAS
BETTER

For Myra,
at Irvington

RICH
WAS
BETTER

Gratefully yours.

Philip

PHILIP VAN RENSSELAER

July 23, 1990

WYNWOOD™ Press
New York, New York

This book is autobiographical, and a few names have been changed to protect the privacy of certain individuals.

The photographs used in this book were taken by Roloff Beny, Cecil Beaton, Fred Eberstadt, Camilla P. McGrath, and Jerry Sacks and are from the author's collection.

Library of Congress Cataloging-in-Publication Data

Van Rensselaer, Philip.
   Rich was better : a memoir / Philip Van Rensselaer.
      p.   cm.
   ISBN 0-922088-30-2
   1. Van Rensselaer, Philip—Family. 2. Van Rensselaer Family.
3. Upper classes—United States—History—20th century. I. Title.
CT275.V388A3 1990
929'.2'0973—dc20   90-32415
                                            CIP

Copyright © 1990 by Philip Van Rensselaer
Published by WYNWOOD™ Press
New York, New York
Printed in the United States of America

For Guido and Joseph, two maitre d's extraordinaire, who gave me endless lunches at L'Aiglon restaurant (now the Italian Pavillion) after the scandal.

And of course, for the last remaining Van Rensselaers: brother Charles and Uncle Steve, friends through the tumultuous decades.

Prologue

In my childhood and adolescence, being born a Van Rensselaer stood for quite a good deal. Many people claimed we were America's royalty, and that George Washington should have given us the title of duke, or at least lord. Whenever my brother Charles and I attended a party in the forties, columnists mentioned our names along with Rockefellers, Astors, and Whitneys. When I came down from St. Paul's School, in Concord, New Hampshire, where rich boys were prepared to take their place in the world, I would read in Nancy Randolph's column in the *Daily News* that I was lunching with Mother at the Café Pierre, or dining with her at LaRue.

During the war years, Charles Ventura, the society scribe of the *Telegram,* made a list of the "new 400," and of course Mother, Charlie, and I were mentioned along with those same Rockefellers, Astors, and Whitneys. Cholly Knickerbocker, whose *Journal-American* column you'd die to get into, called Mother a "social leader," and when he wrote that she was going to marry polo player Rodman Wanamaker, of department store millions, he featured this scoop as the lead article in big bold print.

When I did Mother one better and announced I was going to

marry Countess Caja Palffy, whose castle in Hungary was as big as the Vanderbilts' Breakers in Newport, and whose aunt was Gladys, Duchess of Marlborough, Caja and I even rated a picture on the front page.

Yes, society's staples we were. Big shots!

Of course, I knew it was all a crock, to use Crazy Liz Ellsworth's favorite expression, but I was deep into the disease of grandiosity and a bit of unhealthy narcissism, too.

At an early age, my domiciles were the Waldorf Towers and the Pierre Hotel on Fifth Avenue. A big limousine carried me from one movie orgy to the next. Doormen bowed me through gilded revolving doors. Waiters treated me with respect when they wheeled in the heavy, rattling metal trays from room service. Saks Fifth Avenue and Brooks Brothers gave me lovely clothes when I signed Mother's magic name. Mother's name also brought me some crisp greenbacks when I signed Mrs. Van Rensselaer on a credit voucher at the concierge's desk downstairs in the lobby.

All these things fueled my fantasy that I was a special person, a person of importance, although my other self—the self who saw the truth and was the judge and jury in my head—jeered at me, telling me it was all lies and deceit, that any minute the whole phony show would crumble like a house of cards. I identified strongly with Ray Milland when he was hitting the skids in *The Lost Weekend*, in and out of mental hospitals and finally trudging up Third Avenue under the ominous rumbling El. Goethe wrote, "Two souls, alas, are lodged in my breast, which struggle there for undivided reign." That could certainly apply to me.

Some years ago the long conflict raging in me caused a breakdown; I surrendered completely to my destructive side. On Christmas Eve 1971, I returned to my pretty blue and white island house in Greece. Wearily pushed open the rusty wrought-iron gate, moving slowly up the steep wooden stairs to my studio, I felt like a death row convict on his last mile to the execution chamber. I was forty-three, defeated, a failure. No one took my career seriously; recklessly, I had gambled away my money. I could not face the world without being rich, famous, and important. Yes, grandiose to the end.

I flung back my head, swallowed a bottle of Secónals with a

bottle of vodka, and went to the open window. The studio room on the top floor faced the sea. The night was full of brilliant stars; there was the perfume of jasmine in the air. The moon was making a silvery path on the water, and it seemed to be heading right toward my window. A kind of mystical feeling gripped me.

I remembered my boarding school days with the Malcolm Kenneth Gordons in Garrison on the Hudson, where the sound of organ music reverberated through the gray stone church, St. Phillip's in the Highlands, where we walked every Sunday in our blue blazers and gray flannels. I was Mrs. Gordon's favorite, and I played the coveted role of the Madonna in our Christmas play when I was eight.

I remember singing in the choir, all the young boys' voices singing "Onward, Christian Soldiers" and "Oh, Come All Ye Faithful." I was not corrupt then, not yet tainted.

Mrs. Gordon was forever telling me I must be a strong, manly, and moral human being when I grew up. She constantly stressed the importance of earning an honest living, of having character. She said that all one had in life was one's good name, that I must set an example for others to follow. I knew she was alluding to Mother and, with shame, I'd hang my head.

On that moonlit night in Greece I also remembered Mother, a skeleton at forty-three on her deathbed, hanging on to my hand, telling me that wherever she was she would be thinking of me, and that I must promise to make something of my life. . . .

Much had been expected of me, but I had failed these two women who had loved me deeply and done so much for me. Standing there by the open window, with the scent of jasmine and the sea coming to me, I felt sick with fear. Suddenly I did not want to die. I cried out for help, stumbled to the stairs. My legs felt as if they were frozen in ice water. I fell to the floor. Tears were streaming down my face as they had when Mother died. . . .

In an Athens madhouse I was brought back to life, after three days in a coma and a series of shock treatments that I have never forgotten. In the evening, white-coated orderlies led me around a confined space, shadowed by a huge stone wall. Other tormented souls joined me, heads bowed, eyes haggard, and with skin like parchment. For hours we marched around, the living dead.

As I walked about in the evening darkness, round and round that endless confined space, I wondered how I had reached this point. Diana Barrymore had told me that if I could overcome my background, I could overcome anything. She hadn't, and she died young. I hadn't either. And here I was, literally brought back to life with perhaps thirty more years left. What was I to do with the rest of it?

What had caused this murderous act toward myself? How had I reached this impasse? Slowly, the past returned. As I looked back, some of the darkness faded and I began to see how my early self-destructive patterns had started, and how Mother's had started. Somehow, both of us were tied together in a strange way, as if we were twins. I always felt she and I and Charlie were a team.

RICH
WAS
BETTER

Chapter One

The villain in the piece of Mother's early tragedy was Florence Bonnell. People wondered why newspapers wrote of Mother as being the daughter of the James Brookfields when others said she was the daughter of Florence Bonnell, born Quintard.

Florence Quintard, a spoiled, self-centered, and willful girl, from wealthy parents (Quintard Iron Works) whose Huguenot ancestors stretched far back into seventeenth-century America, had two children by her second husband, John Pratt Richardson, a handsome ladies' man with a Charles Dana Gibson profile. Florence, bored with Richardson, wanted to marry John Rowland, but Rowland did not want to take on the responsibility of two children.

What to do? Florence decided to keep her son, Jack, and sell her daughter, Louise.

Florence approached her childless sister, Adele, Mrs. James Brookfield. Mrs. Brookfield took one look at the baby girl and lost her heart. After signing a check and giving Florence a fur coat, Mrs. Brookfield took the pretty little girl home with her. Mrs. Brookfield was happily married, of gentle and happy disposition— as different from her sister as day is from night. The James Brookfields lived in an old stone house in White Plains, raised dogs, and were very much a part of the community.

Little Louise Richardson was adopted legally by the James Brookfields and, to quote a newspaper, "became the treasure of a luxurious household." Louise's Christian name was now Maude Adele. Maude Adele had her own pony and a pet dog; the Brookfields doted on their only child.

However, these happy days in the stone country house did not last. "Tragedy soon struck," the newspapers reported. Despite her outwardly happy life, Mrs. Brookfield was fond of drinking. One afternoon, in a state of inebriation, she was bending over the fire to turn a log. It was 1908, skirts were wide and full and went to the floor; there were lots of rustling lace undergarments. She fell, and her dress caught fire and went up in flames. She screamed for help. Servants and little Maude Adele ran to offer assistance. They wrapped her in rugs, but it was too late.

Adele Brookfield, now four years old, came into a tidy fortune, and Florence Quintard, now Mrs. Rowland, suddenly finding little Adele most appealing, put in a claim for her. The courts intervened, and a suitable guardian was sought. Soon, Adele went to live with her bachelor uncle, George Quintard, Esquire.

Mr. Quintard, a millionaire playboy, held court in another big Westchester country house. Every weekend luscious Ziegfeld Follies girls made an appearance and and roamed through the hallways. There were parties from noon till the early hours; little Adele often was brought into the drawing room with her governess and presented to the ladies. She was a charming, eager-to-please girl; she liked all the attention. She also liked the easy, informal atmosphere. Uncle George doted on her, but, like his recently deceased sister, liked to tipple.

Mr. Quintard's house was not the proper environment for a young, impressionable girl, so the courts again intervened. A few months later, custody of the eight-year-old girl was awarded to Miss Mary and Miss Ida Hoyt, retired spinster ladies who lived in a red plush Victorian apartment in New York at 103 East Seventy-fifth Street. They were of impeccable background and the highest moral caliber. Adele Brookfield, my mother, lived with the two Misses Hoyt for twelve years. Like Mrs. Brookfield, they adored this bright and pretty girl; she became the focus of their quiet, respectable existence—so quiet and respectable that she was not even allowed to go to the cinema. Movies were considered vulgar, as inconceivable to attend as a prizefight at Madison Square Garden. Adele Brookfield was sheltered, protected, and unworldly.

Her mother, Florence Bonnell, made overtures to the little heiress, but they were not reciprocated. Adele and Florence always remained polite strangers to each other. However, young Jack Richardson, now called Rowland, kept in touch with his sister and told his good friend Charlie Van Rensselaer, Jr., of his "little orphaned sister who lived in a cloister that was pure Jane Austen." This sister had her own money and no parents to hold the purse strings. At twenty-one, Charlie Van Rensselaer, Jr., was eager to leave his parents. To him, they were colossal stuffed shirts, and he loathed the exclusive clubs they set such store in. The whole group, known as Society, was odious to Charles Van Rensselaer, Jr.

Finally, Jack Rowland arranged a meeting between Charlie and Adele. Charlie was hooked from the start. He had never met a girl so innocent, of such a sweet and feminine nature. She thought that men were gods. She looked up to him, hung on his every word, hero-worshiped him. She was plump, not snobbish, not at all like the fashionable, rich heiresses his parents wanted him to marry. She had her own money, and if he married her, he would be appointed her guardian since she was under age. Plus, she was Miss Nobody from Nowhere and had no social aspirations, thank God! She would do anything he told her.

The more he saw of her, the better he liked her. You couldn't help but like Adele Brookfield, people-pleaser without equal. It would be a marriage made in heaven. Luckily for him, she didn't know a thing about his rages and cruelty. Nor did she know that his two first cousins were certifiably insane and that insanity was rife in the Van Rensselaer family.

It was a pity that the two Misses Hoyt did not move in fashionable circles. In truth, they were far more interested in the rise and fall of the Roman Empire than social goings-on on the isle of Manhattan. When they met twenty-one-year-old Charlie Van Rensselaer, all they saw was a handsome, fine-featured young man with his father's courtly manners and soft voice. They had no knowledge of men.

Of course, being consummately well read, the Misses Hoyt were acquainted with the facts of the Van Rensselaer patroons and their feudal domain on the Hudson. They thought it "right" that their Adele should become Mrs. Charles Augustus Van Rensselaer, Jr., and link her destiny with the scion of this ancient and highly esteemed New York family.

Adele herself, well versed in the classics and history, was fascinated by the background of her prospective bridegroom. When Charlie asked his bride-to-be where she would like to spend their honeymoon, she replied St. Jean de Luz in the romantic Basque countryside near the Spanish border. When he asked her what liner she would like to cross on, she replied, in her innocent manner, the *Berengaria*. He had no idea she had social aspirations. Adele wanted to cross on the *Berengaria* because the Russell Forgans, the most dazzling couple of the twenties, would be on board. And she wanted to go to St. Jean de Luz because a classmate's duke had a chateau there.

It seemed Adele and Charlie were at cross-purposes from the very start. They were both too young and inexperienced to marry, but who was to stop them? Indeed, the groom's parents were delighted to be rid of their elder son, a problem since he was five years old. So Caroline and Charles Van Rensselaer breathed a sigh of relief when he married Adele Brookfield and sailed away to Europe. They'd done the best they could. Naturally, they both liked young Adele—"Such an innocent, sweet little thing." Much in her favor was the fact that she had her own money, for the senior Charles Van Rensselaers had no intention of supporting their hateful elder son after Princeton.

They prayed they'd seen the last of this black sheep and resumed their hectic round of social activities in New York and Long Island. Mr. Van Rensselaer had recently closed the doors of his successful wine and spirits business because of Prohibition. Now with young Charlie gone, he raised a glass of fine old English whiskey and soda in the privacy of his library and downed it with an appreciative smack of his thin lips. Good riddance!

Chapter Two

In my childhood and adolescence, I suffered from an obsessive love for my mother. I always called her Mummy, but in this book, I shall call her Adele or Mother, since "Mummy" becomes cloying.

She was a gentle, loving human being; wherever she went she attracted people by her warm and engaging manner. She was extremely popular, good at games, and was never heard to say an unkind thing about anyone. She was extremely feminine, with the biggest, softest brown eyes I've ever seen. She had old-world manners and was graced with exquisite tact. She was generous to a fault and often taken advantage of because of it.

Along with Nannie, who fed, dressed, and bathed me, Mother was the person I loved most in the world. From an early age I idolized her; she was the moon and stars to me. Like her, I was outgoing and forever smiling; I, too, wanted people to like me.

When I was a year old, my parents were divorced. My father told his family that he never again wanted the names of his ex-wife or two sons mentioned in his presence—never would he forgive his great love for leaving him. Mother was that kind of woman; she was hard to forget. Even today, more than forty years after

Mother's early death, I am aware that I have never loved anyone as much.

Divorce was severely disapproved of by the Van Rensselaers, but after five years of marriage, they urged my mother to seek a divorce from their son. It was the first time in the long history of the Van Rensselaers that a marriage split apart. My grandparents themselves loathed each other the last twenty-five years of their marriage, but remained together in the same house because they cared so much what others might say. My elegant grandmother, Caroline, took to her smelling salts because of the odious publicity attached to her daughter-in-law's Reno divorce. My father, brokenhearted, checked into Dr. Riggs's Sanitarium in Stockbridge, Massachusetts.

After this 1930 divorce, which made headline news in the old *Journal* and *Mirror,* Mother took me and Nannie and my elder brother Charles to Europe. During the crazy twenties, when stocks raced skyward, my father had made a killing with my mother's tidy fortune; however, after the 1929 bloodbath, only a fraction of her original inheritance remained. Everyone told Mother it would be cheaper to live abroad; it was not in her nature to scrimp and save. She liked to live well and have servants to look after her. And she always wanted the best for Charlie and me.

Typically, just before we sailed off to foreign shores, my impractical mother lent all the furniture, portraits, and silver from her Fifth Avenue apartment and her Oyster Bay house to a fascinating man-about-town named Dick Hall, who'd been married to Dorothy Schiff. But when she returned to New York in 1935, she learned with horror that all her possessions had been sold at Mr. Hall's bankruptcy sale.

These kinds of things were forever happening to Mother. Everyone agreed that Mother was a careless manager. Even the host of people who loved and adored her agreed that she was highly unrealistic. Undoubtedly that was part of her famous charm. In any case, she was beloved by one and all. She'd overcome so much after her terrible childhood and marriage to my father, and I was proud of her.

Whenever I hear the melancholy hooting of an ocean liner, or a

18

train whistle, my childhood returns to me. We were forever packing and unpacking, moving on to some new place, and to this day,
I continue the gypsy life. For over three years—from 1932 to
1935—we lived a happy, carefree existence, wandering about Europe. Always our villas in Palma de Mallorca, Rome, and Florence
had spacious, flower-filled rooms with balustraded terraces and
great stone urns overflowing with orange geraniums.

The most joyous period was in Florence, where Charlie and I
attended the American school. We spoke Italian fluently and
learned to ride horseback. Mother read Proust in the serene garden, listened to the operas of Verdi and Puccini on the Gramophone, and played tennis. She was a social creature, and there
were many invitations to lunch parties in splendid villas. In the
evenings she liked to go dancing. Sometimes, she'd take short trips
to Venice, or Brioni, or Riccioni, and once even to Paris, but she
always rushed back home to us, often bringing presents and souvenirs.

Every morning Nannie would throw open the shutters of our
villa and the sound of birds twittering blended harmoniously with
the pealing of the church bells. After school Nannie would take me
and Charlie to see the wonders of Florence, to study the pictures
at the Pitti and Uffizi palaces. How I loved Florence! It has always
been a dream to return there and spend my twilight days amidst
the serene cypress trees, listening to church bells.

Mother had many admirers—handsome and dashing men—but
Fred Beckman was her favorite. Fred and Mother had a violent
and physical relationship, often fighting and often breaking up.
They were planning to marry, but something always came up, to
use Fred's expression. Fred came once to the villa in Florence, but
he was jealous of Mother's new admirer, Count Troyberg, whom
everybody called Bubi. Bubi and Fred had a fight, and Fred left
the next morning.

Unhappily, our idyllic times in Florence came to an end. One
morning in early April 1935, when the damp rains were oozing
down our windows and the ancient pockmarked urns and cupids on
the terrace looked most forlorn, Mother received an ominous letter
from the Bank of New York. It stated, simply, that her last stock

and bond had been sold, that they could no longer send her a check.

"What are we to do?" asked Mother.

"I'll go to work for you, Mummy," said Charlie, a manly and handsome nine-year-old, dark-haired and reserved like our father.

I flung myself on Mother's large canopied bed. Charlie lay on one side of Mother's long, slender figure and I lay on the other. Tenderly she put her arms around us, running her hands through our hair. I was seven, golden-haired, energetic, and full of curiosity.

"We can all live in a trailer, Mummy," I said, gazing up at her lovely oval face. Her dark hair was held in place by a blue ribbon and she wore a pink silk bed jacket trimmed with lace at the neck and sleeves. There was a fragrance of gardenia about her, and I marveled at the size and shape of her eyes and the smoothness of her skin. I was always studying her face, and I liked to gaze at her when her head was turned to one side, her profile beautiful and clear. Her lips were full and wide, sensitive, and expressive. When she was angry, they were pulled tight in a taut line. The only time I saw her really angry was when Fred Beckman told her he was going off on Sarah Waterbury's yacht in Mallorca. Mother loved Fred the most. I understood that she had Bubi hanging around only to make Fred jealous.

Fred was wonderful, he looked like Gary Cooper and his sun-bronzed body felt warm when you touched it. I'd overheard Pauline Potter in Mallorca saying that when a man's body is warm it means he wants to make love to you.

My favorite moments came at Mother's cocktail parties when I'd sit on Fred's lap and he'd put his arms around me and let me have a sip of his gin cocktail. It burned my throat and I'd squirm and giggle in Fred's arms, then he'd whisper in my ear and I'd giggle some more. I loved it when Fred paid attention to me!

It was my dream that Mother and Fred would marry and I'd have a real father at last. Mother was furious with me when I asked Fred when he was going to marry her. It was the only time I saw her blush.

Nannie had been watching us for some time with a resigned

smile. She was a thin, middle-aged, gentle woman from Scotland, and her name was Miss Cole. She loved Mother, understood her childlike quality, and liked to give her realistic advice. When the letter from the bank came, she said rather sternly, "Mrs. Van Rensselaer, I think it's prudent we pack and return to New York." She spoke so gravely that we all stared at her.

"I suppose you're right, dear Nannie," said Mother, vacantly. I could tell Mother did not want to return to New York. There would be so many ugly details to face, and Mother hated details.

Presently, with trunks and suitcases cluttering up the villa, the maids were on their knees packing all the things we'd picked up in our travels. We had to leave a lot of clothes and bibelots behind because there wasn't room for everything. Mother was sad that she could not take two portraits of me and Charlie done by Edward Hurst in Mallorca.

Later in the day, Mother viewed the chaos and disorder of our rooms and said, "Packing and moving—the story of my life."

"Mine, too," I whispered.

Mother bent down and kissed me with emotion. "My angel," she said in her lovely, clear voice, "someday very soon, we'll be settled somewhere, for good." But I knew that Mother would never be settled; we'd wander in a gypsy existence, and caravans would be our home.

"We'll always be together, you and Charlie and Nannie and me," said Mother tenderly, drawing me close. Like Fred's, her figure was always warm.

"I suppose, Mummy," I said, kissing her and putting my arms around her neck. I always copied the expressions Mother used, and people often remarked how curious it was that Charlie and I spoke exactly like Mother.

Two days later we were standing amidst a sea of luggage at the Florence Station. The train whistled mournfully, its heavy wheels rotating angrily on the steel track. Many friends saw us off, and Mother was in tears, dabbing her eyes with a lace handkerchief. She wore a brown Fedora hat that half concealed her face and a high-collared mink coat that she had recently purchased in Rome.

"Farewell, farewell," said Mother. "*Addio . . . addio. . . .*"

And then, we were gone. We took lunch in the dining car and that evening arrived at Genoa, where we were to board the steamer to America. Despite Mother's gaiety and cheerful disposition, I felt that there was something tragic about her—which, of course, she skillfully concealed from the world. It was not in her nature to complain; she took everything as it came.

Chapter Three

"Welcome to 300 Park, my dears," said Aunt Winifred. "Stay as long as you want." Winifred Rockefeller was Charlie's godmother and Mother's best friend from their childhood days in Greenwich.

Aunt Winifred slipped an envelope into Mother's hand and said, "Darling, I have much good news for you. Camel wants you to endorse their cigarette, and they'll pay you a small fortune. Don't look so worried, all our friends have given their names—Julia Lowell, the Biddles, Roosevelts, and DuPonts—so you'll be in good company."

Mother laughed, "Nannie promised old New York would come to my rescue."

"And it has!" said Nannie triumphantly, exchanging a look with Mother.

"You look perfectly beautiful, Adele," said Aunt Winifred in her affectionate way. "And this will help you now in these trying times. I told Mabardi, a charming man who sells me liquor at the St. Regis, that you were available for a job, and he said he could use extra help—and he'll pay you a commission on top of your salary."

Mother flung her arms about her old friend. "Winifred, dear, you're a true white knight on a charger."

Winifred smiled. "Pagie Morris and Dorothy Adams have called for you. I think Pagie has a divine white knight for you."

"Heavenly!"

"She's giving a big party at El Morocco tomorrow night, and Dorothy's having a lunch for you at the Colony, celebrating your return."

"Heavenly!"

"We've all missed you terribly, Adele; you're special, you know."

The telephone rang in the large, vaulted marble hall, and Aunt Winifred said, "There! I'm sure it's for you, you'll be swamped morning, noon, and night with invitations, knowing you, you popular puss."

A maid in a black uniform, with touches of lace at the throat and wrist, appeared and smiled at Mother. "Mrs. Van Rensselaer, there's a Mrs. Adams on the wire."

In her impulsive and spontaneous way, Mother blew the maid a kiss and ran to the telephone. "Oh, Dorothy, *heavenly* to hear your voice, so thrilled about lunch tomorrow, can't wait, *counting* the hours!"

I smiled as happily as Mother; it was silly of me to have worried. When you were beautiful, like Mother, good things happened to you.

Aunt Winifred's apartment, almost across from the Waldorf-Astoria Hotel, was spacious and full of old-world antiques. Indeed, it greatly resembled our Florentine home, with the same Fortuny curtains and Aubusson carpets on parquet floors. Only at Aunt Winifred's there was no evidence of distressed gentility. The only things I missed were the birds singing in the garden and the sound of church bells. However, the rumble of the subway far below the gray pavements was energizing, and the sound of El Morocco's dance band replaced the inspiring arias of Puccini and Verdi on the portable Gramophone.

Mother took the job at the nearby St. Regis; she walked to work every morning at nine-thirty and returned at five.

"Just like the rest of the world," said Nannie contentedly.

In the evenings, Mother's many old friends lured her out to dinner parties and nightclubs. She was just thirty, at the zenith of her good looks and charm.

One evening after the Fourth of July, Mother did not go out dancing to El Morocco; she stayed home and dined with us in the Adam dining room. She was dressed in a smart blue and white polka dot dress, and a spring-fresh white hat sat on her dark curls. She seemed unusually excited.

She sipped a glass of white wine and said vividly, "My angels, you'll never guess who I met at a dinner party the other evening! Fred Beckman! Isn't that *scrumptious*, my treasures? He's coming over in a minute, and he's absolutely *dying* to see you. Thank the Lord, he's divorced from Sarah Waterbury, and working downtown on Wall Street as a stockbroker."

Presently, Charlie and I were reunited with our hero from Mallorca. Fred looked as strikingly handsome and vigorous as ever. He sat with us at the table; I couldn't take my eyes off him, nor could Mother. As usual, Fred was in an expansive mood.

"I'll be rich as Croesus if I manage to get some new, rich accounts," he said in his engaging manner. He always spoke to me and Charlie as if we were grown-ups, confiding in us things, we felt, that he would never dare tell another human being. Like Mother, Fred was bursting with high spirits and charm. Like Mother, I found it always a treat to be with him. In his merry way, he told us that he *had* to go about socially a great deal, for there was no telling what millionaire he might chance to meet. And here he winked in his wicked, suggestive way, and Charlie and I laughed.

"But, Fred," I said, staring at him with unabashed pleasure, "but, Fred, you're so good-looking, you don't have to worry."

"Nonsense, my child," he replied with a slow and sensual grin creeping over his tanned face. "I wasn't born good-looking, and I don't have a famous old name like you boys. I just have personality, and go on from there."

How beautiful he and Mother looked together, complementing each other, as it were, he being so blond and robust, and she so dark and boyishly slim.

I told him this, and he flung me a playful, teasing look across the polished mahogany dinner table. "My child, that's all for the best, for your precious mother and I are going out dancing at the Central Park Casino, and hopefully we should break a lot of hearts there. That's the name of the game, isn't it?" he added, with a wink.

Mother smiled an indulgent smile at him, but Nannie was not amused. She led us to our rooms, down the long corridor. After a time, Mother and Fred came down and gave us a good-night kiss. They carried snifters of brandy, and their cheeks were flushed pink. How handsome they looked. I included Fred in my nightly prayers that evening.

All of a sudden, Mother began to receive an excessive amount of publicity.

"I predict that Adele Van Rensselaer, from New York's First Family, will soon relinquish the Van Rensselaer name and become Mrs. Frederick Lewisohn." So wrote the famed society scribe Cholly Knickerbocker in his *Journal-American* column. He went on to tell that Rhoda Seligman Lewisohn, Freddy's wife, had just the year before run off with a Safari hunter in Africa and married him. Freddy, a worldly fifty-five-year-old man-about-town, with a celebrated pink marble villa in the south of France where he gave splendid parties, was much taken with Adele, and they were seen at Manhattan's fashionable haunts—namely El Morocco and the Central Park Casino.

On top of all this newspaper notoriety, Mother's picture was on the back of every national magazine. There was a portrait of her in a dazzling blue evening dress, looking exquisitely lean-hipped, in her Park Avenue drawing room, stating that at home or abroad, she favored Camels. Mother, brought up with old-fashioned manners, hated publicity; being conspicuous went against her grain. She was also nervous about using the Van Rensselaer name; she had phoned her in-laws, and they had urged her to endorse the cigarette, especially when they heard the sum of money she would receive.

Also, the Great Depression was still dragging on, and many old families were feeling the pinch. Even the crème found extra cash helpful during this era of unemployment and hard times. And beautiful ladies with money problems found it most gratifying to have a car and chauffeur at their disposal.

Suddenly, Mr. Lewisohn's conspicuous Rolls-Royce appeared under the awning of 300 Park Avenue. Nannie clucked her tongue wisely and said some important news would be forthcoming. When a man sends his car and chauffeur for his lady love, and she rides in it, then things must be serious.

26

Fred Beckman vanished. His name was no longer on Mother's lips, which was perhaps just as well, for sure enough, Fred Beckman, "handsome and mysterious man-about-town," was seen with Hazel Bache Richards, daughter of financier Jules Bache, in all the same fashionable restaurants and nightclubs as Mother was, and written about in the same columns. And there, bigger than life in Cholly's column, was a picture of the happy couple. Fred, grinning broadly, and Hazel Bache, the great heiress, gazing up at him with the same love and adoration I'd seen in Mother's eyes. She looked much older than Fred, and grumpy.

Early the next year, Fred Beckman married Hazel Bache and sailed to Europe on the *Queen Mary*. We didn't see Fred again for three years.

Mr. Lewisohn was often called "the Copper King" in the tabloids. When I asked Nannie what that meant, she replied that Mr. Lewisohn's family was closely associated with that precious metal, and that he himself was a financier of note and a member of the New York Stock Exchange. She showed us magazine pictures of his art-deco apartment at 726 Park Avenue, which was called a *maisonette*, since it was on the street level and had two floors, rather like a townhouse.

Suddenly, that fateful summer of 1935, our rooms at 300 Park Avenue were flooded with yellow roses. Towering yellow beauties they were, long-stemmed and proud. So many arrived every day that Mother did not have the vases for them, and many times she had to give these amazing roses to maids and doormen, which caused much merriment. Also, pretty little things from Cartier and from Bergdorf began to arrive, exquisitely wrapped, and every woman loves to receive pretty presents.

Despite all these alluring and tempting gifts, and the Rolls-Royce outside at her disposal, Mother looked sad. Her eyes had a faraway look, tinged with pain. I often found her staring out the window, and she sighed a lot. She also paced up and down the rooms, smoking cigarettes endlessly. I had a feeling she was heartbroken by Fred Beckman's treachery. And this fact was made worse because all her friends had warned her that Fred was an adventurer.

One sultry afternoon in late July, Nannie and Charlie and I

returned from walking in Central Park and gazing at the caged lions and tigers at the Sixty-fourth Street Zoo, just off Fifth Avenue. There in front of 300 Park was Grandma Van Rensselaer's handsome black Buick, with two white sidewalls on either side of the motor. Stanley, her young black chauffeur, tipped his hat in a friendly way, and I wondered why he was there.

Upstairs, we found the answer. Mother was pacing and smoking, looked haggard. I was rather shocked by her taut lips and the bluish shadows under her eyes, which told me she hadn't been sleeping. And her eyes were shining with tears.

Mother was never one to show her feelings; she made a big effort to convince us that everything was all right, but I knew otherwise. The night before, I'd overheard her telling Mrs. Morris that she was worried *sick* that her salary was not enough to pay for our schooling. And how on earth was she to afford an apartment of her own with the pittance she received from her liquor store job for Mabardi?

"Most disheartening," she had said, and I felt anxious, seeing the pale gravity of her face.

Mother turned on her charm for us. "My treasures, your grandmother wants to have you for a few months in Oyster Bay." Here we groaned and protested, but she rushed on. "My darlings, you know you don't want to stay in dirty, hot New York all summer long. And you won't be able to be with me, for I'll be at Mabardi's, so there you are. You'll have a lovely holiday! Frankly, I'm *green* with envy, thinking of all those *heavenly* Piping Rock lunches and swims at Mrs. Baker's pool you'll be having. Lucky, lucky boys!" Mother's old enthusiasm and energy did the trick; I began to think that I *was* a lucky boy, and I looked forward to all those club lunches where Grandma's friends would make a fuss over me. And there was nothing I liked better than swimming!

Mother told us that she'd miss us *dreadfully*, but that she'd come down every instant. Nannie packed our bags, and soon we were standing on the pavement of Park Avenue again. And, lo and behold, there was Mr. Lewisohn's fat, disagreeable-looking German chauffeur, Peters, and the astounding black Rolls-Royce, with its basket-weave doors the color of honey wicker. It made Grandma's Buick look quite insignificant. I couldn't stop staring at it.

Pat, the nice Irish doorman, was putting our suitcases into the Buick's trunk. He caught my eye and said, "Isn't that Rolls a beauty? Don't make many like that. And don't make many like your mother, either. She's one in a million, bless her."

Any praise of Mother always made me feel proud and happy. I forgot her pale face and sad eyes, shining with tears. By the time we were crossing the Triboro Bridge and gazing back at the extraordinary Manhattan skyline, I was lighthearted again and asking Nannie a hundred different questions, all concerning Mr. Frederick Lewisohn, the Copper King.

"I've never known such a curious boy," said Nannie, sitting between us in the rear, with our dog, Beans, on our laps.

I admitted I was *dreadfully* curious, using Mother's word, but what did Mr. Lewisohn *really* look like? Was he so old and tired looking? Why would Mummy go out with him if he was so old and tired looking?

"Mr. Lewisohn has your mother's best interests at heart, which is more than I can say for *some* people. Actually, I haven't met him, but I've seen him waiting in that splendid car for your mother, and he wears a pince-nez, rather similar to President Roosevelt's, and he's most gorgeously dressed, the way a gentleman of the old school should look. Besides," added Nannie, giving me a sage look, "a sheltered and protected woman, such as your dear mother, needs a fatherly sort of man to help take care of her problems. You understand that, don't you, you curious boy?"

I nodded sleepily, curling up beside Nannie. It was nice to have a Copper King in your life.

"Poor Mummy," said Charlie, "in that hot, dirty city all alone."

Chapter Four

Grandma Van Rensselaer fell madly in love with me and Charlie. She was a woman of passionate feelings, definite opinions, strong likes and dislikes. She and Nannie did not take to each other. Nannie was accustomed to the soft, passive, pliable nature of Mother, who was only too happy to have someone tell her what to do. Not so Grandma! From the start there was tension between the two women, each used to having her own way.

Charlie and I now saw our father with some regularity. Once a week this "black sheep" came by to collect his allowance—"a pittance," he'd complain.

My father loathed his mother, whom he contemptuously called "the czarina." She called him "the troublemaker," among other things. Mother and son were forever at each other's throats, and both seemed to enjoy a good fight. He'd whine about his ill health, that he was the poorest white man on Long Island, that it was impossible for him to earn a dollar, and that Roosevelt and the Jews were the cause of all these rotten times. Grandma would laugh cuttingly and say that it was all his *own* fault, that he was bone lazy, and why couldn't he have taken advantage of his fine education and all the prominent business people she'd introduced him to.

"Ma, you know I'm not a businessman."

Finally, she'd bait him and ask why couldn't he be more like his younger brother, Steve. Then he'd go berserk, and all hell would break out. He'd down a few too many whiskey and sodas, and he'd slam out the door, muttering vengefully under his breath, his nasty police dog growling in the same fashion. He'd always say he was never coming back, but like clockwork, his angry figure appeared every Saturday afternoon at tea time.

Only once did he smile at me and Charlie. It was the time when Mother sent him the portrait that Camel had used for her endorsement. He was, he said, "tickled pink," and praised the love of his life to the skies.

The next week, though, he was muttering vengefully not only about the czarina, Roosevelt, the Jews, but that Mother was a disgrace. Ruining the family name by carrying on with Mr. Lewisohn. *Lewisohn!* Imagine that! A Jew.

Despite my father's weekly rages, and the tension between Nannie and the czarina, our six months in Oyster Bay were, for the most part, idyllic. Mother was quite right in envying us. Charlie and I lived a privileged and protected English country life that centered around the rambling pillared clubhouse of the Piping Rock Club in Locust Valley and its beach a few miles away on Long Island Sound. Grandma was sixty-five at this time, small and beautifully proportioned, rather formal. Every night she wore an evening dress for dinner and every day she was turned out with style, her thick white hair smartly curled, a strand of large pearls about her neck, and a large and brilliant canary yellow diamond ring on her finger. Even when she was in her beloved garden attacking an odious weed, she was regally attired.

Grandma's house on the outskirts of Oyster Bay Village resembled an old homestead from a Currier and Ives print, of which there were many all over the bedroom walls. The eighteenth-century house was of white clapboard, with a cedar-shingled roof, green shutters, and a deeply rooted wisteria vine covering half of it. There were many fireplaces; hardwood floors creaked and groaned when you stepped on them; and dazzling bouquets of hollyhocks, snapdragons, delphiniums, and roses decorated our rooms, and sometimes branches of forsythia and apple. Peonies delighted me, and I stared with wonder at the pink, white, or red heads whose petals had the texture of silk.

"Your mother and father lived here when you were born," Grandma used to tell me.

"Were they happy here?" I asked.

She laughed bitterly. "If they were, your father ruined it! He ruins everything for himself."

The house, set on six acres, had a garage apartment where Stanley, the chauffeur, lived and a greenhouse where Grandma tended her prized plants and flowers. She had taken first prize for a superb calla lily, and there was a picture of her in the local newspaper displaying it. Also, at this time, there was a picture of Grandma in the rotogravure section of the Sunday paper, standing imperiously between me and Charlie, at the Piping Rock Horse Show, long since discontinued.

Every nook and cranny of this ancient house was cluttered with antique chests, secretaries, highboys, lowboys, and tall-cased grandfather clocks that ticked away loudly, and noisily chimed every quarter of an hour. Every morning we had our tea in a fine old silver teapot, engraved "Harriet Thayer, 1804," one of Grandma's many heirlooms. Nannie remarked that all the silver in the house could have sunk the *Titanic!*

If the garden was radiant with color, so also was the drawing room that housed Grandma's prized collection of French and American Impressionists. There was also a full-length portrait of Grandma in a flowing white dress of the early 1900s, with my father, aged four, sitting beside her, glum as always. Charlie was much taken with this portrait, but our father remarked, in his sour manner, that it was a disgrace that his grandfather, Mr. Fitzgerald, had hired Frank Benson instead of John Singer Sargent.

One afternoon in October, Grandma and I were having tea by the fire. Charlie was out walking Beans, and Nannie was in Oyster Bay, on her day off. As always, I was extremely curious and asked Grandma many questions about the various treasures inherited from her father, Desmond Fitzgerald, a noted collector.

"My father was a friend of Monet and Renoir," she replied in her decisive manner. "Our house in Brookline, Massachusetts, had a gallery attached to it, larger than the house, he never could stop buying." She gave a bright, merry laugh that was one of her great charms. "Imagine, my father had nine Monets, and seven Boudins, many Sisleys and Pissarros, too." She sighed and looked down at me sitting at her feet. "Unfortunately, they had to be sold a few years ago, for we needed to keep the wolf away from the door! Actually, your grandfather closed his successful wine and spirits business in New York, and we needed more income. Thank heaven my angelic stockbroker rushed down to Syosset and begged and implored me to sell out my portfolio of stocks on the eve of the stock market collapse. So, I'm quite all right in these trying times. Comfortable, you might say, unlike your poor mother." She gave me a mournful look and patted my head.

I told Grandma that Mother was too trusting and had too kind a heart. Grandma gave a harsh chuckle. "Your father didn't help matters, gambling her inheritance away on Wall Street."

"Nannie said that Mr. Lewisohn, the Copper King, is a fatherly sort of man, and will help take care of her problems."

"Perhaps," said Grandma, reflectively. "But your mother is so sweet and unworldly—you can't blame her after the way she was brought up!" Ruffling my hair and affectionately hugging me, she said, "How would you like to remain here, with me, my little darling?"

"Well," I said, tactfully, "that sounds quite nice, Grandma."

"Your mother can't look after you anymore," said Grandma.

"Well, Nannie will, then," I said lamely.

"Grandma's face hardened, her eyes became more intense. "Who do you love more, me or Nannie?"

I gulped. The fire was dying out with low, sputtering noises. I heard the maids in the dining room putting plates on the table. The many clocks all began to chime. I stood up and flung my arms around Grandma. "I love you both! But you know, Nannie's been with us such a long time, since I was a baby, and—"

Grandma stood up and said she must dress for dinner. I knew I hadn't fooled her. I did not like the look in her eye. A wintry mood proceeded to fall over our old homestead. The lawn was full of mud puddles, the flowers in the garden had dried up and withered, the oaks and elms stood naked with their barren limbs stretched up to a dismal gray sky. One morning in early December there was snow on the ground. I raced out with happy cries and rolled about in the fluffy whiteness, like a madman. In Mallorca and Italy, we never saw snow.

I ran back into the dining room, a stately chamber with seventeenth-century ancestors from floor to ceiling. Portrait lights glowed dully on the ancient canvases. Grandma sat at the head of the table, and Grandpa at the other end, facing each other in stony silence. Even Nannie and Charlie, facing each other in the middle of the mahogany table, looked solemn. For many years my grandparents had not gotten along; they rarely spoke a word to each other. Most of the time, Grandpa was off in the Far East, traveling or visiting his younger sister, Mathilde, in Palm Beach, Florida. Like the dining room, he was stately in appearance, reserved, tall, and spare. I often gazed at him with interest, but the interest was not returned.

I flung myself on Grandma, making ecstatic observations about the altered landscape. Grandma looked down at me indulgently. The cold air had made my cheeks pink, and she remarked what a pretty little boy I was, just like my mama.

Nannie glared at the czarina, "Boys are not pretty, Mrs. Van Rensselaer."

Grandma bristled, ready for a good fight, and the spare, formally dressed old gentleman chuckled with pleasure. He'd like to have seen his wife routed! Without a word, he stood up and vanished out the door. His quarters were as far removed from his wife's as possible, on the far end of the house. He was only "visiting" till Christmas.

Grandma directed a fierce gaze at Nannie. "Miss Cole, you've driven poor Mr. Van Rensselaer away!"

"I did nothing of the sort," replied Nannie, returning the hostile stare with her customary spirit. I sat on a high-back chair beside Nannie, and ate my Cream of Wheat cereal. A dreadful silence fell over us. Those ticking grandfather clocks sounded fearfully loud!

Our happy days in Oyster Bay ended as they had in Florence, in a flood of tears, emptied drawers, and packed suitcases. On the move again. Abruptly, a few days later, Nannie was fired, and she departed on the afternoon train to New York. Mother telephoned and said she would be down that weekend to take us back to the city. She was living at the Hotel Westbury at Madison Avenue and Sixty-ninth Street.

On that last Saturday afternoon, my father suddenly appeared, smelling bad news. At tea time he sat in the drawing room and stared gloomily into the fire. He was a figure to be pitied, and I felt sorry for him. Yes, he *was* handsome, but his posture was poor. He carried himself as if a cross were on his shoulders. His thin lips were held in a bitter line; they looked cynical when they smiled. His mother made things worse for him that day by pretending she didn't know why he was there—to collect his weekly allowance from the czarina, of course!

As usual, he was dressed in gray flannels, a bow tie, a murky tweed sport coat that was probably a hand-me-down from his father or brother. Yes, Uncle Steve was there by the fire, too. He came down every weekend, debonair and attractive, with the same merry laugh as his mother, and the same gregarious nature.

Unlike his older brother, Steve was immensely popular, outgoing, social, and his mirror was filled with engraved invitations to dinners and dances. He held a good job at National City Bank in New York, was a member of good standing at the Racquet Club at 370 Park Avenue and, of course, Piping Rock, where he played an excellent game of golf. Often, on his free weekends, he took me and Charlie to swim at Mrs. George Baker's pool, or at Jones Beach. Steve had a dashing V-8 Ford convertible like President Roosevelt's, and Charlie and I and Beans sat in the rumble seat.

My father went to the drinks tray and made himself another whiskey and soda. His pale face flushed a bit, and a hostile glint appeared in his eye. Steve had always been his mother's pride and joy. She was always mentioning all of Steve's successes to the world. Why couldn't he, Charles A. Van Rensselaer, be like him? Steve had just been promoted and had received a nifty raise.

"Steve, always Steve," said Daddy.

Grandma had told me that Daddy had also had a wretched temper as a child. Once when they were living in the New York house on East Fifty-fifth Street, Daddy had attacked Steve and hit him on the head with a hammer, so savagely that Grandma had packed

36

him off to Fay School, in Southboro, Massachusetts, where he boarded till he was twelve. And then he was sent to St. Mark's School, also in the same New England town.

Suddenly, there was a commotion in the hall, and a uniformed maid rushed in and said that Mrs. Adele Van Rensselaer had arrived in a splendid car.

Grandma stood up, and directed a glance at the troublemaker. "Charlie, I think you'd better make yourself scarce. It's not appropriate that you be here with your former wife, all things considered."

Daddy stood his ground. "That's not fair, Ma," he said in his whining voice. "You know how I feel about Adele."

"Yes, I know!" returned Grandma fiercely. "The whole world knows, thanks to your Reno divorce that brought us all that vulgar notoriety in the newspapers."

My father looked the pathetic figure, whipped and beaten down. "I didn't want the divorce, Ma," he said quietly with dignity, but I could see that ominous glint in his eyes. "I went out to Reno and begged Adele on bended knee to come back, but she refused."

Grandma moved over to her elder son, her small, slim figure tense and straight. "Of course she refused!" she snapped. "Any woman in her right senses would have left you, the way you behaved. Now, kindly leave this room this very minute." Daddy hesitated, and she hissed, "If you stay, you won't receive your weekly check!"

Without another word, he took the envelope pressed into his hand and moved in his slow, defeated step out the back door.

The front doorbell rang. Charlie and I clapped our hands with excitement, and Grandma said sorrowfully, "Say hello to your pretty mama, then vanish upstairs to your room. Your mother and I have to have a long talk."

So ended our stay with Grandma in Oyster Bay. Years later—more than a half a century later—I visited Teddy Roosevelt's house in Sagamore Hill. As we were driving through the atmospheric town of Oyster Bay, I asked Uncle Steve to pass by Grandma's old house, the place where my parents lived in the late 1920s. We were dismayed to find a large and ugly condo development there. No trace of that rambling old white-shingled homestead with its

green shutters and pretty garden. The barn and greenhouse were
no more, either. Even the little hill behind the house where Charlie and I used to sled on our Flexible Flyers had vanished.

"All gone," said Uncle Steve, eighty-one, gray-haired, and slow-
moving. "All gone. . . ." He peered out through his thick specta-
cles.

"Well," I said, "it *was* more than a half a century ago."

"Was it?" asked Steve, frowning at the time passed.

The afternoon we left Oyster Bay, we had a joyful reunion with
Nannie at the Westbury. She promised us she'd never leave again.
So did Mother, but I had my doubts. There were trunks and
suitcases all over her rooms, all richly labeled with the hull of that
new transatlantic ocean liner *Normandie,* the pride of the French
Line, touted as the most luxurious ship afloat.

When I stared at these telltale labels, Mother said, "I'm taking
a little voyage next week to France, to see a Brearley friend, now
married to the Duke de Nemours. You can write me care of the
Nemours in Paris, my precious ones." She exchanged a quick
glance with Nannie, and I had a feeling she'd be traveling abroad
with Mr. Lewisohn and staying in his villa at Cannes.

Everywhere there was evidence of Mr. Lewisohn and his devo-
tion. His car had driven us to New York, his gold-framed picture
was next to ours on her bedroom chest of drawers. The hothouse
gardenia and orange plants, the vases of towering yellow roses
mixed with white tuberoses, white fresia, and white stock.

Almost the minute we arrived in her sitting room, the phone
began to ring and Nannie announced that His Lordship was on the
phone.

"Can't wait for our Colony dinner tonight, Freddy dear!" said
Mother with such exaggerated enthusiasm that Charlie and I
smiled. "Yes, Morocco sounds *divine.* True regulars we've become. Who? The more the merrier. You know I *adore* new faces!"

"What will Madame wear this evening?" asked a sleek young
woman with a foreign accent, whom Mother introduced as her
personal maid, Elena, who would accompany her on her crossing
on the *Normandie.* Elena's arms overflowed with sumptuous
evening dresses, of taffeta and satin, chiffon and tulle, some black,
some white, some lavender, some silver, a few embroidered with

little diamondlike stars. Mother picked out a black satin one, and Elena, smiling in our direction, vanished into the bedroom again.

It was six o'clock in the evening. I went over to the lavishly festooned window and stared out. Mother's sixteenth-floor apartment faced Fifth Avenue. The rooftops of five-story townhouses were all that stood below, so there was no obstruction to the Central Park view, now glittering with warm lights. Across the park were the towering apartment houses of Central Park West, also glittering with warm lights. The winter winds blew outside, but our rooms were pleasantly steam-heated, fragrant with tuberose and gardenia. From Mother's bedroom drifted the intoxicating perfume of Moment Supreme of Guerlain, mixed with her face powder and bath oil.

"Rather a pretty apartment, wouldn't you say, my sweethearts?" said Mother, in a most animated mood, sipping a champagne cocktail. "Such fun to press a button and have room service day and night, and a concierge to get you theater tickets. By the by, what are you going to have for dinner?"

She took up the menu and started to read aloud all the tempting specialties from the cuisine downstairs. Every now and then the phone interrupted her, and she spoke briefly to Mrs. Moffet and Mr. Post, who I gathered were making up the El Morocco party that evening. Presently, our dinner was wheeled in over the thick carpeting, and two waiters prepared the entrees over a little flame, then asked us if we wished them to remain and serve dinner. Nannie smiled and said she could take care of everything and they bowed out of the room.

To make it a gala celebration, Mother turned on some dance music. On a Chinese coromandel low table was a portable white leather Gramophone from Liberty Music Shops, and Chauncey Grey's El Morocco band played the lilting refrain of "Won't You Change Partners and Dance with Me?" An appropriate melody, I thought, for I was certain many tall, white-tied admirers would cut in on Mother tonight in her lovely new black satin and lovely new hairdo. Her chestnut hair was now ash-blond and seemed fuller and fluffier. Her face was more carefully made up, and her nails were now lacquered a deep, mysterious Chinese red. I noticed the hollow in her cheeks.

Mother kept us company at the dinner table, asked us a flood of questions. How was Grandma, Steve, Daddy? When we told her the sad state our father was in, she looked mournful, and sighed, "Makes me sad to think he's suffering so. Wish there were something I could do."

"There isn't," said Nannie, cracking open the meringue shell that covered the vanilla ice cream.

Elena entered and said that Madame must prepare for dinner. Mother flung out of her chair, said please excuse her, but she would come down later on and give us a good-night kiss.

"So *thrilled* you're here," she said softly as we were led out the door by Nannie.

Mother had rented us a pretty suite of rooms down the hall from her. Maids were everywhere in the corridor. I'd never seen so many maids and valets and waiters. Like Mother's, our rooms were fresh and spotlessly clean, decorated in the voluptuous rococo style. Our bedsteads were cream-and-gilt upholstered in a charming red-and-white toile de Jouy, and so were the armchairs and curtains. Our cream chest of drawers had a marble top, in the Louis XV style, with gilded bronze handles, and the writing table was also cream and had gilded bronze feet at the end of its spindly legs. Cupid clocks chimed the hour, and naughty pink and blue cupids were painted on the gilded panels over the tall mirrors and doors.

Nannie got us ready for sleep. After a time she was sitting on the edge of my bed and answering a lot of questions. I was mystified by the sharp contrast the Westbury Hotel made with Grandma's house. Nannie reassured me that Grandma's house was a real home, whereas a hotel was merely an impersonal stopover.

"Then we'll move again?" I whispered.

Nannie's eyes clouded. She looked uncomfortable. "Your mother will be here in a moment. She'll tell you," she replied evasively.

"She's certainly changed," I persisted.

Nannie forced a laugh. "It took me a while to get used to her blond hair, but its becoming, I think." I could tell Nannie was as disturbed as I was, and uneasy.

I was asking Nannie if she was going to accompany Mother on the *Normandie,* and, right on cue, Mother appeared, striking in her black satin evening dress and smart cape of silver foxes about her shoulders. Two diamond-and-ruby clips flashed in her hair. Her large eyes appeared even larger, and she laughingly explained that it was the mascara she applied to her lashes.

She restlessly moved her tall, lean figure about for a moment, puffing on a cigarette in a holder and inhaling deeply. I knew she was uncomfortable and that there was something she didn't know how to tell us. Finally, she took a deep breath and blurted out that Charlie and I were being enrolled the following week at the Malcolm Gordon School, up in the highlands of the Hudson, where our ancestors had come from, so we'd feel right at home.

Once again she spoke with that exaggerated enthusiasm, telling us how beautiful the school was, fifty rolling acres and the schoolhouse itself, my dears, built in 1854, was a marvel of Hudson River Gothic architecture! There were also eighteen other charming and absolutely delicious little playmates for us, and Mr. and Mrs. Gordon were a most distinguished pair, rather like our grandparents, and we'd have tea with them every afternoon by the fire. Mr. Gordon would teach us Greek and prepare us for St. Mark's or St. Paul's.

For a moment, she sat on Charlie's bed, then she moved across to mine. We both stared at her with accusing, resentful eyes, but she gave us many hugs in her loving fashion, and continued to paint a dazzling portrait of our future home. When I asked her how long we'd be there, she replied with alacrity that it was only till summertime, then we'd all spend the holidays in Europe together. And Nannie would be there, too.

While Mother was talking, I fingered the long chiffon handkerchief tied to her platinum-and-diamond evening case. The fragile handkerchief was black and embroidered with her name, *Adele*, in slanted writing. A gardenia was pinned on the evening case, which she told us came from France, and was called a *minaudière*.

Finally, Mother floated out the door, blowing us kisses. There were tears in her eyes, and there was a tragic quality about her. The image she made lingered in my mind: the seductive black satin dress, the silver fox cape clinging to her shoulders, the diamond-and-ruby clips flashing on her ash-blond head, the gardenia pinned onto her platinum-and-diamond evening case, the heavily madeup eyes tinged with pain.

Just before I slipped off to sleep, the dull roar of the Madison Avenue bus came to me, then the shrill whistle of the doorman blowing for a taxi. Mother, of course, would ride in great style in Mr. Lewisohn's top-heavy black limousine, her knees covered with a robe of mink bellies decorated with mink tails. She'd pick up Mr. Lewisohn at his maisonette around the corner on Park Avenue, he'd embrace her, and they'd be carried down to the Colony Restaurant, sit on a corner banquette, and gaze adoringly at each other.

A stab of anger startled me. Mr. Lewisohn had stolen Mother away from me! Stolen her with his yellow roses and gardenia plants, diamond clips and silver fox coats, limousines and chauffeurs and personal maids. Stolen her with doormen, chambermaids, and room service, Elena, and the crossing on the fabulous oceangoing palace, *Normandie*. Mr. Lewisohn had bought Mother!

Even at that young age, I knew the power of money. Mr. Lewisohn would pay all our bills for the next thirteen years. It was too bad that every time I saw him I felt that stab of anger, especially when I saw Mother playing that false role for him, killing her true self.

Chapter Five

It was a winter afternoon in early January 1936 when Mother left us at the Gordon School. It was a stormy day, with a cruel wind coming off the Hudson and the river coated with ice. Mr. Lewisohn's black Packard limousine, or town car as they were called in those long-ago days, progressed slowly and carefully over the slippery roads. Peters, the chauffeur, cursed the weather often, and the heavy iron chains covering the white sidewalls made a loud crunching sound. Despite these heavy chains, which symbolized a kind of prison to me, the grand car often skidded. Peters would growl, like my father's dog, and wrench the wheel in the opposite direction.

After an hour and a half of this grueling ordeal, as Mother called it, we ground to a stop. Mother leaned forward and peered out the side window, which was covered in black leather like that of a carriage. A sign informed us we were at last at our destination, Garrison. Mother said she recognized the gray stone church, St. Phillips in the Highlands, and the adjoining graveyard.

Mother rapped on the glass partition that separated us from Peters. "It's just a little farther," she said, trying to keep her voice cheerful.

Our recent farewell with Nannie had brought on a flood of tears, and my throat still had a lump in it. A feeling of dread hung over me; I sat, unusually still, by Mother's side. She, too, was ominously still.

A moment later we viewed a sign on Route 9, "Malcolm Gordon School" it read, and a gray fieldstone fence marked the entrance.

"We're here," said Mother, in a queer, strangled voice.

The heavy, twelve-cylinder Packard started down the long, narrow drive banked with spruce and pines, their branches drooping with snow. It had snowed the day before, and the low, forbidding sky looked as if another storm were on the way.

Suddenly the thick-walled, three-story schoolhouse appeared through the mist. The initial sight of this Gothic manse brought a chill to my heart. It seemed like the punishing institute of *Jane Eyre*. When Peters stepped out in his high-laced boots and opened the door for us, the white countryside seemed strangely still. As we moved up the steps of the old-fashioned porte-cochere, a solitary crow screeched. From far away came the wail of the Grand Central train clattering along the river track.

Mr. and Mrs. Gordon and their son, David, received us in the warm library off the hall. It had high ceilings and fine moldings, and a fire was burning cheerily in a black marble fireplace. As at Grandma's, there were portraits on the walls, beautifully bound leather books in the shelves, and stiff antique Chippendale chairs. And like Grandma, Mrs. Gordon was a handsome and imposing woman with a no-nonsense manner—a lady of the old school, grayhaired and about the same age as the czarina.

Mr. Malcolm Gordon was small and athletic, with neat sandy mustache and eyes. He was dressed in a blue blazer, with his coat of arms on the breast pocket, and gray flannels—the uniform I would soon wear. He smiled at Charlie and me, puffing every now and then on his pipe.

His wife gazed at Mother's figure critically, sniffing the air around her as if it were polluted—Mother sported a great deal of flowery Guerlain perfume, and as she stood by the warmth of the fire, the jasmine fragrance permeated the room.

And I could see Mrs. Gordon was shocked by Mother's appearance. At that time of the Great Depression, American ladies of the upper class did not dye their hair and wear clothes from Paris; and only film stars, celebrities, and flamboyant heiresses of the international set wore mink coats. It was a time of pulling in and dressing down; one certainly was not supposed to *look* rich. Not good form, you know. Far better if Mother had worn old clothes and driven up in a battered station wagon as Mrs. Rockefeller and other parents did.

Through the tall window, Mrs. Gordon glanced suspiciously at the Lewisohn limousine and the Lewisohn chauffeur stamping angrily about in the snow. I did not care for her knowing smile. On the other hand, Malcolm Gordon and his tall, handsome son, David, whom I would soon call Mr. David, beamed at Mother's alluring figure, veiled face, and blond curls. Ham Gregg, a fellow schoolmate, was to call Mother "the essence of glamour," and obviously the headmaster and his son felt the same. Suddenly, watching Mr. David paying court to Mother, a fantasy was born in my mind: He would marry Mother and I'd have a real father whom I could look up to. That would fix Mr. Lewisohn, all right!

Mrs. Gordon stared disapprovingly at Mother's voluminous mink and the heavy shawl collar that was turned up to frame her face.

"Won't you take it off, Mrs. Van Rensselaer?" Mother carelessly flung the fur over a chair. She stood with her back to the open fire, warming her chilled figure.

Mrs. Gordon asked Mother if she cared for history, as this spot was famous for historical happenings. Mother nodded her head graciously, and Mrs. Gordon explained that once, long ago, all the land about us had belonged to the Philipse family, who also had a manor like the Van Rensselaers, but not so large. She added that the house itself was a summer place for the Philipses.

"How fascinating!" said Mother, with that phony enthusiasm.

"Grandma said we were Dutch boys long ago," I piped up, and Mrs. Gordon stared at me and inquired where I had picked up that foreign accent.

Mother smiled. "We lived in Florence a few years, and both boys speak Italian quite fluently."

"Really?" intoned the imposing lady. "And I dare say you took them to the Pitti and Uffizi every day to study the paintings."

"Naturally," said Mother, staring back at her, not intimidated at all.

Presently, Mr. Gordon explained to us that he had been a master at St. Paul's School for twenty-seven years, had taught hockey there, and had even coached the famed Hoby Baker. He showed us a picture of the golden-haired athlete who died so tragically young in World War I and told Charlie and me that we'd soon be playing hockey in his own skating rink. Mr. Gordon was standing quite close to Mother, feeling strong and manly next to Mother's frail and feminine silhouette. She coughed a bit, delicately, and he asked her if the smoke bothered her.

"Good gracious, no," she replied, smiling at him in a sort of flirtatious way, as she did with every man. She pulled out a gold cigarette case and Mr. David an agile and muscular fellow, sprang to her with a light.

Mrs. Gordon's eyes narrowed and she asked me if we'd like to see our rooms upstairs. Mother said she'd stay behind and discuss last-minute details with the two Gordon gentlemen.

Mrs. Gordon led us up the long, dark staircase to the second floor, showed us the large, drafty dormitory, definitely Spartan in feeling, with six beds and six chests-of-drawers, and told us this would be our new home. It was a far cry from Grandma's cultivated clutter and the splendors of the Westbury.

Looking at me with pity, Mrs. Gordon remarked that I was such a tiny little fellow, that I would be the youngest boy at school. I smiled up at her hopefully, eager to please. In a few weeks I would be her favorite; indeed, I was the boy closest to her heart for the five and a half years I boarded there.

When we returned to the warmth of the library, Peters's bulk was standing there, stomping his high leather boots. "We'll have to return to New York, Mrs. Van Rensselaer; Mr. Lewisohn will be worried."

At the mention of Mr. Lewisohn's name, the two Gordon men looked embarrassed and Mrs. Gordon shocked to her core. In this WASP bastion, Jews were unknown. Many Jews at the time changed their last names, concealed their backgrounds, even became Catholics. Years later Mr. Lewisohn's daughter, Eve Palmer, who became my dear friend and confidante, confessed that she had been brought up in the Episcopal faith, even baptized at birth with Episcopal holy water. She had been sent to snobbish, restricted WASP schools where a nasty little girl told her who she *really* was.

For the Gordons it was unthinkable that a Mrs. Van Rensselaer should be the companion of a Mr. Lewisohn, and their liaison marked me as wrong. I was considered different.

Mother's farewell was concluded through a mist of tears. I felt strangely numb; the reality of the situation had not yet dawned on me. Mother would never abandon us! As if in a dream, she knelt down before me and wrapped me in her arms.

"Good-bye, dearest Philip," I heard her say, and I clung to her, not wanting to let go. She told me not to cry or she would, too, and promised to send me a raft of postcards and souvenirs from the *Normandie* and from Paris. She started out the door but then returned to hug and kiss us once more. Then she was gone.

I heard the great car start, then watched it slowly move ahead, the iron chains making that fearful grinding noise on the icy road. I stood there by the hall window, watching the black car vanish down the drive until the oval window in the rear was a tiny speck on the horizon. Tears streamed down my face. I clung to Mrs. Gordon and cried deep, wrenching sobs. "You'll see your mother again at Easter time," comforted Mrs. Gordon. I wiped the tears away with my hand.

Later, Mr. and Mrs. Gordon tucked me into bed; windows were opened and lights turned out. In the darkness I lay awake on the cot and stared at the ceiling. My dormitory room faced the Hudson, and I heard the haunting echo of an endless freight train clattering over the river track. Mother had abandoned me, as her mother had done her. Mr. Lewisohn's money had indeed triumphed. How was I to survive on my own? For many years I felt that fearful sense of abandonment.

Mother stayed on in Europe. We wrote her care of the Duke and Duchess de Nemours in Paris and received weekly postcards. They became our most treasured possessions. Receiving them reassured us that we had not lost Mother forever.

Once I showed Mrs. Gordon a postcard from the Ritz Hotel in Paris. It pictured some splendidly dressed party goers in evening attire having a good time in the Ritz garden that looked like Versailles. One of the women looked rather similar to Mother, sumptuous in a fur cape and a satin evening dress with diamond clips in her hair.

"Mother has the same diamond clips, Mrs. Gordon," I said proudly.

"Does she?" replied Mrs. Gordon meaningfully.

"And doesn't she have the same pretty smile?" Mrs. Gordon said nothing, and I rushed on, saying that Mother also had heaps of friends who loved to go to parties and dancing at El Morocco. Mrs. Gordon gave me a severe look.

"Just remember, dear boy," she said in authoritative tones, "that there are far more important things in the world than a pretty smile, fancy clothes, and fashionable, idle people going to parties. A life devoted to pleasure is draining and self-centered. Pity the people who live like this. They are incapable of true love. And love is the most important thing in the world."

"Yes, Mrs. Gordon," I swallowed.

"Remember the school motto: *Non Nobis, Sed Aliis*—Not for Ourselves, But for Others. Remember that, dear Philip, and become a strong, manly, and moral human being. Also remember, you must look after your mother."

"Yes, Mrs. Gordon."

She also reminded me, like Grandma, that the original Van Rensselaers who came from Amsterdam were wealthy, highly respected people and they were the *first* to arrive in the New Land. They had not arrived on a cattle boat, nor were they immigrants. I had a lot to live up to; my name stood for something good, something honorable, for the old principles and standards that I must live by and uphold as a *true* Van Rensselaer.

"Yes, Mrs. Gordon," I invariably replied with my courtly manners, despite the fact that the frivolous and amorous goings-on at the Villa Corne D'Or, Mr. Lewisohn's pink-marble palace in Cannes, had made an indelible impression on me. Had hooked me for good!

Chapter Six

In the summer of 1936, Charlie and I had a dazzling time with Mother on the Riviera. Daily we lounged on canvas mattresses and oiled our bodies with Bain de Soleil beside Mr. Lewisohn's enormous blue-tiled pool, while white-coated butlers shook up frothy cocktails in the bar and dance music played on the Gramophone. Russian grand dukes like Dimitri, and Austrian counts like Ludi Salm, great ladies' men with the record to prove it, took us to lunch at Eden Roc in Cap d'Antibes. We water-skied behind a powerful Chris-Craft speedboat, the Honorable Charles Winn took us up in his private plane, and we often lunched and dined in the gilt and chandeliered dining room of the Hotel de Paris in Monte Carlo. Eve Lewisohn said we were so snobbish we'd ride only in a Rolls!

Several times Mr. Lewisohn allowed us to accompany him to the Palm Beach Casino, half a mile from his villa at the end of the Croisette, and we were given chips to play on the chemin de fer tables. We watched Mother dance the rhumba and were exhausted.

Everywhere we were exposed to the game of love; the most exciting flirtations were carried on beneath our very noses: in speedboats, casinos, hotel lobbies, planes, tennis courts, on the red rocks of Eden Roc, at Lanvin, and Hermes, and Van Cleef and Arpels. And most definitely at twilight in the Terrace Bar of the Carlton overlooking the jasmine-scented Mediterranean, where singing Charlie played the piano.

Yes, Mother and Mr. Lewisohn's friends *were* fashionable, beautifully dressed, and idle people, some bearing the most illustrious names of England, France, and Italy. Despite their impressive titles, some were even penniless, but one and all had style. Definitely, all were drained, as Mrs. Gordon had said, by an excess of love and infatuations.

Perhaps they were to be pitied for their self-indulgent, narcissistic ways. However, I'm here to tell you, *they had one hell of a good time.* Parties and love affairs were a way of life for them, as were business careers and hard work for the rest of the world.

The seductive palm trees and pink oleanders of the Mediterranean sure beat the scrub pines and oaks along the Hudson! Dr. Chorley, our minister at the Church of St. Phillips in the Highlands, had fine organ recitals and choir practice, and I was moved, often to tears, by Mr. Gordon's daily reading of the evening vespers. The words afforded me much solace, but they couldn't hold a candle to the lively strains of the "Lambeth Walk" and "Dipsy Doodle," those catchy tunes that never left my head at the Villa Corne D'Or.

To please Mrs. Gordon, I had become a thoughtful and responsible student, that paragon known as "a good boy." Unfortunately, the other part of me sprang passionately alive when I stepped off Le Train Bleu at Cannes, smelled the sunburned bodies on the beach, saw the vivid stretch of Mediterranean blue dotted with white yachts, and entered the gates of that vast pleasure dome known as the Villa Corne D'Or.

As soon as I saw all those gorgeous, almost naked bodies lolling about the enormous pool, flirting, drinking cocktails, and discussing last night's escapades at the casinos, I switched into the role of the bad little boy. Oh, polite and sweet to be sure, but devilish, greedy, cunning, listening to the gossip and spreading it to get attention. My favorite role was that of a winged cupid shooting a love dart into a sex-dulled pair.

Eleanor Young, in exotic silk beach pajamas, arrived at the villa one day with New York art dealer Carroll Carstairs. She was the most beautiful 1936 debutante, from Newport and Palm Beach, and I became her confidant during the two weeks she was there. I listened to her problems and helped her out so successfully with a complicated love affair that she rewarded me with a star sapphire ring I'd had my eye on. I often reflected that my keen perception could earn me an honest living when I was grown up, but I didn't tell Mrs. Gordon that!

Ravishing Lady Ann Mappin rewarded me with a wooden horse whose limbs moved, all because I helped make her realize that her infatuation for the Russian tennis pro at the Carlton, whose bulging muscles obsessed her, was leading nowhere. Especially since I knew, and she knew, that what she *really* wanted was a Mr. Lewisohn or an abdicated king. At this time, Wallis Warfield Simpson was hiding out from the press in a nearby villa, waiting till she could wed the man who had given up the throne of the largest empire in the world for her. But Mrs. Simpson wasn't half as tempting a dish as Lady Mappin. Milady predictably ended her days as rich Lady Rootes, beautiful and pampered 'til the end.

As the years progressed, Mrs. Gordon must have sensed my dual nature, had an inkling of my chameleon personality. She often wrote me warning letters at Cannes, saying that I must not take on the colors of everyone just because they were charming and pretty, that the devil wore strange and baffling disguises, and that I must remain armed with that strong moral code she had given me. She also said I must be true to myself.

Actually, I did not have a clue who "myself" was. Besides, it was simpler to be like Mother and not to think too much. Simpler to lose myself in the dramas of the Villa Corne D'Or, or the dramas of novels like *Gone With the Wind* and *Vanity Fair*, my favorites.

Mr. Gordon was astonished that I had read all the fiction books in his copious library. I don't think he understood why I devoured those books so hungrily. I was not like other boys, any more than Mother was like other mothers. I was different. With little effort, I managed to give an impression of being a carefree, outgoing, bright little fellow. But then again, playing a role came easy to me. I *was* like Mother.

As for love, I had the notion that love meant selling something

precious you had, like good looks and charm and energy, and
getting well paid for them. My role models, besides Mother and
her friends, were Becky Sharp, Scarlett O'Hara, and Wallis Simpson, born schemers all. They went after what they wanted—and
what's more, they got it.

Money was the trump card; that's what *really* was important. For
all my acting so wide-eyed, I was not innocent at all. Mother was,
unfortunately. Everyone at the villa said she was gentle and wonderfully sweet-tempered, but hopeless in the ways of the world.
The Victorian parlor of those two maiden ladies Mary and Ida Hoyt
had not prepared her for a reckless career in the competitive playground of the Riviera.

The end of the Thirties was our most extravagant period. Money
seemed to slip through our fingers like water, and I used to hum
"We're in the Money" as I swanked through the marble halls of the
Pierre, the Waldorf Towers, and the Villa Corne D'Or—enhanced,
of course, by a retinue of servants and Mr. Lewisohn's Packard that
carried us to fashionable restaurants, the theater, or the World's
Fair on Long Island. I liked to think we were little princes of the
realm.

As I walked breezily but somewhat anxiously through those
beautiful stage settings, I played the role of Fred Astaire. In my
daydreams, I saw Mother whirling about with him, bending and
dipping to the Carioca or the Continental, dressed in feathers and
furs, and I gave myself up to fantasies in which *he* was my father.

Eve Lewisohn Palmer saw through me and my facade. A lonely
and unhappy childhood had made her perceptive, and she was well
versed in Freud and Jung. She begged and implored Mother to
keep us away from the corrupting atmosphere of her father's pleasure palace in Cannes. She said we should be learning some trade
to prepare us for earning our living, training for a career.

"How clever you are, Eve," Mother would say, vaguely.

She also begged Mother to find a real home for us. It was neither
healthy nor harmonious, she said, to lead a permanent transient
existence in hotel suites that changed every holiday. We needed
continuity and a sense of family life.

"You're so right, Eve," Mother would say, again vaguely.

She also pleaded with Mother not to allow us to sign for cash at the concierge's desk at the Pierre or the Waldorf Towers, or we would not understand the value of money and how hard it was to come by.

Mother would listen intently, and nod her head. "So true, Eve," she'd say, vaguely.

But hotel life was addictive. Hotel life was easy, carefree; there were no housekeeping problems, no servants to hire or fire, no dinner parties to plan, no decorator to change the decor, no laundry to send out, no grocery shopping. Hotel life enabled you to be a pampered child—or adult—whose every whim was gratified by the pressing of a button or picking up of the telephone. Mother was drained by her nightlife; she did not have the energy to cope with the day's boring details, which she called "the tyranny of trivia."

Plus, Mother had a nature as restless as Mr. Lewisohn's, and hotel life enabled her to fly off here and there without much planning and certainly no stress. Elena was there to pack for her, and Eric, Mr. Lewisohn's valet, took care of all the tiresome travel arrangements and reservations. All Mother had to do was have her hair waved, her nails done, buy a few more dresses or shoes or hats, and she was off on a fresh adventure. "Free as a bird," she would say.

There were always trunks in Mother's hotel bedrooms, often lined up out in the hall. When she departed for the intoxicating casino-nightclub world of the Riviera's Gold Coast, these massive trunks were carried to the basement by porters straining under their weight.

Life with Mother was one of extremes—from the Spartan-spiritual world of the Malcolm Gordons in the highlands of the Hudson, to the narcissistic playground world of European resorts. Our transient existence confused me. I often had the sickening feeling of falling. I got the same falling sensation when the mirrored elevator picked us up on the fortieth floor, closed its doors and plummeted us down to the street level, often with no stop. The palms of my hands were invariably wet when I stepped, dizzily, into the lobby.

Ocean liners sometimes disturbed me, too. I told everyone at school that Charlie and I were booked on the fabulous French liner *Normandie* for June 1, 1938. Avery Rockefeller, an older boy, said,

"Make hay while the sun shines." I didn't want to think what that meant.

Later, out at sea on the vast eighty-thousand-ton vessel, I lay down to nap before lunch. I closed my eyes and saw a pair of lethal torpedoes racing toward us under the water. Then the ship exploded, broke in two, and it was a catastrophe like the *Lusitania!* People were screaming and I was drowning, immersed in water, struggling, gasping for breath. I awakened in my stateroom filled with terror, my heart racing, drenched in sweat.

But the transatlantic ocean liners, those grand floating palaces, were very much a part of our lives. In 1937, Charlie and I raced over to Europe on the *Ile de France* and returned on the Italian liner *Rex* by the southern route, passing through Gibraltar and then across the clear blue horizon to New York.

In 1938 we crossed on *Normandie*, whose only rival in speed was Cunard's *Queen Mary*, and then returned on the sleek *Conte di Savoia*, stopping at Cannes and then gliding on through the Straits of Gibraltar.

My favorite liner was the Edwardian monarch *Aquitania*, a *Titanic*-type beauty, faded somewhat, with past glories behind her.

All these splendid ships were described in the feminine gender, as *she*. Perhaps that was one of the reasons they reminded me of Mother: sleek, beautiful, filled with trunks, suitcases, and hordes of people. Always moving till they were too old. And in a state of limbo, detached from the rest of the world.

The most exciting year of our youth was 1939. Charlie was thirteen, and I was eleven. We had a greater capacity for enjoyment— God knows there was plenty to enjoy—and the pace of our life had accelerated.

The very day after Commencement Exercises at Malcolm Gordon's, we were racing across town from the Waldorf Towers to the West Fiftieth Street piers on the Hudson River. Mother and Mr. Lewisohn sat in the rear, with Charlie and I in the jump seats trying not to stare at the obscene ridges of fat on Peters's neck.

Mother was dressed in a dashing traveling costume, an intricately tailored yet simple gray flannel suit from Captain Molyneux's skilled hands, up-pointed lapels, a cream silk blouse with bowknot at the throat, and a mass of bracelets dangling with ruby, diamond, and sapphire charms. A black lizard handbag and black lizard pumps completed the ensemble.

Mother was thirty-four, still fresh and youthful. Her face and figure still caused a stir, and the Paris suit revealed there wasn't a break in her pencil-slim line. No ugly lumps or bulges for her! It was an obsession with her to remain thin as a rail; she knew that clothes looked elegant only on such a frame.

Mr. Lewisohn begged her to eat more, but she'd laugh and say that the stomach was only as large as a fist, and the most people ate like swine, giving them those repulsive potbellies and gross behinds.

Mother exerted extreme effort of will about her figure, but somehow you sensed that her whole persona was very precariously maintained. She was overly high-strung, complained of the jitters, and her hand shook when she lit a cigarette.

Mr. Lewisohn, almost sixty, looked more than ever like a drowsy Buddha. His hooded lids kept closing over his eyes. Of course, like Mother, he was wonderfully turned out, with a fresh red carnation in the buttonhole of his expensive and deftly tailored gabardine suit, a cream silk shirt from Sulka, and a matching tie and handkerchief of yellow silk foulard from Charvet. When you have this bandbox elegance, your clothes help conceal an unmentionable state of weariness and give you a lift.

"Wasn't it too sensational, watching Larry and Peggy do that rhumba?" Mother was saying vivaciously.

"My little girl was pretty good, too," said Mr. Lewisohn in his slow, tired voice.

"Darling, you're too sweet," laughed Mother. He treated her like a child, often calling her his "little girl," which embarrassed me no end. She raced on about all the glorious activities in store for them on the Riviera and in Paris. Mr. Lewisohn perked up.

As for me and Charlie, Mr. Lewisohn treated us with indifference. But he was a good provider and often pulled out his blue lizard billfold with gold edges, handing us a twenty-dollar bill. My eyes would linger on the roll of greenbacks, some fifties and some hundreds. I wanted them all.

Suddenly, we pulled up before the bustle and activity of the Cunard Line pier. A roar of voices greeted us as we moved through the shed. Many passengers stared at Mother with interest; she was quite lovely, and she carried her five feet eight inches with pride and dignity. Just from the look of her, you knew she was someone. Yes, Mother gave good value for the money, and I could see Mr. Lewisohn was gratified by the stares as we made our way to the mammoth ship.

Trotting behind us was the usual entourage. As we crossed the gangway and stepped onto the promenade deck of the *Queen Mary*, several strapping sportsmen gazed appreciatively at Mother, and I wondered who her summertime romance would be this year. Anything was possible on the Riviera! It was a pity that Lord Louis Mountbatten and Averell Harriman were taken; I'd heard Mother say these two gentlemen were her ideal of perfection.

A fleet of stewards and porters greeted us, and we were led to our cabins. In a short time we were steaming majestically past the Statue of Liberty, New York's skyline receding in a summer haze. The peeping of the little tugs, the screeching of the gulls, and the roar of voices all faded behind us; blessed peace reigned. We were outward bound, luxuriously ensconced in our staterooms. Dimly, pleasantly, came the whoosh of the waves against the hull and the throbbing pistons and turbines below, driving us with all possible speed to foreign shores.

Peters was too old to accompany us on these voyages. At Cherbourg, a smart French chauffeur met us, whisking us easily through customs officials who treated Mother and Mr. Lewisohn like royalty. Then we were off to the most beautiful city in the world.

If Paris was the most beautiful city in the world, then the Ritz was surely the most beautiful hotel. Right on the Place Vendôme, formerly an eighteenth-century mansion, its cream-and-gilded rooms glittered with crystal wall lights and crystal chandeliers, Turkish red carpets, and blue Chinese temple vases.

Mother was grateful for these civilized rooms. She was never jaded or world-weary like so many of her friends, and her eagerness and enthusiasm were infectious.

That evening we boarded the sleeping cars of Le Train Bleu, took supper in the dining car, and retired for the night in our plush compartments. The next morning I pulled up the blind and there, spread out before me, was a world of enchantment, like a Cézanne landscape. A grove of gnarled, silvery olive trees, orange-tile-roofed houses, balustraded French windows and balconies. The verdant tropical shrubbery of cactus, palms, and orange trees, all outlined against the purplish mountains of the Alpes Maritimes. The sun felt hot on my hand.

As we started over to the waiting car, a flower stall caught Mother's eye, or perhaps it was the dignity of the decrepit old vendor. He wore the Legion of Honor, won in the Great War, he told us, and had a welcoming smile. Mother bought an enormous bouquet of white stock and pink carnations, freshly picked that morning, and handed him a lavish roll of franc notes, and he gave her God's blessing.

We settled into the rear of the long Packard, and Mother pressed the fragrant flowers under her nose with girlish cries. Mr. Lewisohn chuckled, amused by her intense eagerness. Mother was moved by the vendor's blessing and said, "It's an omen that something wonderful is going to happen." Her face, bathed in the flowers, was radiant.

Mother's hunch was right. Two days later, tall, suave André Lord was staying at the Corne D'Or, and Mother was gazing at him with that same desperate hope and longing with which she looked at every handsome man. My most glamorous summer on the Riviera had commenced.

Chapter Seven

Where but on the Riviera could you find Russian grand dukes, notorious American heiresses squandering their fortunes to find true love, the king of Sweden, the king of the Belgians, the maharaja of Kapurthala, Somerset Maugham, and adventurous playboys and playgirls, some bearing historic titles dating back to Charlemagne or Edward the Confessor?

If yachting was your preoccupation, you could party aboard the *Cutty Sark* of the duke of Westminster or *die Schwester Anna*, Daisy Fellowes's yacht. If you didn't make these dizzying heights, perhaps you could manage to get on board the *Alva*, the white, oceangoing steam yacht of William K. Vanderbilt and his wife, Rose. Madame-Queen Vanderbilt had a boyishly slender figure like Adele's, lived on soda biscuits, oysters, champagne, with an occasional grapefruit or half an orange. Adele's diet was much the same, give or take a few clams and some tiny mounds of cottage cheese.

Mr. Vanderbilt's sister was the legendary Consuelo, now Madame Balsam, and happy as a clam after her forced marriage to the duke of Marlborough. For twenty years she lived in the palace of

Blenheim until true love, in the form of a dashing French aviator, rescued her and made her a happy woman in France. Like all Vanderbilts, she had a passion for building, and her house in Eze, called Lou-Sueil, was predictably palatial. My World War II hero, Churchill, often stayed with her and painted there.

In Antibes frolicked the "most romantic couple of the century," the Duke and Duchess of Windsor. Wallis Simpson felt the Riviera "had a cheap air about it," so she did not choose to marry the former King of England there. Nevertheless, after successfully capturing His Majesty, she chose to party there nonstop.

Michael Arlen, author of *The Green Hat*, and his wife, the splendid Greek Countess Atalanta Mercatti, had a villa in Cannes. They were often at the Corne D'Or for buffet lunches or bridge afternoons. Mr. Arlen was the best dressed man I've ever seen, small and thin, with a waxed mustache. He looked rather like Adolph Menjou, surely the most urbane man on the silver screen.

The Corne D'Or rather resembled the Frick House on Fifth Avenue. It was a neoclassic, eighteenth-century-style palace built in the Gilded Age. The villa's twelve-car garage, hundred-foot-long swimming pool, and Fragonard-type rose gardens all helped to make it a perfect background for a never-ending gala. Roses, by the way, were especially magnificent at the Corne D'Or, because of its proximity to the sea. Apricot-colored tea roses were in abundance.

The rooms of the villa were large and beautifully proportioned, with a network of gilded moldings lining these rooms, silk-covered Louis XVI chairs, and a triple layer of silk curtains draped over French doors and windows. People often remarked it was like the Ritz Hotel, having its same towering mirrors, marble dining rooms, marble floors, vast marble halls, and sweeping staircases decorated with curly, black wrought-iron balustrades.

People also remarked that staying at the villa was like being a guest at the Ritz, because so many people were forever coming and going. Mr. Lewisohn loved to entertain. He was fortunate that he had his youngest daughter, the pretty Eve, to take over the tedious details of running the villa like clockwork.

It was to Eve we owed the scrumptious lunches and dinners, the servants pressing our clothes and doing our laundry at a moment's notice, the elaborate stationery and postcards in our desks, the fresh flowers and latest books in our rooms, the use of the car and chauffeur to take us to Eden Roc or the Hotel de Paris in Monte Carlo, in case we craved a change of scene, as most of the guests did.

Once, a few cars took us all down the coast to St. Tropez, then a simple, undiscovered fishing village with Colette as its only celebrity. That was certainly a startling contrast to the Belle Epoque extravagances of the winter and summer casinos of Monte Carlo, and that Arabian Nights fantasy down the road from us called the Palm Beach Casino. That voluptuous hangout seemed like a bordello, there were so many amorous couples. Mother dancing was a sight to behold.

An air of grandiosity and decaying wealth lingered over the Corne D'Or. Despite all of Eve Lewisohn's efforts to keep me untainted, I picked up a lethal whiff. Ruined fortunes and waste seemed rather heady stuff to me, and later I thought that Scott Fitzgerald recklessly squandering his talent was romantic.

Eve must have sensed what was happening in my head. That summer Charlie and I were banished to the little folly at the far end of the property called the Chateau d'Amour and told to develop inner resources. In our miniature castle with its poetic turret, we whiled the hours away gorging on chocolate soufflés and salmon mousse, endlessly playing honeymoon bridge.

My favorite pastime was lying on the cool, flowered linen sheets that smelled of fresh ironing and verbena sachet and turning the pages of Jane Austen's novels. I often hoped that André Lord's figure would materialize into Darcy's clothes and we'd all live happily ever after in his country house surrounded by rolling fields, dogs, and horses—a real home. I also dreamed of being showered with ropes of pearls and egg-sized emeralds, indulging in endless buying orgies of eighteenth-century French pieces of furniture, signed by the master ebonistes, of course.

Despite Eve and her father constantly telling us to, "Run along, boys," we lounged by the pool at high noon, watched the ladies' half-naked breasts, listened to gossip, and hung over the afternoon bridge tables making pests of ourselves.

Early mornings were my most treasured times at the villa. This was the only time Mother and I were able to be alone—the only time she wasn't playing that false role of court jester or siren to amuse Mr. Lewisohn.

Early mornings in Cannes were lyrical. These hours were enchantment to me. At eight, the great pink villa lay shuttered and still. The rose gardens with their basins of water were empty. The large awninged terrace off the drawing room, graced with tubs of blue and white hydrangeas, was deserted. The air was cool and had the exhilarating freshness of the nearby sea. The hot Mediterranean sunshine burned through the fragrant eucalyptus and umbrella pines.

Mr. Lewisohn and his guests were never visible till noon, with Mother the sole exception. Always she was awake at eight-thirty and having her breakfast in bed at nine. Not much of a breakfast at that, the usual half grapefruit or orange, a thermos of black coffee, and cigarettes. Mother told us we could visit her after nine.

So at exactly nine, Charlie and I would race across the gravel paths through the roses surrounded by boxwood traceries, through the front door, up the grand staircase and down a long corridor. We'd knock softly on her door; Mr. Lewisohn's room adjoined hers, so for once we were quiet as mice.

"Entrez, entrez," came Mother's vibrant voice, and then we'd fling ourselves onto her large bed.

Mother would be sitting up in bed, reading the Paris *Herald* or frowning over the crossword puzzle. She adored doing these puzzles, and she was good at them, gifted as she was with a plentiful vocabulary. Elena would be patiently pressing some flowered chiffon dress Mother would wear in the evening or the white linen dress or sharkskin shorts she'd wear to lunch. Sometimes, when Mother had won at the casino, she'd tell us to go through her evening case and take some franc notes.

Mother seemed rather quiet and calm these early mornings, although as the day progressed, with crowds of people, she became overly animated, nervous, and distracted. She'd ask us what we were doing, how our French lessons were progressing, and had we written the Gordons or Aunt Bessie Ellsworth, who regularly sent us postcards or letters. Then she'd go back to her puzzle, sometimes asking our aid in a word.

The view from Mother's windows was spectacular. The villa occupied an enviable position in Cannes, situated right on La Croisette, the main boulevard of the resort, which ran along the sea. Just right of the villa stretched the line of great hotels: the Miramar, the Martinez, the Carlton, the Grand. In front of them was the yellow expanse of beach, La Plage. Brightly colored flags and pennants fluttered in the ocean breeze, and white sailing yachts skimmed across the azure blue. For me, the scene was like a Raoul Dufy, Mother's bedroom like a Matisse with its arched balustraded windows and flowers, and the bedroom interior, a Vuillard.

At noon, Eric would knock and enter, announcing that Mr. Lewisohn was up and feeling well or not well, according to the day. Mother would fling back the silk-and-lace bed covers and tell us she must dress and that she'd meet us in a second down at the pool.

Charlie and I would move down the marble stairs, remarking on Mother's astounding energy. She never returned to the villa till three in the morning, or later, and yet was always up by eight-thirty. And after lunch she usually rushed onto the Chris-Craft and water-skied over to Eden Roc, or sometimes two hours away to Monte Carlo.

Mother was an indefatigable water-skier. At one Monte Carlo gala she raced by the Summer Casino on water skis, dressed in evening dress and flanked by two men holding torches. One of the gentlemen was the athletic, bronzed Captain Darcy Rutherford, another great friend of Adele's and a famous seducer on the Gold Coast from Monte Carlo to Marseilles. Milady Ann told me he had flawless technique, whatever that meant, and sighed deeply.

"Do you think Mummy looks well?" I asked for the hundredth time.

"Why do you keep harping on her looks?" Charlie asked, impatiently.

"It's important that she look well," I said.

"How come?" Charlie inquired with nonchalance.

"Well," I said, "if she doesn't look well, then it's curtains for us."

A little later the villa's guests would parade down the steps with boisterous good mornings and head for the dressing rooms. The ladies disrobed on one side of the bar, and the gentlemen on the other.

Already, Carl was shaking up a fresh round of delicious cocktails, the ice clattering against the crystal shaker. The Gramophone was playing "Lambeth Walk," and Milady Ann was showing André Lord how to do the new dance craze.

Mr. Lewisohn sat under a round canvas umbrella. His body in bathing costume was not appetizing: gray flesh hung off his arms, his legs were spindly, and his pectorals sagged. Eve's husband, Paul Palmer, sat next to our host, staring disagreeably at the *Wall Street Journal*. Paul was a big, handsome fellow, from an old New England family, with a strong intellectual bent. He'd worked for H. L. Mencken, started *The American Mercury*, and his enormous house in Ridgefield, Connecticut, was crawling with every famous writer you could think of.

Paul himself attracted the fair sex like flies, and he and his father-in-law shared many young damsels. The only time I ever saw Mr. Lewisohn really enjoy himself was when Paul was around; he had a dry, pungent wit that was irresistible.

Mother always did a dozen turns back and forth the hundred-foot-long pool, intent on her exercise. Then she'd fling off her bathing cap, shake her curls, lie down on a canvas mattress, and attend to her smooth golden tan, sipping a champagne cocktail, or a Pimms Cup, or a Vermouth Cassis.

If Mr. Lewisohn looked bored, she'd gaily challenge him to a game of backgammon. Charlie and I would watch their every move on the board, eager to pick up some tips. Now and then Mr. Lewisohn would grin at his "little girl" and possessively touch her hand. His hands were soft and old, ugly with liver spots. I shuddered to think of those hands touching Mother's flesh.

André Lord was always in fine form, the perfect guest. He had a physique like Hercules, and Continental sophistication. Mother was head over heels about André and he with her. I often caught them gazing starry-eyed at each other. Often, they'd vanish in his convertible to Eden Roc or wherever, and sometimes Charlie and I were invited along on these amorous excursions. The wind blew Mother's hair about as she laughed radiantly, sitting next to her beloved Adonis.

That summer I fervently prayed to God that André would be walking up the aisle with Mother, she in a long white dress with a veil over her head, and he in a morning coat and striped pants.

Someone like Malcolm Gordon would marry them, then we'd all shower rice over them, and they'd vanish into the sunset the way couples did in Hollywood films.

Our lavish days on the Gold Coast were bound to end. After the fireworks display on the fourteenth of July, there were ominous portents that we would soon be banished to a more wholesome ambience, to use Eve Lewisohn Palmer's hateful expression. If she'd had her way, Charlie and I would have been in convict's garb on a chain gang in Mississippi.

We were greatly looking forward to the month of August when Mr. Lewisohn took the whole villa to Monte Carlo. That Hotel de Paris was as much a bordello as the Palm Beach Casino. Naughty men and women behind every potted palm, to the strains of tea music of Strauss or Lehár. Champagne corks exploding. Sounds of love, like a passionate aria from *Norma, Turandot,* or *Aïda.*

One afternoon at the end of July, our fate was revealed to us.

It was during the mistral, when a furious wind blew day and night. During this period, crimes of passion were excused from Monte Carlo to Marseilles. Everyone in the villa had the jitters, and sensual appetites reached alarming peaks.

We were all in the Louis XVI drawing room. After lunch, we'd trailed nervously out of the dining room and taken our seats at the bridge tables. Now five tables of four were intensely concentrating on their cards, playing for high stakes.

The atmosphere was rather like a casino; heavy smoke hung over the tables, and waiters brought fresh trays of drinks or coffee. Greed, cunning, and lust were the three emotions that these faces wore, and all and sundry were high-strung.

The hellish wind was banging the tall French doors, rattling the shutters, making a disturbing sighing sound through the pines and eucalyptus trees around us. All at once, a terra-cotta vase on the terrace was overturned, and a gardener cursed, "Merde alors!"

Mother and Mr. Lewisohn gave a start. Mother ground out her Marlboro, with its tip smeared with crimson lipstick, and stared vacantly at her cards. "Too vile this weather," she said, sighing deeply. Then she drummed her long, lacquered nails on the green felt table and lit another cigarette.

Mr. Lewisohn took forever to bid, closing and opening his cards.

Through his pince-nez, he stared at the bending trees outside, at the sky that was an ominous silver-green. Similar, Mother remarked, to a Van Gogh landscape at Arles.

Charlie and I were hanging over the bridge table, making our usual obnoxious remarks, living up to our reputations as undisciplined brats. We raced around and looked at everyone's hands, rolling our eyes or groaning loudly, depending on the cards.

A white-coated waiter passed silver trays of brandy and coffee. Mother took an espresso, and smiled tensely in my direction. "Philip, dear," she said in her clear, distinct voice, "can't you take a swim or something?"

"Mummy, it's raining." I said.

"Is it?" she said, drumming her nails again, then glanced out the tall, arched French windows. All the windows were closed tight, the room was suffocating. Mother's heady jasmine perfume mixed with the odor of tuberoses. Through the tall windows fell an eerie, sickly light. Bronze-and-crystal wall lights glowed dully in the dimness. The rich Persian carpets were the only color in that muted room.

Suddenly, Mother gazed yearningly at the handsome figure of André Lord in a neat blue blazer and cream-colored flannels. Feeling her eyes, he turned to look at her. He smiled at her with so much tenderness that I wished he'd turn over the bridge table, grab Mother's arm, and fly her off to Corsica. That's what Claudette Colbert had done at the end of *It Happened One Night*, when she fled from an insufferable suitor into the arms of Clark Gable.

At five, Eric appeared and said it was time for Mr. Lewisohn's rest. Mr. Lewisohn had not been in good health; in his day he'd been a big drinker, and now he was paying for it. He'd been under a doctor's care for some time, and on the wagon.

"All right," said Mr. Lewisohn, reluctantly putting down his cards and pushing away from the table. He'd once been strong and virile, Mother told me, with the physique of a boxer. I'd heard him say many times that he'd made his first million by the time he was twenty. That impressed me more than anything, although Milady Ann pooh-poohed that and said he'd inherited it from his father.

Mother gazed compassionately at her best friend. With her customary tact, she, too, stood up and said, "I'm tired, too, I must confess." She crossed over to Mr. Lewisohn and playfully took his arm. Her nearness seemed to be like a blood transfusion for him; his eyes gleamed behind the pince-nez clipped onto his fleshy nose.

Eve, too, put down her cards; the mistral and the Van Rensselaer brats had been too much for her. She closed her eyes in her customary way, and I knew something significant was going to come out of her pursed lips when she opened her eyes again. Sure enough, she said, "Scotland will be a perfect place for you, boys."

Charlie and I protested with loud groans, looking at Mother for verification of Eve's statement. Mother nodded her blond head and smiled. "Yes, my loves, the day after tomorrow, you're off to Paris, and then to the old moors of Aberdeen. Imagine the thrill of dressing up in kilts and dancing to bagpipes!"

"You boys will like Myrtle Farquarshon and her little girl, Zoe d'Erlanger," said Mr. Lewisohn wearily.

"Her castle on the River Dee is *staggering*," added Mother, "and she has her own clan and her very own plaid!" Charlie and I glanced at each other. Our banishment didn't sound so bad after all.

Presently, Mother and Mr. Lewisohn crossed the length of the drawing room and moved slowly into the hall with its tessellated black and white marble floors, up to their rooms where Mother would do whatever she had to do to please her lord and master.

Chapter Eight

Hitler's blitzkrieg smashed through Poland on the morning of September 1. For the next two days we huddled over the radio waiting for news. On Sunday, September 3, we heard Churchill's voice announce that England and France were in a state of war with Nazi Germany.

Poor Mother and Mr. Lewisohn were in the Ritz in Paris when war was declared; she was scared to death, unable to communicate with us. The telephone lines were blocked, but finally she managed to get through to us at Invercauld House. We would all meet at the Ritz in London the following day. We would soon all be on the *Aquitania*, the last ship to leave war-torn Europe.

The *Athenia* had been sunk by U-boats, casting a pall over us all. But secretly, Charlie and I hoped we'd be torpedoed like the *Luisitania*, for we did not want to return to Malcolm Gordon School on the Hudson. Much more dangerous and exciting, we thought, to stay in England, wearing gas masks and fighting Hitler.

Invercauld House was a huge pile of stone overlooking the winding River Dee. Mother was right: We had attended Highland dances dressed in kilts and danced to the music of bagpipes. On some rainy afternoons, we also enjoyed dressing up in Myrtle's evening clothes and parading about the castle. Myrtle was a cozy human being, and we loved her. It was quite a shock to hear of her death in the London Blitz the next summer. She refused to go to the air-raid shelter, and her Mayfair house was blown to smithereens.

We took the Flying Scot to London and went to the Edwardian splendor of the Ritz Hotel in Piccadilly. It was a little scary being in London with blackouts and people carrying gas masks, but the lobby and luncheon room at the Ritz, complete with marble columns and potted palms, swarmed with diplomats in striped pants and swallowtail coats, and patrician ladies with pancake hats and silver foxes stepping into stately Daimlers and Rolls-Royces. An air of intrigue and suspense pervaded the Ritz corridors and I got lost in the drama. Charlie and I became so excited that we rushed out and bought two Scottie pups.

In Southampton, the *Aquitania*'s four red funnels rose up above the white superstructure and black hull. It was built in the *Titanic* period and resembled that ill-fated liner, so there was much speculation about that tragedy, and the later one of the *Lusitania*, another look-alike. Our mountain of luggage was piled onto a wheelbarrow, and an overburdened porter wheeled it off, up the gangplank and into the crowded ship packed way over capacity.

We had wanted to return to New York on the famous Lisbon clipper, but it was too difficult to get on her. So instead, we were packed like sardines into the majestic old Edwardian ship. People were sleeping on cots in the public rooms. Charlie had to share a cabin with Adele, and I with Mr. Lewisohn.

My heart sank at the idea. Frankly, I was terrified of Mr. Lewisohn. I felt he was uneasy in my company as I was in his. I pretended I was sound asleep whenever he appeared at midnight; I did not dare watch him being helped into bed by trusty Eric, for fear he might look up and catch my inquisitive eyes. Poor Eric and Elena, by the way, were in the bowels of the ship.

Ambassador Joseph P. Kennedy, the United States ambassador to England, came down to the *Aquitania* and warned us that the trip would be perilous, that German U-boats were in the Atlantic. Mother exchanged despairing looks with Hazel and Fred Beckman, who were also making the trip. Mr. Lewisohn shrugged. The

Beckmans explained they had to return because of Mrs. Beckman's middle daughter's debut. Hazel's sister, Best-dressed Kitty Miller, said the Duke of Kent had warned her to flee.

That afternoon the misty coastline of England vanished. Three destroyers escorted us out through the choppy channel; then we made a dash for it. We were on our own, making a fast zigzag course, hoping the submarines would not find us in their periscopes.

On that voyage home aboard the *Aquitania*, Charlie and I fell under the spell of wicked Fred Beckman, a spell that was to last many, many years. Fred's detractors said he could charm men, women, children, and dogs with equal ease, and such was certainly the case with us and our hounds.

Fred was bigger than life; he had a prima donna quality. Mr. Lewisohn used to say, in his dry, humorous way, that it was a pity that Fred hadn't tried Hollywood, for God knows he had tried just about everything else under the sun. Mr. Lewisohn also liked to tease him about his amazing collection of gold cigarette cases. Cigarette cases were much in vogue then. Adele had a few gold ones and a few blue enamel ones with matching match covers in suede cases. Fred, bless his heart, had a Vuitton suitcase full of these treasures that had been gifts from satisfied members of his fan club.

In any case, Fred was exhilarating company for a pair of children, especially two children who were hungry for a male image to identify with. Naturally, we did not have an inkling of Fred's sinister reputation, although he exuded an aura of sensuality.

For years friends had warned Mother that Fred was dangerous, but she refused to hear anything ugly about those she loved. And when she did hear anything, she'd put up her hand and say, "I forbid you to go any further." Of course, Fred had been a peerless lover; Adele was too naive to understand that men such as Fred could be sexually insatiable. Mother often remarked on people's cruelty, especially in response to Fred, who roused jealousy and who had so much to be envied for. For Fred was a child of the gods, and the gods had certainly endowed him well.

The only criticism that Adele ever leveled at Fred occurred a few months before she died. "Dear," she asked me, "don't you think perhaps Fred wears a little too much Knize cologne?"

Fred was born in Kankakee, Illinois, and like so many people born in the Middle West, in the middle class, he was determined to get away from his background. He charmed his grandfather, and the old man sent Fred to Princeton, where he got his first taste of the high life and of the heiresses in Scott Fitzgerald's and Louis Bromfield's novels. From then on, Fred was off and running, determined to win the big sweepstakes.

Like Louis Bromfield, Fred had originally wanted to be a writer, so he'd gone to Paris and lived in a writer's garret to do just that. But soon, to use his words, there were too many temptations and he was too weak to resist them. His writing was shoved into a drawer. Fred was wonderfully good-looking, fresh on the scene, and soon, he, too, was swept up into the world that the Louis Bromfields and the Michael Arlens moved in.

The Ritz in Paris became the base of his operations, and here he met the rich and famous who moved restlessly from Deauville, to the Côte D'Azur, to Venice and Biarritz. Fred was taken up by a lot of these grand couples, and soon he was their favorite. They paid his bills. He lived just like the rich, in their grand houses, but had none of their headaches and responsibilities. For a time, he was content to be a houseguest; he had a talent to amuse and satisfy. His enormous energy made him a bed partner without equal.

By the time he was thirty, it dawned on him that he must make a killing and marry well. He was smart enough to know that after thirty, one's days as a favorite are limited.

Fred first married Sarah Waterbury, who had all the right credentials in Newport and New York. In Newport, Fred and Sarah had their moment of truth. She learned he had no money and he learned she had no money. Both were living behind fronts. They parted good friends, after a few months, each a little wiser.

Fred then went back to Adele and they resumed their on-again, off-again romance, but while Mother was being wined and dined by Mr. Lewisohn, Fred was singing for his supper with Hazel Bache.

Hazel was plain, dumpy, and short, with a nasty disposition, and ten years older than Fred, but he hooked her with his personality. Soon she agreed to become Mrs. Frederick W. Beckman.

Hazel *really* was a great heiress. Her father, Jules Bache, of 814 Fifth Avenue and Palm Beach, Florida, lived in the grand manner reminiscent of Otto Kahn and Mr. Lewisohn. Fred was fond of his old father-in-law and affectionately called him Mr. B. Mr. B left him $50,000 when he died, and Fred went through it immediately. Whenever Fred got any money in his hands, he spent it. He always felt that his magical good looks would ensure him a fresh high wave of greenbacks. He died broke. His good friend Countess Dorothy di Frasso, an American heiress who lived in a Roman palace, also died broke. Barbara Hutton, too. The 1930's were over.

Chapter Nine

It was interesting to note how Adele and Freddy Lewisohn handled their living together in Puritan America. It was a ticklish problem, no doubt about it.

Late in 1939, Mr. Lewisohn rented a large, Italianate stucco house on the ocean in Palm Beach and Mrs. Van Rensselaer leased a Spanish colonial–style apartment at 240 Phipps Plaza around the corner. Quite discreet, all things considered. Charlie and I spent Christmas and Easter holidays at Phipps Plaza, swam daily at Mr. Lewisohn's, and rode in his limousine to the Palm Beach Playhouse for our movie orgies.

Later, Mother said Palm Beach was not for her. What had happened was that they hadn't been invited to join the Bath and Tennis Club or the Everglades; there were not any other couples like them, so they didn't fit in. Quite simply, fashionable people in America did not live in sin in those days. They married and that was that.

Fred and Hazel Beckman were also spending these holidays in Palm Beach, at the opulent Mediterranean-style villa of the rich and social Mr. Bache. But no invitations were forthcoming from them. Jo Hartford Douglas, the A&P heiress and Adele's old friend from her Oyster Bay days, was in residence in Palm Beach, but no invitations came from her either. Years later, a dear friend of my mother's said Adele suffered a lot of slights and put-downs, but was courageous and gallant about the whole thing. She'd made her bed and she slept in it.

The summer of 1940, we all lumbered up to Silver Shells, a red-brick mansion on the water at Marion, Massachusetts.

God only knows why the Beckman–Lewisohn–Van Rensselaer ménage chose this austere New England town. Newport or Southampton would have suited their gregarious natures better, although Newport was severe about those of the Jewish faith and the Southampton Beach Club was equally strict.

In any case, the grand, shiny black limousines arrived in this quiet and respectable New England town by the sea in a conspicuous blaze. Suddenly, there was no place to go, and no invitations to accept. Both Hazel and Adele had stunning summer outfits from Schiap in Paris and that year's styles from Bergdorf but they remained in the closets most of July and August, in clammy darkness.

Boredom set in. The house faced the sea, and a huge pier stretched out into a flat, colorless, and uninteresting sea. A few sailboats glided by. What a letdown after the sparkle of Cannes and Monte Carlo! There were no bars like the Terrace at the Carlton or Eden Roc, no hairdresser, no Lanvin, no Van Cleef, no Cartier. No casinos! No one to flirt with. No water-skiing! No handsome gentlemen callers. No complicated love affairs or scandals to dissect. What to do, my darlings?

Outside talent was imported. The beautiful Audrey Emery and her son, Paul Ilyinski, saved us for a week. Then, the slim and clever Eve Lewisohn arrived with her best friend, Mrs. Amos Tuck French, in a cartwheel hat, silk dress, and sling-back pumps, and groaned.

Finally, in desperation, Mother's brother, Jack Rowland, his wife, Ruth, and their child, Cynthia, were summoned for the Fourth of July. Adele adored Ruth, who was good-looking and loved to laugh, but brother Jack was a heavy piece of furniture and was always giving her unwanted advice and gloomy forecasts for her future.

Jack was a bit unnerved that I'd never heard of a YMCA or the WPA. He was also rather shocked by everyone's indifference to the Depression, which was still going on. Charlie and I were described, as usual, as spoiled brats, with no sense of discipline, being allowed to do anything we wanted. Not quite. A tutor had been imported for us from Harvard, and a sailing boat had been purchased so we could learn about things nautical. We were dragged out in this little boat and we loathed being covered with salty spray and tacking this way and that. "Phooey!" as I noted in my diary.

At Silver Shells there were endless croquet matches on the endless emerald lawn, endless lunches and dinners, endless movies for me and Charlie. But I recall most clearly about that summer the bored expression on Hazel Beckman's face as she vengefully attacked her needlepoint, and Fred Beckman making me giggle by throwing out his big, muscular arms and saying, "Give till it hurts, I always say!" He and Hazel played backgammon for huge stakes, most of the time in ominous silence.

At the end of the summer, the shiny black limousines lumbered back to Manhattan with their jaded loads. Back to autumn in New York. Back to seductive piano bars, like the Café Pierre, and back to the alluring zebra stripes of that exciting nightclub, El Morocco. Back to sipping frozen daiquiris at the Colony Restaurant Bar, staring into a new admirer's eyes with a desperate hope as he lit your Marlboro. Back to Xavier Cugat and his Latin-American delights.

Mother gave a sigh of relief as the uniformed doorman at the Waldorf Towers tipped his hat and we were bowed through the gilded revolving doors and carried swiftly and soundlessly to our spotless all-white apartment on the fortieth floor, with its majestic view of the skyscrapers spreading out in all directions and the faraway George Washington and Triboro bridges.

Back to our beloved room service, with the heavy trays rattling over the thick carpeting of our luxurious room, and the black Packard carrying us to movie matinees at the Plaza or Normandie theaters.

Back to signing for cash downstairs and lunches with Mother at the nearby Voisin with the yellow canaries singing in their cages. Back to making paper airplanes out of dollar bills and sailing them out the windows, and listening to Mother talk on her two bedroom telephones all morning long about the excitement of the night before at El Morocco.

Mother's huge eyes regained their luster, and she treated us once more with her teasing, playful manner, as if she were flirting with us. Diana Vreeland, who always admired Adele, said that whenever she saw the three of us out dining or nightclubbing, Charlie and I seemed like Mother's beaux.

How tiresome to return to the morally correct and highly principled Malcolm Kenneth Gordons. How tiresome to be lectured about having values, being a strong and manly character, and earning an honest living. I was sick to death of hearing that all you had in life was your good name and you must not dishonor it.

Nevertheless, after a time, the ordered routine of the Hudson River days was soothing, and I quickly fell back into my role of the good little boy to please Mr. and Mrs. Gordon. I'd grown to love the yellow-brick Gothic-style schoolhouse and all the Gordon family. I never tired of sitting on the veranda and gazing up and down the Hudson River, which always seemed to me rather like a romantic Italian lake, like Como or Maggiore.

Charlie was graduated from the Gordon School in May 1940. A year later, I won the Langhorne Gibson Prize for Best Public Speaker and was also graduated.

Later in May 1941, Mother arrived in a blaze of glory for Parents' Day and Commencement Exercises. Audrey Emery, now the Princess Djordadze, accompanied her. Both women were fashion-plate thin, sported big black cartwheel hats, flowered silk frocks, and white gloves, and both were heavily doused in Guerlain. After Mr. Gordon handed me my diploma, Mother embraced me radiantly and said, "Darling, I'm so proud of you." She gave me a fourteen-karat-gold Hamilton wristwatch with a classic Roman dial, and I hugged her to death.

It was hard to say good-bye to the Gordons. Mrs. Gordon had been like a mother to me, as had young Mrs. David. Malcolm Gordon and Mr. David were parental figures, too, and I still nursed a wild dream that Mother would run off with either one. All of them had given me guidance and a sense of continuity that I desperately needed.

As Mr. Lewisohn's car pulled away from the schoolhouse, I saw many mothers staring with curiosity at Adele. And as we made our stately progress back to New York, a station wagon passed by us, slowly, and all its passengers took a good long look at Mother, half concealed by her black picture hat and the black leather covering the rear window. Such long looks!

On June 1, Mother and I moved down to Easthampton. She had rented a house on Egypt Lane within sight of that spreading stucco-and-timbered English manor with the thatched roof called the Maidstone Club. We promptly became members, and Mother started to play golf again on the splendid course that surrounded the club facing the ocean.

Soon there appeared on the scene the thin, gentlemanly form of shy George McAlpin, who lived with his mother, Blanche Benjamin McAlpin, an old dragon and one of the resort's leaders. He also shared a large Park Avenue apartment with his mama.

George was mad about Adele, and they were seen everywhere together. He was on the committee of the snobbish Maidstone Club and warned Mother not, on any account, to invite Mr. Frederick Lewisohn down for a weekend. It would cause too much talk—and Easthampton was not Cannes, or Monte, he said, although a bit more sophisticated than Marion, Massachusetts.

As luck would have it, Mr. Lewisohn had been in poor health; indeed, he'd been in the hospital for many months, and the only thing that cheered his gloom were the daily visits from his little girl. Years later he told me how touched he was that Mother had made the effort to come and see him faithfully, every afternoon, rain or shine. She was the only person who did.

And so, one sunny day before the long Fourth of July weekend, the big black 1941 Cadillac limousine that Mother and I had picked out in the West Fifty-seventh Street GM store, drew up on our front lawn at Egypt Lane. Peters opened the door and out stepped Mr. Lewisohn, a familiar figure in his elegant olive gabardine suit, yellow foulard tie with matching handkerchief, and pince-nez. He looked thin and pale, but grinned wanly, as Mother ran girlishly from the doorway with happy cries of welcome. But, as so often happened with Mother, her happy, girlish cries were soon to be followed by a rivulet of tears.

The next day, Saturday, there was a big buffet at the Maidstone

Club. Mother was determined to go with Mr. Lewisohn as her guest. Behind the Olds wheel, Mother was dashing in a trim double-breasted blue blazer studded with gold buttons, sleek white sharkskin pants, and a striped matelot shirt from St. Tropez; her hair was styled in a sleek pageboy. She was unusually talkative on the way to the austere club.

I sat in the rear next to Mr. Lewisohn and tried also to be lively and engaging. Charlie sat in the front. He'd shot up so quickly I hardly recognized him. He was six feet tall, broad-shouldered, and looked like a man, and I felt most inadequate beside him. He was also bored to death with me; I'd lost my childhood playmate.

Finally, we drew up before the timbered Tudor outline of the Maidstone. We all stepped out of the car and made our way into this exclusive club where Jews were not permitted. Mother had a fixed smile on her face and kept up an animated conversation. Suddenly, the thin figure of George McAlpin appeared; he was pale and trembling with rage.

"You know the rules of the club, Adele," he reminded her in a distinct, carrying voice.

Mother flushed under the insult. Then, she took Mr. Lewisohn's arm and walked with dignity out into the gravel drive and back to the car. I felt a host of eyes watching us, and I lowered my head.

To this day I cannot return to the Maidstone Club, I have never joined any club with those kinds of rules, and I've always felt uncomfortable at the Racquet or the Knickerbocker club.

Chapter Ten

In mid-September 1941, something terrible happened.

Mother always lunched out. Her favorite restaurants were the Colony, Voisin, Giovanni's, and Passy. Passy was located at 28 East Sixty-third Street, and its matchbooks said it had a cuisine that epicurians applaud. It was also expensive as hell. There was a glittering mirrored bar off the dining room—like *Normandie*'s.

After Charlie and I gorged on a tremendous lunch and Mother sipped a frozen daiquiri and nibbled on some lettuce leaves, she paid the bill and we started to leave. Instead of going out onto the gray pavement between Park and Madison, she pushed open the door that led into the Lowell Hotel. The hotel had a simple lobby and a concierge's desk, behind which the telephone operator sat.

It was definitely not a grand hotel, like the Westbury, the Pierre, or Waldorf Towers. No marble. No gilded columns. No sweeping paneled lobbies, blazing with shops, no Belle Epoque exuberances. The Lowell was known as a residential hotel, used as a pied-à-terre for rich folk who came in only once a week for the opera or the theater. I asked Mother why we were here, and she replied that this was going to be our new home.

A small metal elevator rattled up to the sixteenth floor, then Mother opened the door to another door marked 16A. The sitting room was so dreary that Charlie and I looked at each other with shock. There was no gilded French furniture, no marble-topped chests, no crystal wall lights, no heavy damask curtains quivering with tassels and ball fringe. Our eyes were offended by lumpy upholstered armchairs and sofas. The two bedrooms had Early American maple bed frames, matching chests, and drab chenille bedspreads. Skimpy chintz draperies. For peasants!

"Don't you like it, my angels?" Mother said, gazing at us hopefully.

Charlie and I curled our lips. "Really, Mummy! It's awful!"

"I have a wonderful new maid called Jessie," Mother persisted in that hopeful tone. "She'll make you breakfast every morning; you'll adore her, my treasures!"

"You *bet*," said Charlie sarcastically.

"You mean, we won't have room service anymore, Mummy?" I glared at her.

"Well," she replied, avoiding my eyes, "Room service is so fearfully expensive. What with the war and all, I have to cut down."

Cut down? What did that mean?

Charlie and I exchanged a frightened look. This was the first time Mother had ever mentioned things being expensive or the need to cut down. Something must have happened between her and Mr. Lewisohn. Insecurity gnawed at me.

Two days later, suitcases and trunks were packed, drawers emptied, closets denuded. Just before we departed for the Lowell, I stood for the last time in the Waldorf Towers sitting room, looking about with confusion and feeling lost. Worst of all, Mother looked tired. There were lines under her eyes, and her color was poor. The freshness had gone. That dreadful downhill period had started.

In panic, I quickly called Duncan Ellsworth to test his reaction to our new quarters. Duncan Ellsworth was my best friend at Malcolm-Gordon. He was a figure of envy for me; I looked up to him for many reasons. The main reason was that he had a loving mother and father sitting at the head of the dinner table; they were secure with old money, and the Social Register listed a dozen or so clubs next to their names and address.

These much-envied Ellsworths had many addresses! One was a summer house in Southampton, rather like the Maidstone Club in appearance, with the same thatched roof and facing directly on the ocean. If that wasn't enough to break the monotony of the Hamptons, they had an ancient red-brick house in Chester, Vermont, which I had visited the previous summer, and which I would have killed for. Some people had all the luck.

I nervously awaited Duncan's arrival in 16A. Suddenly, the doorbell rang, and there was young Duncan, full of high spirits and that dry sense of humor I admired. I gave him a tour of 16A and carefully watched his reaction.

"Is this all there is?" he asked.

"Yes," I gulped.

"It's rather small," he observed, and my heart sank. I could tell by his pinched expression that he thought it was Tortilla Flat.

Mother joined us for lunch at Passy downstairs. She looked smart in a severely tailored blue suit, lace blouse, and a flowered straw hat, with veil, resting on her forehead. A diamond flower pin flashed on her lapel.

Duncan fell for Mother's light and easy charm. My hopes for approval rose a little. After lunch, Duncan and I stepped into the Cadillac limousine, and I accompanied him back to Sutton Place and Fifty-seventh Street. He asked me if Mother's diamond pin was real. I knew it was false, but I lied and said that Paul Plato had designed it. Mother *did* have a diamond pin from Plato, but it wasn't this one.

"My mother has a *real* diamond one," he said. I could tell he didn't believe my lie.

Peters drew into the impressive porte cochere of One Sutton Place, and a doorman rushed to open our door. Duncan thanked me for lunch and said we'd soon meet at St. Paul's up in Concord, New Hampshire.

"Are you dreading it?" I asked.

"A little," he smiled with a shrug. He took everything in his stride, like the Rock of Gibraltar.

"I've got butterflies in my stomach," I confessed.

He stepped out onto the street, his eyes examining every inch of the Lewisohn car. The cream-colored initials *FL* glared on the black door. I knew the words he would ask even before he opened his mouth.

"Is this your mother's car?" he asked.

I swallowed hard. "It belongs to Mother's best friend, Frederick Lewisohn," I replied, the words catching in my throat.

He gave that same knowing smile as Mrs. Gordon, then waved and said he'd soon see me in Concord. I watched his tweedy figure vanish into the vast lobby, where about a hundred doormen and elevator men made a fuss over him. And this "old money" lobby was not like that of the Pierre, the Waldorf, or the Ritz: There were discreet and conservative pieces of antique furniture, no French curves or opulence. Louis forbid!

As we drew away from the East River, I sank despairingly back into the rear. I knew the Ellsworths would never accept me as a first-class citizen.

The awful first day at St. Paul's finally arrived. There were no kindly Gordons to greet me. I unpacked in my little alcove, feeling abysmally forlorn. I couldn't even play a part. The sea of unknown faces frightened me. I felt as frail as Mother. On December 7, the Japanese bombed Pearl Harbor and Roosevelt announced we were in a state of war. This didn't help matters.

By Christmas, I had made a new friend, Hartley Ramsay. We had much in common; his father had died three years earlier, and he and his twin brother were being brought up by their mother. Hartley was as thin as Fred Astaire, danced as well, knew all the Astaire-Rogers movies by heart, and could sing all the lyrics of their songs. He could also imitate all the masters and their wives, play the piano like José Iturbi, and was as shy and overly sensitive as I was.

Whenever we appeared, older boys would whistle, and make a sound of rushing wind or the roar of an airplane. "There they go," came the contemptuous voices. We were called fairies, and our critics said we were so light on our feet we could fly out the window. This hurt me. I withdrew further and further and felt very isolated.

Mother wrote me weekly letters, filled with her news—the latest novels she'd read, the latest party she'd been to, the latest plays or musicals she'd seen. She missed me, of course, but she and I never discussed anything of a personal nature; unfortunately, I didn't know how to ask for help. Going into my teens, I had many problems that a father should have aided me with. But no advice, no support, was forthcoming.

Mother believed things take care of themselves. I suppose she felt older boys at school or a Mr. Chipps–type headmaster would mold my character and shape my identity.

The war years slipped by; I slipped deeper into the morass.

My first year at St. Paul's ended, and we had no summer plans. No more Easthampton disasters!

Mr. Lewisohn was not well; he wanted to be close to New York, so he rented a large house with a swimming pool in Mt. Kisco, an hour away. The Van Rensselaer jesters spent a few weekends there, then Charlie and I were shipped off to St. Mark's summer camp in Southboro, Massachusetts, to keep us out of the suffocating metropolis.

My growing anger was simmering on a low burner; somehow, I managed to keep it from exploding.

I did not want to become like Crazy Liz, Aunt Bessie's raging, middle-aged daughter, whom I glimpsed every vacation. She chain-smoked, tiger-paced the rooms, was dressed like a teenager with bobby sox on her muscular, weather-beaten legs. Crazy Liz had wanted to marry the groom at her mother's Bernardsville, New Jersey, estate, but Aunt Bessie forbade it, and Liz never forgot it.

I was beginning to resent Mother. Our apartments at the Lowell were sinking to lower and lower floors until I began to think that we'd soon be on the street. By Christmas vacation in 1943, Mother was existing in 3B, almost on street level, and she stayed there for two more uncertain years.

During our vacations she'd rent a little room for us, sometimes across the hall and sometimes on a different floor.

To compensate for not having a home of my own, toile de Jouy curtains and Regency silk embroidered country fantasies were hung on my schoolroom walls. You can imagine this did not help my reputation as a winged freak. My roommates shook their heads and said I was pathetic.

I used to dread my Christmas, Easter, and summer vacations. When our train was slowing up in the smoky tunnels of Grand

Central, fear would paralyze me, and the old anxiety sweats would start. By the gate, Mother would be standing more pale and ethereal than ever, showing her age. Her frailty filled me with anger. Why didn't she eat more?

Another thing that irritated me was the steady stream of male figures passing through the doors of 3B. Why couldn't she get married?

Every vacation, she'd say, "Oh, I'm so in love and we're going to be married very soon and live in the country." Getting married and living in the country with the beloved one was Adele's perennial fantasy. Fred Beckman and Mr. Lewisohn mercilessly teased her about this, to which she'd retort triumphantly, "Wait and see."

Invariably, Mother's fatherly beaus would ask me, dear boy, what was I going to be when I grew up. My answer depended on the last movie I'd seen. I didn't have a clue who I was. I snatched at people's identities and then pasted them on myself for a trial period.

In 1940, after seeing *Rebecca*, my answer would have been I wanted to be a country squire like Max deWinter and own a house like Manderley.

In 1941, after seeing *Sergeant York*, I replied I wanted to be a war hero.

In 1942, after seeing *Pride of the Yankees*, I said I wanted to be Lou Gehrig, also played by my hero, Gary Cooper.

In 1943, after seeing *Casablanca*, I said I wanted to own a café like Rick.

Mother would clap her hands and say how clever I was—but the gentlemen looked a bit worried.

Chapter
Eleven

Flying down to Mexico for the summer of 1943 to visit the
Beckmans, Mother sat next to me on the plane. The slightest
turbulence seemed to frighten her; her nervous system had obviously collapsed. I was fifteen now; I'd shot up like Charlie had two
years before, only I was bone-thin, like Mother, and weighed about
the same as she did.

Fred Beckman was quite a famous figure in Mexico during the
war years. Hazel's enormous Bache income enabled him to entertain lavishly and hold open house every day, not only in their
Cuernavaca hacienda, but in their large Paseo de La Reforma apartment in Mexico City. Hazel, by the way, won the lottery that year
and $50,000 was handed over to this woman who spent $800,000
every year and yet was always in hock because of Fred's extrava-
gance. The dolce vita had put a lot of weight on Fred's big-
shouldered, six-foot-two-inch frame; he was up to two hundred
pounds but he could carry it. He was drinking a good deal, as
usual, only now he was showing it. Before and during lunch, he'd
consume shaker after shaker of gin-and-Dubonnet cocktails and
then stagger off with Hazel for their siesta.

Cole Porter and Howard Sturgis appeared several times by the pool in Cuernavaca that summer. Over lunch there were sly reminders of Fred's pleasure-boy days when, apparently, he could satisfy an army of women in an evening. His sexual energy was still strong; every few days he'd vanish to Mexico City and rumor had it that he and Joan Fontaine were having one hell of a time.

As in Cannes, our life in Cuernavaca centered around the pool. Hazel and Fred had their quarters on one side of the pool, and Mother and Charlie and I on the other; a big garden with a lawn separated us. As at Cannes, there was a bar by the pool; Fred was forever shaking up a fresh round of cocktails. He loved playing the host, loved being on center stage; with his flamboyant personality, he kept things moving along at a merry pace, and there was never a dull moment.

Mexico City attracted much royalty and many big names during the war: King Carol and his red-haired mistress, Magda Lupescu, were favored guests of the Beckmans. His Majesty was the son of Queen Marie of Rumania and the great-grandson of Queen Victoria. Other guests were Jock and Betty McLean and Hollywood's Bruce Cabot. Jock's mother owned the ill-fated Hope Diamond and loved to play backgammon with Hazel.

When life in Cuernavaca grew tiresome and the need for new faces and new surroundings became urgent, we took off for Mexico City. There, we stayed at the new Reforma Hotel and nightclubbed at Ciro's where you saw a lot of glamorous film stars dancing and flirting. A Boston debutante called C. Z. Cochrane cut quite a swath in town. She was painted nude by Diego Rivera, and this painting was hung for a time in Ciro's bar. She'd had a fling with Victor Mature, "the body beautiful." He was a figure of envy for me, because Rita Hayworth was insane for him. For me, Rita was the most exciting film star, and I avidly read every detail of her career and romances in *Photoplay*, which I hid in the closet.

One weekend, we flew down to Acapulco. It was a quiet little fishing village then, with no grand hotels, no skyscrapers, no yachts in the harbor. It was beautiful at night, with the lights twinkling along the coastline. Memories of the south of France flooded me. The fuschia bougainvillea and yellow hibiscus struck me with their exotic beauty. Poor Adele! She suffered so on that tiny one-engine plane to Acapulco. A high wind over the mountains had the light plane bouncing around like a toy. Mother grew paler and paler, beads of perspiration dappling her brow. I comforted her as best I could, and she gripped my hand tightly.

Back in Cuernavaca we oiled our bodies with Bain de Soleil, lay in the blazing sunshine by the pool, and enjoyed lunch parties and bridge.

The only discordant note in this Latin American paradise was Hazel Bache Beckman. She was a bully, so I tried to keep out of her way. One afternoon, during one of their endless bridge tournaments, Mother was staring dreamily at her current lover, oblivious to everyone else. Hazel snapped, "Concentrate on your cards, birdbrain!" and glared at Adele.

"Shut up, you filthy slut!" I yelled at Hazel, and my glare was as fierce as hers. I'd been absorbed in *Moll Flanders* and other bawdy, Restoration novels, and their language was always going through my head. Mother was stunned by my tirade and told me, severely, to remember my manners and apologize to Mrs. Beckman. I did, but sulked for the rest of the day. It was the first time I had expressed any anger.

Strangely enough, Hazel was friendly to me after that; indeed, we became quite intimate and corresponded until her death three years later. She wrote perspicacious letters about life in Mexico, in which she described details behind the threads of the social tapestry. Hazel was no fool; she was her father's daughter, all right. Her weak point was her obsession with Fred. Her first husband, by whom she'd had three daughters, had been cruel to her. Fred was always polite and agreeable with her, and he certainly didn't neglect her. Of course she saw through him, but his fleshy muscular body obsessed her. Heaven knows, you couldn't blame her. Fred was strong as a horse, tremendously physical, and his body was built along the heroic lines of a Rubens war god. He was, also, most of the time, in a good mood—if he had his own way.

That summer I felt different, out of step with the rest of the world. There was a kind of mist over me, and what I observed had the dullness of a sepia drawing. A sense of loneliness was constantly with me. Oh, I laughed at all the right moments and even flung out a clever remark, but I knew something was wrong. I didn't dare talk to anyone about my feelings. Every now and then, my eyes would rest on Mother, or Hazel, or Fred, with a pleading look. But I got no response.

For me the landscape was tinged with melancholy. Perhaps it was my state of mind or perhaps it was the lewd aura surrounding the Beckmans. Or, it might have been Mother's love affairs ending, as always, in tears. This time, when her latest passed out the garden gate that early September morning, and the tears were streaming down her face, I felt a special bond with her. In a way, she was as alone as I was—lost in a dreamworld.

Things went from bad to worse those last two years at St. Paul's school. The New Hampshire winters seemed endless. So did the hissing, banging radiators, my cold, wet feet, red nose, and grippe. So did the snow and walking through this snow to different class-rooms and endless chapel services.

I no longer participated in sports as I had neither the energy nor the inclination. I joined an effete group of lads who did not care to exercise and who were known, contemptuously, as the Grub Squad. My body remained thin and undeveloped, and I dreaded the afternoon shower room where I'd have to display my naked-ness.

Mother was in that grisly period of "cutting down," and my clothes reflected this state of economy. As with Blanche DuBois, clothes have always been my passion, but suddenly I looked rather shabby and hated it. My gray herringbone Brooks Brothers over-coat was threadbare, green, and shiny, from too many dry-cleanings. One afternoon my eyes lingered on a dazzling polo coat. It belonged to a good-looking Southern boy. His polo coat obsessed me; I had to have it! Why should he have it? It would look much better on me. Like Mother, I knew how to wear clothes and would give it the style it craved.

The next time the other boy was off playing hockey, I crept into his room and stole his coat. I took it to my room and breathlessly examined it on the bed; then I tried it on and was delighted with my image. Quickly, I ripped out the label, sewed in a Saks Fifth Avenue one from a tweed sport coat, and tied a belt around it. That evening, quite brazenly, I wore the polo coat, belted, with a heavy

silk scarf, to chapel. He looked at it, with a puzzled stare, but
didn't say a thing. I'd gotten away with my plunder!

That term I also started to write stories. I still read voraciously,
all the while managing to concentrate on my homework and do the
necessary studying. One of my stories, "Audrey," appeared in the
school magazine and won second prize.

Over the summer of 1944, Eve Lewisohn decided it would be a
good thing for me to join her in a trip out West. She told Mother
I needed "toughening up," that I appeared "too soft, too pale."

The A-Bar-A Ranch in Laramie, Wyoming, was our destination.
Early in July we boarded the luxurious sleeper at Grand Central
Station. Mother came down to see us off. It was a sticky, humid
day, and humidity did not agree with Adele. She looked tired; her
hair was thin and lifeless and there were hollows under her eyes.
Her smile was not so pretty. Her gums were receding.

When our train was pulling out of the Grand Central tunnels into
the gritty daylight, I looked at Eve sitting across from me and said,
"Eve, Mummy doesn't look so pretty anymore. I wonder what's
the matter?"

Eve fixed a knowing eye on me. "Your mother's not as young as
she used to be," she replied in her slow, thoughtful voice, "and we
all have to get old, you know."

"We do?"

I had dreaded the thought of Mother's getting old. I frowned
darkly. Mother was losing her looks! Disaster. What would happen
to us now? Would Mr. Lewisohn find a younger, prettier companion? Such men usually did, I'd heard. Look at Edward VII, Louis
XV, and Louis XIV. Those jaded gents soon got tired of their
favorites.

My thoughts wandered to the Rowlands and my father. Both
lived in small, cramped Long Island houses and had small, old cars.
And my father's voice was lifeless and defeated, and his clothes
were a disgrace. No way did I want to be like Uncle Jack or my
father! Failure was not for me. The good, easy life of Fred Beckman
was what appealed to me. Endless amounts of money to burn, huge
closets full of London suits, Peal shoes, and Charvet shirts and ties.

Fred had a hundred thick and lustrous cashmere sweaters from
Scotland and forty silk dressing gowns like Noël Coward's, some in

satin with velvet lapels and long sashes with fringe. He had polka-
dot ones in all colors—blue, red, gray, black, green; all bore his
monogram *FB* in large, fancy stitching. Fred had all his shirts
custom-made, and they, too, bore his monogram, even his pajamas
and undershorts. I've never seen a man with more monogrammed
clothes.

Fred also had more cuff links and dress-sets than Cartier and
Arpels displayed in their Fifth Avenue windows; he loved to pull
down his French cuffs and reveal his loot. Fred had it made, all
right. His whole existence was like a Fred Astaire–Ginger Rogers
musical, dancing from one continent to the next, one fabulous
party after the next. What more could a man want?

The A-Bar-A Ranch was everything Eve said it would be. West-
ern people *were* nicer, simpler, more sincere than hard, materialistic, snobbish Easterners. I enjoyed my early-morning rides with
Michael and Audrey Palmer, Eve's two children. Sometimes we
had evening cookouts and sang "The Tumbling Tumbleweeds" by
an open fire. The smell of sage was pleasant. Cowboys in their
jeans, denim shirts, and boots resembled Gary Cooper and had his
slow grin.

Returning home after Labor Day, the train was packed to overflowing with marines, sailors, and soldiers. I remember we stopped
off in Denver and had a lunch at the Brown Palace Hotel. A few
days later, in Chicago, we enjoyed a sumptuous meal in the Pump
Room of the Ambassador.

Charlie and Mother had spent the summer in New York and had
taken some rooms in a boarding house on Hill Street, in Southampton, for weekends by the ocean. Charlie had been drafted and was
to leave any minute for Fort Dix, New Jersey.

We all drove back to New York in mid-September and stopped
off to have lunch with Grandma Van Rensselaer in Jericho. She had
become quite senile, and I was shocked and saddened by her
behavior. My Uncle Steve was now a captain in the army. My
father ran a little antique shop around the corner. He'd married a
woman named Vera Baer, who, fortunately, had a little money and
a dreary cottage on her mother's estate, where they lived.

We returned to our shabby little room at the Lowell. We went
to La Rue a few times. I loved to get drunk on Cuba libres, which

were a mixture of Coca-Cola and rum, a very popular drink during the war. Feeling drunk agreed with me; I acted silly, made people laugh, and told some grandiose stories fraught with exaggerated details.

We occasionally lunched with Mother at the Passy downstairs, and she became quite tearful talking about Charlie's imminent departure for war and Europe. Mother had been working hard at the Salvation Army Canteen. She looked sweet in her little green uniform and she also looked worn-out. Once, when Charlie and I picked her up, she fell into the taxi and burst into tears from sheer exhaustion.

Finally, the dreaded day arrived. Jessie packed Charlie's duffel bag and made him a frozen daiquiri. Then Charlie had a tearful farewell with Mother. She had wanted to come down to Penn Station with us, but was so overwhelmed by emotion that she could not. It was five o'clock, and the streets were full of shadows. I took Charlie down to the dirty station and walked him down the concrete platform to his waiting train. We embraced shyly.

"Look after Mummy," he said.

"Yes," I said, with a gulp.

"Take care."

"Yes."

Then he was gone. When I returned to the Lowell, Jessie was comforting Mother with her usual tenderness. She loved Mother and could not bear to see her unhappy. Mother canceled a dinner that evening, didn't go out. She told me she was convinced Charlie would die in the war, like Jean Mixell's son, Donald.

In the dark bedroom, she closed her eyes. "Who would think it would all end like this?" she said. Then, she gave a queer little laugh. I felt distinctly apprehensive. I'd never seen her like this.

The next day, she returned to the Salvation Army Canteen. Later that year, when the war ended, they honored Adele with a medal stating that she had devoted five hundred hours of her time. I had this medal until recently, but it must have been lost during my last move.

When I left St. Paul's in mid-June of 1945, I was asked not to return. My grades had slipped; I no longer bothered with my homework. Besides, nothing I read penetrated. Worst of all, I'd become openly hostile, especially to some headmasters. My general attitude was, Who gives a damn? and I often spoke these words. During an English exam in May, I'd written a foulmouthed composition full of sex and graphic images.

My English teacher summoned me to his office. "Did you think that I wouldn't read your disgusting paper?"

"Yeah," I replied.

"You imagined you could get away with such filth?"

"Yeah."

"You're not sorry, Philip?"

"No."

The distinguished-looking, gray-haired English master stared at my sloppy attire. I no longer cared how I looked, and my hair was too long. However, my face had become strikingly handsome, and I saw many people gazing longingly at me.

When I returned to the Lowell, I didn't dare tell Mother of my expulsion. I avoided her company, went to LaRue, and got drunk as much as possible.

One morning at the Lowell, an anxious Jessie appeared in my room. She said that Mother was angry as a hornet, had just received a letter from St. Paul's School, and wanted to see me.

"So what?" I laughed. But I dressed with trepidation, wondering what story I could tell her. When I slouched into Mother's room, with my hands in my pockets and a cigarette dangling from my lips, she paled with fury. She started on the letter and demanded an explanation.

"Nothing," I said, with a hostile intonation.

"How dare you talk to me with your hands in your pockets!" she said severely. "Have you no respect for me?"

"No," I said rudely.

She flung me an exasperated look. "What *is* the matter with you? I demand to know!" She spoke in a grand manner.

Mother was still in apartment 3B, but it wasn't as grim as it could have been. The sitting room had a fireplace, flanked by a built-in bookcase, and casement windows that opened onto the street. It was the period of *Laura*. I'd dragged Mother to see that movie with Gene Tierney at the Plaza Theater during Christmas vacation, and

every fashionable woman had a portrait of herself in that style.
Mother's hung over the gray sofa, flanked by two big red lounge
chairs; her face had two enormous eyes staring sadly, that perfect
nose, wide red lips, slightly turned down at the corners, with a
shade of disappointment.

Talking about portraits, Mr. Lewisohn had one of Mother at the
Drake Hotel, where he spent the war years. Servants were scarce
as hen's teeth (Mother's expression), and most everyone we knew
had moved into the Plaza, the Lowell, the Volney, or the Alrae.
Mr. Lewisohn's portrait of Mother hung in his sitting room; it was
painted in the French Impressionist style and was done in 1941, at
the Maisonette at 726 Park Avenue. Mother looked graceful,
pretty, and untormented, with her enormous soft brown eyes staring out at you through the blond waves of her siren hair.

Mother said she was appalled by this ghastly news and that Mr.
Lewisohn was pondering this very minute what the solution should
be for the spoiled Van Rensselaer, scion of a great family, as the
newspapers often called me. Great family, indeed!

I gave her a long, disagreeable look. "No," I said, turned on my
heel and walked out the door and back to my little room. I switched
on Marlene singing soulfully, lit a cigarette, and started to read
Frederic Prokosch's latest novel, *The Conspirators*. It concerned
war-torn Europe. Hedy Lamarr, in white turban and ropes of
pearls, had slinked around in a white convertible Rolls in the
Warner Brothers movie.

After lunch I was still lying in my bed, reading Prokosch and
listening to Marlene. Mother knocked on the door and in she
came, followed by one of her suitors, Alex McLanahan. I didn't
bother to get up, and she rebuked me for my bad manners. Sul-
lenly, I stood up.

"It's a lovely day," Mother said. "Aren't you going out?"

"No," I said. I caught Mr. Mac's eyes and felt ashamed. He knew
how sick and depraved I was. His son Mike must have told him I
was on the Grub Squad.

"Are you going to stay in all day and listen to old records?" asked
Mr. McLanahan in his deep voice.

I blushed angrily and lowered my eyes. "Yes," I answered.

"Why aren't you out in Central Park, playing baseball with the other boys?" Mr. Mac persisted. I winced. Mother and her beau exchanged looks and closed the door behind them. For two years Mother had said she and Mr. McLanahan would soon wed. But I'd seen his gorgeous wife and knew there was no hope.

Two days later, Jessie informed me that plans were being made for me to go to Louis Bromfield's famous Malabar Farm in Lucas, Ohio. I'd read *Mrs. Parkington* by Bromfield the previous year and seen the movie twice at Radio City Music Hall. Of course, I knew all about Louis: That year, Lauren Bacall and Humphrey Bogart had been married at his Malabar Farm, and I'd read that one of my idols, Joan Fontaine, had recently been a guest.

I had devoured every biography about the Fitzgeralds, and Louis's name cropped up with Hemingway's and Gertrude Stein's. Louis was also a friend of Edith Wharton, whose best friend was my distant cousin, Walter Van Rensselaer Berry. Also, Fred Beckman had told me he and Louis had been chums in the Twenties in Paris, had gotten drunk at Hinky Dinks and the Ritz Bar, and had listened to Mabel Mercer sing with Jimmy Daniels at Bricktop's. Louis had been a hero, driving an ambulance, and had won the Legion of Honor.

Yippee! I jumped out of bed and danced Jessie about the room. "How did all this Bromfield stuff come about?" I said.

"Paul Palmer," replied Jessie, smiling happily. "Eve told him he had to do something constructive about you this summer!"

"Gee, Eve saved the day, again!"

Chapter
Twelve

I loved Malabar Farm, Mary and Louis Bromfield, the dozen boxer dogs running after Louis, and the fertile Ohio countryside. The exuberant music of *Carousel* flooded the spacious, flower-filled Bromfield rooms at the big house.

What a contrast these thirty-one rooms were from the dark, airless, low-ceilinged two rooms of 3B at the Lowell! Mary and Louis quickly became my Perfect Couple. And Louis Bromfield became my hero, without equal.

Thank God, Louis came along at that crucial time in my development from boy to man. If he hadn't, I would have continued to follow in the footsteps of Fred Beckman. Now I wanted to be a heroic ambulance driver and be awarded the Croix de Guerre.

Fred Beckman's fleshy Rubens body faded momentarily from my fantasies and Louis's frame took prominence. Instead of day-dreaming about being a blond playboy shaking up gin-and-Dubonnet cocktails to appreciative guests and satisfying a rich old mate with lizard skin, my reveries centered on becoming a rich and successful writer who entertained the crème of Hollywood, traveled the world, and spoke French and Italian fluently.

Malabar Farm was named after the Malabar Caves outside Bombay and within the view of the Taj Mahal Hotel where Louis met every maharaja from Baroda, Cooch Behar, and Jaipur. He had stayed in their colorful palaces, driven their Rolls-Royces, and swayed on elephant backs during tiger hunts.

Louis also had a mill outside Paris, in Senlis. This was where he parked his wife Mary and their three daughters, Hope, Ellen, and Anne, when he took off for his wanderings around the globe with his handsome male secretary, George Hawkins. Mary Appleton Wood-Bromfield was a noble and long-suffering wife. She worshiped Louis, and the large headboard of her bed was made up of the dust jackets from her husband's numerous novels.

Louis spent a lot of time that summer on a tractor, tending to the endless details of the thousand-acre farm. Like Fred, he exuded energy, but his was disciplined and controlled.

Returning to one's roots was a constant subject in his novels. He told me that his favorite pastime those twenty years abroad was dreaming of his return to the Ohio farm where he was born. That summer of 1945 on Malabar Farm, I felt for the first time the strong attraction of nature and came to understand its healing force. Indeed, I seemed to grow stronger and healthier, both in body and in spirit. I awakened those summer mornings with "the corn is as high as an elephant's eye" from "Oh, What a Beautiful Morning," running through my mind (a wholesome change from Marlene's songs).

Louis also adored the lyrics of this Hammerstein song. He kept mentioning values to me, but I had no idea what he was talking about. He also kept mentioning the feeling of belonging—belonging to some place and some person, which gave one strength and stability. And he stressed the importance of being part of the community and taking pride in civic and political matters, the importance of voting and standing up for the things you believed in.

It was strange hearing all my unconscious problems aired like this. For a long time I had felt rootless, as though I belonged nowhere. My heritage meant nothing to me; I seemed a misfit Van Rensselaer. As boys at Saint Paul's often reminded me, I took no pride in those long-ago ancestors, illustrious citizens and patriots all, founding fathers of America. They had integrity, stood for something, as Louis talked about, but somehow I was not part of them. It occurred to me, sadly, that I had none of these things to sustain me.

That summer I lived in a Quonset hut, inhabited by a dozen other young men interested in agriculture. Malabar was a model farm, and these boys came from all over the country to study soil, irrigation, erosion. Just like the values Louis talked to me about, these things to do with the earth seemed Greek to me. My roommates regarded me as an alien creature, but I kept smiling Mother's smile at them, and nodding in an intelligent way whenever they spoke of things I didn't understand. My ability to adapt to new situations served me well.

From nine to five, we boys worked in the fields, picking corn and gathering hay and throwing it up on the wagons. It was hot working in those fields, and some evenings we cooled off in a pond. Other evenings I lay on my bunk and read.

One day Louis gave me *The Rains Came*. I returned to the Quonset hut, and I couldn't put it down. Its heroine, Edwina, made a strong impression on me. Her opening scene had her lying in a luxurious sleeping car of a train moving through India. She was a beautiful, empty, bored aristocrat of thirty-seven. She'd lived the good life in Cannes, Monte, and Deauville and was woozy from too much sleeping medicine, which put her in a kind of an erotic coma, dreaming of muscular coolies and wondering what it would be like with them. Edwina's fantasies were a lot like my own, and she acted rather like Mother and some of the other inhabitants of the Villa Corne D'Or. She was married to the rich and powerful Lord Esketh, a man she loathed and feared—and cuckolded constantly. All this rang a familiar bell; I was hooked.

All during those hot, sweaty days in the fields, I'd think about Edwina, Mother and Mr. Lewisohn, Fred Beckman and Hazel. I looked forward to returning to the barracks and the adventure-drama in Ranchipur, where Lady Esketh lived in the maharaja's palace, similar to the palace of the Jaipurs, in fantastic luxury, surrendering to her husband's odious lust and scheming to have a sexual interlude with the "copper Apollo" who was the maharaja's favorite doctor. This gorgeous Indian doctor was played by Tyrone Power, complete with turban, in the 1939 movie, and Myrna Loy played the "fashionable slut," Milady Esketh, complete with chiffon dresses and diamonds. I'd seen it, like so many of my favorite films, three or four times; now, I hungered to discuss these characters with their author.

Louis and Mary would often invite me up to the Big House for dinner. Their three daughters would be there and usually some interesting guests. Invariably, there was conversation about the war, my heroes Roosevelt, Churchill, and DeGaulle, and the danger of Stalin. Louis also liked to talk about American bankers, lawyers, and stockbrokers, of whom he had a low opinion.

Mary Bromfield took me aside and gave me a mother's love and concern. She often looked at me with pity, especially when I asked her what she thought of Mother and Mr. Lewisohn. Mary was discreet in her answers. She said that Adele was the most alluring and attractive woman, but that the life she'd chosen for herself was somehow futile and gave back nothing, and didn't I agree?

Mary, who came from an old New York family, had grown up with the Ellsworths and gone to school with Crazy Liz. She felt sorry for Aunt Bessie because she'd had all those looney children. I told her, quite dramatically, that there was a terrible strain of madness running through the Van Rensselaer family tree—that they'd too many times intermarried into other Hudson River dynasties, like the Livingstons. The blood had run a little thin. She nodded her head sympathetically.

The end of the war with Japan came in mid-August, and we celebrated V-J Day by driving all the way to the big town of Mansfield, where there were fireworks and much drinking. We returned to Malabar at break of day. My days with the Bromfields were drawing to an end, and I felt a sense of finality during those last days of August.

Two days before my departure for New York, Louis and I had a memorable talk. We sat on the porch in back of the kitchen of the Big House. It was a hot summer night. The frogs were croaking, the crickets chirping. Over the fields and meadows hung a strong but not unpleasant scent of manure, hay, and damp earth.

Below us were some barns and silos, some with plaques on them reading "Courtesy of MGM" or "Warner Brothers," and I could hear the cows moving restlessly in their stalls.

We talked of *The Rains Came*, which I'd just finished, and Edwina's end, which had made me weep. Edwina, sensual and corrupt, had lived a worthless life, but her decadence was redeemed by a force of goodness and courage. She became a nurse after the dam-burst disaster, when Ranchipur was flooded and a cholera epidemic broke out. The Maharani wanted Lady Esketh to leave, but she stayed on in the hospital and died.

Louis told me he'd modeled Edwina after Edwina Mountbatten, who had quite a dramatic history and was said to be Nehru's lover. Then we spoke of his life among the rich and famous "International Garbage Set," and he recalled Eddie Wassermann, later Waterman, bringing Adele Van Rensselaer alone, sans Mr. Lewisohn, to one of his Sunday lunches at Senlis. Apparently, Louis said, Mr. Lewisohn was having an amorous interlude with a pretty young thing.

"Did Mr. Lewisohn have many love affairs?" I asked.

"Are you mad?" Louis exclaimed, and then he recalled a crossing on the *Normandie* when two young girls caught Mr. Lewisohn's eye in the bar. They had quite a romance. Years later, Eve told me about a crossing on the *Queen Mary* when she caught her father and husband with some girls they'd picked up.

"It all sounds pretty decadent," I said, feeling uncomfortable.

"Your mother and Mr. Lewisohn live a corrupt and decadent life, Philip," Louis said gravely, never taking his eyes off mine. "And you must break away from them—or you'll be tainted."

I hung my head, feeling depressed. If only I could stay with Louis and Mary Bromfield forever. They understood me; some of my feelings of strangeness and isolation had faded that summer. I enjoyed working in the fields and I looked forward to every new day. Now I had to return to that New York life, only now there was no school to go to. What should I do? I looked at Louis with desperation.

Louis began to talk about my future and the necessity for a career. He had such a strong personality that his words mesmerized me.

"You must have a career, Philip," he kept saying.

"Career?"

"Every man must have a career," he said.

"Well, Fred Beckman doesn't."

Louis was shocked that I knew such a "worthless, shallow" character and told me that Fred was hardly the right role model. "I'd avoid hanging around Fred Beckman!" Louis concluded grimly. "He's a narcissist."

"He's mother's favorite beau," I ventured, hoping to hear more about Fred.

"The blind leading the blind," was all Louis said. Then he went into the kitchen and returned with a book. It was a copy of *Pleasant Valley*. On the title page he'd written, "For Philip, hoping you'll remember some of the things we talked about. With the friendship and best wishes of Louis Bromfield." I kept my head buried in the book, so he wouldn't see the tears in my eyes.

Presently I stood up and Louis embraced me affectionately. "You're a strong, wholesome young man," he said. "Sign up for Columbia School of Journalism. You have the sensitivity, curiosity, and awareness needed for a writer's life; now you must develop the discipline."

"Remember," Louis continued, "I believe in you; don't let me down. Don't be sad. You can make use of your loneliness; it will stand you in good stead. And keep in mind: Your mother has made her life; she's done the best she could. Now you must make yours. Don't take the easy way out, like Fred and Adele; don't sell out."

"I won't," I replied.

"Be careful of your chameleon quality." He spoke so gravely all I could do was stare at him.

I headed back to the Quonset hut. I felt charged by his supportive words; I'd have an identity: a writer! The triumphant waltz from *Carousel* was playing in the sitting room. The figures of Mary and her three daughters made a picture of family unity as lovely as a Bonnard. Yellow lights from the Big House gleamed in the darkness as brightly as the fireflies around me. A heat mist lingered over the avenue of trees and the fertile, fragrant farmlands. With wonder, I gazed up at the stars. In New York, you never saw them—or perhaps I never looked up. Louis said the secret of enjoying New York was looking up; if you looked down you saw the soot on the pavements.

On the train back to New York, Louis's face rose before me, and the haunting strains of *Carousel* would not leave me. A delicious fantasy swam into my mind. In a few years I would be a rich and successful writer with a place in the country like Malabar Farm, a warm, loving wife like Mary, and three pretty daughters like Hope, Anne, and Ellen. A dozen boxer dogs (Audrey Emery had given Louis his first two) would be following my footsteps, and music would be playing in my spacious sitting room full of French Provençal chests and cabinets in warm walnut and beechwood. A marble bust of Voltaire by Houdon would repose on my writing table. And this large writing table would have a boxer dog on it, looking at me with love and affection, and my hand would be on his paw. Tall French windows would overlook flower beds, bright with red zinnias, yellow marigolds, white stock, blue delphiniums, lavender gladiolas. All my rooms would be overflowing with these flowers, fresh from my garden, as Louis's were.

Thus was born my fantasy of being a writer. I overlooked the fact that much hard work, discipline, and love had created this appealing picture. I even neglected the fact that Louis had been a child prodigy. Typically, I overlooked the truth and distorted the reality of Louis's situation. And of mine, too.

The next morning I was in a manic mood. I raced through the station, bounded up the endless flight of stairs, two at a time, and into the street. I sprang into a taxi and told the driver to take me uptown, and through Central Park, please.

At the Lowell Jessie was warmly receptive, and my dark, impersonal hotel room facing the brick rear wall only momentarily depressed me.

I asked Jessie the usual questions: How was Mother? Was she looking pretty? Was Mr. Lewisohn in good health? Who was the new flame? Jessie laughed in her merry way, unpacked the two Louis Vuitton suitcases I'd stolen from Mother, and hung my clothes in the closet. Louis had humorously called my wardrobe more appropriate for Monte Carlo or Palm Beach. Thank God for Mother's charge accounts at Saks Fifth and Brooks.

Jessie couldn't keep her eyes off me. She kept touching my shoulders and arms, saying, "You've filled out so, dear Philip!

You're brown as a walnut, and what muscles! Louis Bromfield has worked miracles."

I smiled and started the lies: "Louis Bromfield said I'm a *genius* and will make a *terrific* writer. I showed him some stuff I'd been working on, and he said I was so sensitive, so aware, so curious—all the ingredients that make up a successful writer, Jessie! And that I must start my important career!"

Jessie looked surprised.

"Well, your dear mother will be very pleased to hear you talking like this. She dined with Mr. Lewisohn last night at the Colony, and they discussed what should be done with you, young man. How handsome you are! I bet all the girls are crazy about you, aren't they?"

I gave a humorless laugh and made a gesture as if I were brushing off all the girls. "Can't keep them off me, Jessie!" I winked. "Hah-hah. How is that wicked Fred Beckman, by the way?"

"Mr. Beckman gave a cocktail party yesterday at his new apartment on Park Avenue. Your mother said he's become so grand she can hardly recognize him. He sent your mother some pretty roses yesterday. She's up, by the way, and wants to see you."

My elation continued. "I'm going to look after Mother when I'm rich and famous, Jessie. I'm going to have a big country house like Louis's, thanks to MGM and Warner Brothers! Mother will live with me, and we'll be so happy, with lots of dogs, and cows, and horses! With you, too, of course, Jessie, you gorgeous creature."

She kissed me on the cheek. "I do hope you stay in this mood, Philip. Your mother was upset by your rude behavior before you left, you naughty boy."

"That was *before* I understood what a genius I am."

Mother, as was her custom every morning, was lying in her double bed, a breakfast tray over her lap, a ribbon through her hair, talking on the telephone.

I moved restlessly about Mother's bedroom, and her soft brown eyes followed me uneasily. Presently, she hung up and gave me a shy smile. We hadn't parted the best of friends. I crossed over to her bed and as I leaned down to kiss her, I caught the fragrance of her Guerlain jasmine on her pink silk and lace bed jacket. I thought her looks had been restored, and I smiled.

Swiftly, with much drama, I told Mother of my great success on Louis Bromfield's farm, and how I, too, was going to write best-sellers that, of course, would be made into movies. Mother's slightly anxious look faded and she took a deep breath. She said she was proud of me, and that I looked so strong and handsome. I blushed with pleasure. She added that she and Mr. Lewisohn had decided that I should start classes at the Hun School, and——

I impatiently interrupted her, giving her an intense look. "But, Mummy, Louis said I *must* start college at Columbia School of Journalism immediately."

She gave a little laugh. "But, dear, how could you start college, when you haven't even graduated from high school?"

This took me back some; I frowned a puzzled frown at her. "Well, Mummy, Louis says I'm a *genius* and that I must make a life of my own and have an important writing career."

"That's all very well, dear," she explained, "but Peters is driving us down to the Hun School next week."

I felt a trifle let down about the Hun. I'd heard some disagreeable things about it, that it was nicknamed Café Hun and known as a country club. And that really wasn't the correct place for a budding Shakespeare like me, now, was it?

Suddenly, she decided a change in conversation might help matters. How were Louis and Mary? Was their house charming? Did Louis still have that peculiar haircut?

I flung her a bored look. "Mummy, Louis has a crewcut, because he has no vanity and doesn't spend hours in front of a mirror, like Fred Beckman, who's a narcissist! Heavens! Louis has values, Mummy!"

Mother looked vague. "Does he?"

My voice began to rise as I became angry. "Louis said Fred is a worthless, shallow creature, Mummy!"

"Really?" The telephones started to ring, and she made her usual distressed face. "I think we should have lunch and talk things over." She picked up the receivers and explained, in the sweetest tones, that she'd call them back in a sec.

"The Problem Fox and Mr. McLanahan will be awfully upset if you don't have lunch and a matinee with them, won't they?"

"And what," she said in an icy voice, "do you mean by that remark?"

"You're decadent and corrupt!" I shouted.

"Go on," said Mother in a low, tense voice, her lips taut.

"Louis said you and Mr. Lewisohn live a corrupt and decadent life and that I must break away or be *tainted! You're disgusting, Mummy!"*

Mother's wide red lips smiled thinly. "Well, in that case, why don't you pack up and leave, if you feel this way?" Her voice was taunting; her eyes narrowed as she watched me. "I'm not stopping you."

Icewater froze my veins. What could I do? I had no profession, could not earn a living. I was utterly dependent on the slender, pretty, blond woman reclining on the double bed in pink satin and lace. And she was utterly dependent on the Copper King. The blind leading the blind.

Futility and despair swept over me. I could never break away. In my heart I knew I was as shallow and luxury-loving as that lazy hunk of beefsteak, Fred. At least he could sing for his supper and get paid a lot for his services. I'd even failed at making a woman happy this summer. Two boys from the Quonset hut had taken me up to the see the local prostitute. She was young and voluptuous, but I couldn't do anything. That was the worst moment of my life! That was something that I was never going to tell a living soul. Defeat and failure would never be in my vocabulary. They might apply to my failure of a father, but not to me!

I slammed out of Mother's room, shaking with fear. Like father, like son.

The following day, Mother and I lunched in the art-deco splendors of the Passy Restaurant, reconciled. Mother never harbored a grudge; it was not in her nature to remain angry with someone she loved. Her way of dealing with a difficult situation was to overlook it.

One weekend I was asked out to a dance on Long Island and was to stay the weekend at Susan Norton's. Her parents were the Skeffington Nortons, old friends of my grandparents'.

All went well on Saturday. I got drunk and danced with everyone. I felt secure, everyone was nice to me, and I was voted the best-looking boy there. I don't remember too many more details of that dance. I *had* to drink! God knows, if I didn't, I wouldn't, couldn't, dance, couldn't make those foolish jokes or spin out those grandiose tales!

I woke up in a luxurious room the next morning in the Norton's big house on Piping Rock Road, across from the club. There was a commotion outside my door; I heard voices whispering in a frantic way and I felt uneasy. Suddenly, Mrs. Norton, an extremely lovely blond woman, burst in. "I want you to pack your things and leave," she said cooly, in her very proper manner.

I gulped. A terrible fear gripped me. "Why, Mrs. Norton?" I asked faintly. What had I done?

Mrs. Norton, slim and petite, every hair in place, kept staring at me. "Your mother's the scandal of New York," she said, "and I don't want my daughter tainted." Her clipped Locust Valley drawl continued, but I didn't hear anything else. *Tainted.* The word Louis had used to describe Mother and Mr. Lewisohn. I didn't know what to do. Panic swept over me. Then I had a brainstorm.

"Can I call my father?" I asked, pale and sweating. My fragile voice sounded like a stranger's.

Mrs. Norton flung me a disdainful look. "As you like," she snapped, "but please pack your things."

A further humiliation was having my father, the failure, drive up in his dirty old Plymouth coupe. The arrogant butler gave him a condescending look.

My father came up to my room. I hadn't dared move. "Well, Phil," he said in his tired defeated voice, cultivated as hell, however, "what's happened?"

No one *ever* called me Phil. I was not the Phil type. Now, wouldn't you know, my father was calling me this hated name. Well, how could he know how I felt? I'd seen him few enough times since I was a year old. It was rather embarrassing to be put in this vulnerable position with him, for I'd played high and mighty with him, with the Lewisohn largesse. Now he eyed me with a kind of cynical contempt.

I burst into tears. He comforted me as best he could, ill at ease. Somehow, we managed to get out of the Nortons' big house and then I was in his horrible old Plymouth, crunching down the

Nortons' long, long drive, headed toward Jericho. In silence we drove past large, fancifully curved wrought-iron gates and brick manors, every lawn and shrub immaculately maintained.

It was a shock to wind up in my father's dilapidated, white-shingled cottage, where Vera Van Rensselaer spoke in the same tired, defeated way as her husband. Their house was dark, and quiet as a tomb. I could tell they hated each other; hate lingered in every gloomy corner.

"What happened with the Nortons?" my father kept asking me. Finally, I was able to answer. I told him, between painful sobs, what Mrs. Norton had said. Who was Mrs. Norton to *dare* to say such horrible things to me?

"Well," said Charles Van Rensselaer, Jr., with his customary thin smile, "Mrs. Norton is a very proper woman. Daughters of the American Revolution and Colonial Dames, great friend of the Czarina, wouldn't you know. She's right, of course, about your mother. Your mother *is* a scandal and has ruined our fine old name by her amoral behavior. You boys and your mother are to be pitied; your easy days on the Lewisohn gravy train will soon come to an end."

I glanced up at him with fear in my eyes. "What do you mean?"

He laughed unpleasantly. "Your mother and you boys are all living in a fool's paradise."

Again, I asked the same question.

"I hear your poor mother's lost her looks. No wonder, after the playgirl life she's led, burning the candle at both ends. I hate to think how you boys and your mother will end."

I laughed wildly. "In the Bowery, probably."

My father nodded his handsome head, his eyes glittering at me. "Probably," he seconded.

Suddenly I realized he hated me, was jealous of me. I could not escape his dark, silent cottage too soon, and be on my way back to New York. As the Long Island train crept through the ugly suburbs, banging and clattering, I looked at the poor stucco houses, certain that's where I was headed. A terrible fear pervaded me, and with it, a sense of inevitability. Why fight it? We were all ruined.

The next day I went into Mother's bedroom to say good-bye before I left for the Hun School. She was on the phone as usual, talking to a suitor. I never mentioned the Norton incident to Mother. Let her live in her fool's paradise. We were all steaming toward disaster, like the ill-fated liner of my earlier fantasy. Yes, that nightmare had returned in full force. Only now, I awakened in a cold sweat, as the waters filled my lungs and suffocated me. I struggled in the water. I wanted to live, but I was going down in the ship. I was being buried alive like Lady Madeleine in *The Fall of the House of Usher*.

Chapter Thirteen

Mother began a romance with Rodman Wanamaker. He was to be the Great Love. Rod, or Roddy as he was called, divorced his second wife and searched for a country house where he and Adele could live quietly. He had a poodle named Saint, and he gave Adele one called Sinner.

Rod Wanamaker exerted a positive influence over Adele (she did everything he told her). He did not like her dyed blond hair, so she quickly returned to her natural chestnut; he did not like her lunching at the Colony with Mr. Lewisohn or dining with him at El Morocco, so, she rarely saw Mr. Lewisohn anymore. Roddy and Adele spent weekends in the country, and during the week, they walked in Central Park. Mother even knitted him a pair of socks and started to cook him meals! This was serious.

Mr. Wanamaker presented his bride-to-be to his family, to all the fashionable and rich Warburtons and Munns. The Vanderbilt princess, Miss Rosemary Warburton, was presented to Adele, who thought her "lovely" although she didn't relish "having Mr. Lewisohn's girl as a family member."

Years later, when I was Rosie's Southampton houseguest, she

told me how her mother, Big Rose Vanderbilt, had crossed over the length of the Colony Restaurant one evening when Mother was dining with Mr. Lewisohn, and kissed Adele Van Rensselaer so the whole world would know that she did not disapprove of what "poor Adele Van Rensselaer was doing, sacrificing herself for her two boys." Rosie used to tell me, "Adele was a Christian martyr, sacrificing herself as she did with that lewd Lewisohn man."

Mr. Wanamaker, as I always called him, possessed all the requisite credentials for a perfect stepfather. He was Adele's age, had a huge apartment at 120 East End Avenue overlooking the East River, was a member of the Racquet, Brook, National, Southampton Beach, and Metropolitan clubs, and more. He'd been a polo player, was a great friend of the Duke of Windsor, dressed with style in Savile Row duds, and had been quite a ladies' man, too. What more could I ask?

Meanwhile, I was off on my brief, six-month Hun School interlude. The school was set in the midst of some Constable-type woods outside of Princeton, and I enjoyed the country club atmosphere, where I could escape my violent thoughts. My fellow guests all seemed out of the decadent pages of *Brideshead Revisited*, my favorite book that fall. Some of my friends had the depraved look of those hollow-eyed figures painted by Schille or Klimt. I fell into the role of playboy Philip.

At the Café Hun, only a few exercised and even fewer studied. Pleasant self-delusion took over. I adopted Mother's motto: "Let things take care of themselves." It suited my mood to perfection. I no longer wanted to think of what Louis or my father had said. I blocked out Mrs. Norton. The only books I studied were novels like *Forever Amber* and *Kitty*. I vastly improved my knowledge of the cinema and sat through every movie at the Princeton Playhouse, once if not thrice.

I had dreams of restoring the Van Rensselaer fortunes and putting gold back into the greatly depleted family coffers, and I intended to get what I wanted, come what may! And what I'd always wanted most of all was to own a bigger Rolls than Mr. Lewisohn's, the one with the basket-weave doors. After all, *the* Mrs. Vanderbilt had a Rolls parked outside her palace at 640 Fifth Avenue, so why shouldn't Philip Van Rensselaer, Esquire, the scion of a famed Hudson River dynasty and New York's "first family," have one?

Mother finally moved out of the odious Lowell and into a grand five-bedroom apartment at the Volney Hotel, at 23 East Seventy-fourth. This had been Eve and Paul Palmer's; they'd divorced after years of an unsatisfactory union. Eve had married Irving Baer, a psychiatrist, and moved with him to Topeka, Kansas.

So Eve saved the day again and gave me a momentary reprieve from the madness that was about to descend on me. Her Volney apartment was lovely, wonderfully furnished all in modern, and it momentarily changed my dark mental outlook. It was a real home. A thirty-foot living room, complete with piano and big windows, had an unobstructed view of Central Park. I now had a room of my own and had all my books around. Dear Jessie was replaced by Eve's maid, Olga. Olga was as sweet and motherly as Jessie, and I felt secure and protected.

Mother and I got along quite well that Christmas of 1945, the last Christmas we'd be together. Unquestionably the most stimulating event of this period was my purchase of a Rolls-Royce on February 16, 1946. For months I'd been devouring the "Cars for Sale" column in the *New York Times*. I didn't want just *any* Rolls; I wanted a grand chariot. During the war years, Grandma Van Rensselaer had been giving me hundred-dollar war bonds for Christmas and my birthday, April 29. Now the bonds were worth a cool two thousand.

Without consulting Mother, I answered a *Times* ad from New Jersey that read: "Magnificent Phantom Rolls-Royce limousine, black, 1935 model, with luxurious interior; perfect condition. Sacrifice, $1950."

I arrived, cash in hand, drove the huge black monster around the block, then handed the owner the greenbacks. I didn't know a damn thing about cars—pistons, cylinders, batteries. I didn't even have a license or registration. But those were boring details. I had to have that Rolls—now! Driving back to Café Hun, I hummed "We're in the Money," then parked the Leviathan-on-wheels in a secluded place in the woods.

Tyler Smith and Art Scully, my two best chums, viewed the

monster with amazement and delight. The silver grilled front, the two white sidewalls on either side of the bonnet, the winged figure topping the motor, the delicious purr of the engine, and the soft muted sound of the closing door were all pure *bliss* (my favorite word that year). I felt as rich as Mr. Rockefeller.

Every weekend was spent in New York with Tyler, Art, and my Hun gang. We camped out in the luxurious modern decor of Eve Lewisohn's. Mother was a little annoyed with all the company, but she rose to the occasion in her gracious manner. She viewed the mammoth car parked in front of the Volney canopy with some consternation.

"Darling, are you sure you have a license and registration?"

I made a bored face. "Of course, Mummy," I lied.

Mother kept staring at the Rolls. "Wasn't it fearfully expensive?"

"It was a real bargain, Mummy. I cashed in Grandma's war bonds, and there you are!"

Mother glanced at me. "Was that wise, darling?"

"Mummy," I replied in an exasperated tone. "Mummy, this is an investment, it can only go up in value. It's cheaper than your mink coat and will last longer."

"Really, dear?"

One Sunday in late February was unusually quiet. Mother had no invitations. I asked her if she'd like to take a spin through the park. She smiled, and then we went downstairs. Mother, in her mink coat and mink hat, gazed at the huge car with some trepidation. People stopped dead in their tracks to stare at us. Mother loathed being conspicuous and became nervous. I opened the rear door for her, but she hesitated.

"Darling, I really can't sit in the back. I'll sit next to you, in the front."

"Okay," I smiled.

The powerful engine purred, and we headed toward Fifth Avenue. I turned into the park at Seventy-second Street. Mother gave a merry laugh and said she felt just like a maid on her day off, sitting next to the chauffeur. We had a lot of laughs, playing maid and chauffeur, and had a fine time. Indeed, it was the happiest moment of my life. Mother was sitting beside me on a cold winter afternoon and we were safe and warm. She was slim, pale, delicate, deliciously fragrant, dressed and looking like Anna Karenina. Best of all, Mother was saying, "Darling, it was *too* brilliant of you to think of this outing in the park. Haven't had such a *lark* for ages! Thank you so much, dear, for asking me, you adorable creature."

Mother was thanking *me*. I was doing something for *her*. It was the first and only time I ever did anything for her.

One day in early March 1946, Mrs. Hun summoned me to her rooms. With my keen intuition, I instinctively felt something was up; with dread I opened her door and slinked in. Madame Hun fixed accusing eyes on me. She'd been informed that I had a Rolls-Royce in the woods. Cars were forbidden at the Hun School, she reminded me, never taking those eyes off me.

"Now, Philip," she kept saying, "do please tell me the *truth*."

I shuffled my feet, remembering how Coop and Jimmy Stewart acted the simpleminded good guys.

At age seventeen, about to be eighteen, I was a cretinous-looking fellow with long, untidy, blond hair over my face. Huge China-blue eyes stared out emptily—or wildly, depending on my mood. A slow smile was constantly on my face, and my wide, slim, girlish lips—Mother's lips—were forever in a pout or hanging open.

Mrs. Hun, the witch, kept staring at me as if to read my thoughts. And I kept smiling my slow, dopey smile at her.

"I swear, Mrs. Hun, on a stack of Bibles, I don't own a Rolls."

Finally, Mrs. Hun asked me, with a significant stare, if I was telling the truth. She kept emphasizing that damn word *truth*, and I kept looking moronic. She would pardon me, dear boy, if I owned up like a man and was honest. Stupidly, stubbornly, I held to my innocence.

That same afternoon I shot out of the Hun woods in a frenzy. My beautiful black beast, the twelve-cylinder P. 111, raced in the direction of New York. I sat at the wheel in solitary splendor. The richly purring engine, the spinning spoked-wheeled tires made a hypnotic sound on the asphalt beneath me, lulling me into my usual daydreaming state. I liked to drive fast, like Michael Arlen's heroine, Iris March, in *The Green Hat*. Now I brooded about *her* end, wrapping herself and huge Hispano around a tree.

With a wild laugh, I pressed the accelerator down to the floorboard, watched the speedometer climb to fifty—sixty—seventy—eighty—ninety! A reckless sense of self-destruction filled me as the car surged forward, careening slightly. My hands gripped the wheel, trying to keep the car on a straight line. I was out of control, but it didn't matter. That was how it should be, wasn't it? Not giving a damn! *Out of control!*

Really, a Rolls was the only car on the face of the globe! I glanced around the highway. Why didn't more people own one? Who on earth, in their right mind, dear boy, would *choose* to drive a ghastly Chevy or Plymouth (Daddy! Ugh.), when they could lord it over everyone in a car fit for a king?

Fred Beckman had just recently told me he was sure he was going to die behind the wheel of a Rolls. He had made me giggle when he related his favorite Rolls-Royce story to me: He and Lady M., a highly publicized duke's daughter, were driving through Regent's Park in 1925, when the theater doorman opened the car door, and Milady, in white satin and a diamond tiara, was discovered flagrante delicto. Fred's reputation was made in the fashionable world.

Fred loved to give house tours of his "cottage" in Princeton. The last time I had been there he'd put his arm around me and told me Uncle Fred was going to take me on an extensive European trip very soon. But not to tell anyone. "That would be *our* secret, my child, *comprenez?*"

"Oh, yes, Fred!"

"Make hay while the sun shines, my child!" He laughed that old insinuating laugh.

"Oh, I will, Fred!"

"Use your personality."

"Oh, I will, Fred!"

"Don't do anything I wouldn't do, and think of me while you're doing it . . . I know! I know!"

Suddenly, my daydream of Fred and me in Europe was shattered. I became aware of a shrill siren. Then a crude-looking man in a blue uniform rode by me on a motorcycle, signaling *me* over to the side of the road. Some nerve. I glared at him. How *dare* he? Didn't he know who I was?

"Let's see your license and registration." The ruffian in blue was peering at me through the window, sizing me up. He had sort of a John Wayne appearance with the same massive shoulders and square face. I fluttered my dark lashes at him.

"Just one moment, officer," I said, fumbling awkwardly in my breast pocket for my blue pin seal wallet. "Where, oh, where are you, you little devils? Hah-hah!" All the time working my charm and giving him sidelong glances.

"Did you know you were going over eighty-five miles an hour, buddy boy?"

"Eighty-five? Meee? My goodness gracious, officer, fancy that."

"You might have killed someone in this hearse, buddy boy," he growled.

I registered horror, shock, disbelief.

"Okay, smart-ass, let's cut all this crap. *License and registration!*"

Out of the blue, I concocted a wild tale of leaving my license and registration in New York by mistake. "With my mother, officer, Mrs. Brookfield Van Rensselaer. She's beautiful, and her best friend is Mr. Frederick Lewisohn, the Copper King, you know? Well, you *should* know, if you don't, hah-hah!"

His craggy face turned to stone, and my bowels quaked.

"Have you been drinking, smart-ass?"

I grinned from ear to ear. "Mercy, no, officer, I never, uh, imbibe. I'm Philip Van Rensselaer, by the way, and we Van Rensselaers, uh, uphold all the laws and traditions, have *for centuries!* Do you know my uncle is a four-star general down in old Washington? A *great* friend, natch, of sweet Franklin D. Roosevelt. Such a great man, dear Uncle Franklin! Come to think of it, he'd like you, and I *must* introduce you."

"Yeah?" he replied with a sinister connotation. "For your information, Phil, your dear Uncle Franklin died last year."

I flushed scarlet. Roosevelt, my hero, dead? It couldn't be possible! Of course, I hadn't been following current events.

In a haze his voice came to me. He now spoke in a condescending manner, as if he were talking to a sick and confused child. "Well, Phil, unless you can find your license and registration, I'm going to take you for a little visit to the judge, at the nearby courthouse."

Three hours later I was in Mr. Lewisohn's limousine, seated between him and Adele. The judge said that I was a menace to mankind but perhaps a good long stretch with Uncle Sam's army might straighten out my criminal character. I was profoundly ashamed. In the dimness of the pearl gray upholstered rear, I kept gnawing the flesh around my nails. It was twilight outside the Cadillac windows, and we were approaching Manhattan from the ugly flats of New Jersey.

Mother looked like part of the ethereal mauve dusk. She seemed unusually fragile, all in black with a scarf of dark furs twisted around her neck. A dark, wide-brimmed Fedora hat half concealed her face. Her eyes were shining from all her tears, and her wide, expressive lips were trembling with emotion. Now and then she sniffed into a lace handkerchief that she had brought out from her black lizard bag. Her initials A VAN R were stamped on it in gold. She kept sighing, and the sound wrenched my heart.

I felt swamped with guilt. After the judge passed the army sentence on me, Mother stared at me with reproachful eyes. *How could you? How could you?* That haunting sadness of hers that was always there under the surface struck me with force. In the courthouse, she stood erect and still, with great dignity, but when she stepped into the car, she collapsed.

When I dared look at her, I saw an entirely new look of understanding on her face. There was gravity there, as though she was aware for the first time what had happened to me.

Suddenly, her voice broke the awful silence. "Philip, how could you lie to the police and tell them all those preposterous stories of the Roosevelts?"

"I guess I have a vivid imagination, Mummy," I said weakly.

"And you lied to Mrs. Hun about the Rolls," she continued in the same tone. "That's why she has just expelled you from school. She told me she'd forgive you anything, but not lies. Why on earth didn't you tell the truth? What *is* the matter with you?"

"I guess I'm a juvenile delinquent, Mummy."

"Don't you know right from wrong?"

"I'm afraid I have a criminal character, Mummy," I replied miserably.

"I had no idea you had no license or registration; it's appalling." Mother was every inch the great lady, and I felt a fresh wave of shame. "You might have told me the truth, at least. Whatever were you thinking, driving about like that?"

I hung my head, with my queer smile. I had a wild idea to tell her I was thinking of Fred Beckman and about going to Europe with him. That would really cause another drama! As it was, I mumbled, "I don't know, Mummy."

Mother suddenly became angry. "I can't begin to tell you how humiliated I was standing there before the judge and having him stare down at me with that insolent, accusing manner of his. As if I hadn't brought you up properly."

Mr. Lewisohn leaned over and took Mother's white-gloved hand. "It's all right, Adele; it's all over now," he said soothingly.

Mother kept after me. "Really, Philip, it was quite selfish of you, too, to drag Mr. Lewisohn out on this cold day. He's just gotten over a bad case of the grippe."

I mumbled an apology to Mr. Lewisohn.

"You must feel some sense of responsibility for your actions, Philip. Really!" Mother concluded severely. Then she took out a cigarette and put it into a holder. "I hate to tell you, Philip," she went on, her anger now mixed with irony, "but if Mr. Lewisohn hadn't contributed, quite generously, to the Police Athletic League, you'd be in some vile cell of a reform school this very minute. I can't very well see you with those poor, underprivileged boys from broken homes."

"You don't think our home is broken, Mummy?"

Adele glared at me. "I'll thank you to wipe that idiotic grin from your face."

"Yes, Mummy."

"It's not comic, Philip!" she glared.

"Our broken-down family sure is," I replied.

Mother flung up her hands. "I've done the best I could!"

All my resentment and rage toward her burst out. "Things don't just take care of themselves, Mummy! You have to spend some time with me. You always promise we'll have a talk, but we never do." Then I burst into tears. Mother and Mr. Lewisohn looked at each other helplessly.

We drew up before the canopy of the Volney on East Seventy-fourth Street. I followed Mother's tall figure into the long marble vestibule and then into the somber, paneled lobby, dully lit by pink-shaded crystal wall lights that gave a fashionable gloom.

In the elevator Mother stared at her reflection, and I stared at her. She was always extremely proud of her figure; she was joyful when people remarked there wasn't a break in the line anywhere. Mr. Lewisohn often scolded her on her dieting, cautioning her to go easy, but this evening I thought that all the discipline and strength of character to maintain such a silhouette was worth it.

Olga opened the door of the luxurious ultramodern interior. The fragrance of faded rose potpourri and the jasmine of L'Heure Bleue floated around me. There were white tuberoses in a Steuben crystal vase on the sleek, white piano. Olga smiled knowingly at Mother. "Mr. Wanamaker sent the flowers, madame; he just called this minute."

"Did he?" said Mother. She flung off her furs and hat and fussed with her dark hair in a mirror. She was transformed by the news. Color suffused her pale cheeks. Her eyes sparkled, and a smile crept up her face.

Olga watched her lovingly. "I just put the flowers in water, Ma'am."

Mother embraced her with a cry, "You're an angel of light, Olga dear!" She half ran down the long, narrow corridor that led to her bedroom–sitting room. The door slammed. Of course she was going to quickly call Rodman Wanamaker.

Olga made me a drink and we sat in my room. She was full of news about Adele's great love. They were going to be married in a year or so. He'd found an old brick house in Charleston, South Carolina. It was antebellum, with lofty rooms, fireplaces, mahogany wainscotting, and superb moldings.

"And what about me?" I asked.

"Well, you're almost a man," said Olga in her cheery manner. "And you will be, after the army!"

"I suppose," I said bleakly.

"Your mother told me that when you get out of the army, she's going to put you on an allowance. Then you can find a little nest of your own. Won't you like that?"

I swallowed some more whiskey. The lights in the room seemed to fade. Anticlimax settled over me. I felt a terrible exhaustion. My headache was blinding. I heard Olga's voice going on about Mother's happiness and I felt envy and rage.

"Your mother's whole life is going to change now. She'll have everything she's always wanted. Isn't that wonderful?" Mother's high heels made a clatter as she came down the corridor toward us. Olga smiled and added, "Be kind to your mother; you've been an awful strain on her."

A vision stepped into my room and said, "Dear, I must dine out. Olga will make you some scrambled eggs or hamburger." She laughed radiantly. "I can even make a hamburger myself these days; they're sublime, aren't they, Olga?"

"Sublime, Mrs. Van Rensselaer."

Mother looked exquisite with a broadtail coat over her shoulders, a flexible necklace of ribbed gold studded with diamonds and matching bracelet flashing richly. She was heavily made-up, and her skin was lovely. (A far cry from the tragic creature at the courthouse.) She was adjusting some lace about her head.

That evening General Bill Donovan accompanied me to the Palm Court of the Plaza. After I'd decamped school, Mr. Lewisohn had hired General Donovan, the wartime OSS hero, to look after me and make sure I wouldn't abscond. I'd been terrified at the prospect of meeting him, and shuddered at the thought of being in the charge of this potential Gestapo-like inquisitor. As it happened, Donovan and I got along like a house afire, as diverse personalities often do. At the Palm Court that night, he listened appreciatively to the Strauss and Franz Lehár waltzes the band played. He also listened to my grandiose tales of high life, here and abroad, with an indulgent grin.

"Dear Philip, how are you?" came a fascinating voice. I looked up, and there was my idol, Jeanne-Marie Schley, with her brother, Barney, in a nifty uniform. I sprang to my feet and introduced General Donovan as my father. Since no one had ever met my father, they seemed to believe it! Donovan didn't correct me, either. I was proud as Lucifer to be seen with General Donovan and I laughed in a manic way.

I glanced at Bill Donovan. If only I'd had a father I could be proud of. Unlike that bitter, mean-spirited failure in that dark, silent cottage on Long Island, who hated my guts and hungered for my downfall. And Mother's too.

Chapter
Fourteen

Being brought up to have good manners, I looked around the crowded barracks of Fort Dix and thought politesse was the answer.

"Hi, everyone, I'm Philip Van Rensselaer." I shook hands with each boy. "I'm awfully pleased to meet you." This performance was followed by a lot of catcalls, whistles, and groans. Half the boys in the barracks were blacks from the South, and the others came from Brooklyn, the Bronx, and the Amboys. You can imagine the Brooklyn wisecracks.

Then Ralph Lamo stepped forward, and I grinned from ear to ear. He was as dark and powerful as Anthony Quinn, just as handsome, of Italian descent, and very well built. He had the biggest muscles I'd ever seen.

"Hey, listen, you louses," said Ralph in a voice that could stop a dozen trains. "Hey, listen, lay off my pal." Ralph was the leader, and what he said was law. Suddenly, everyone became friendly, and Ralph chuckled in his good-natured way. "Listen, you assholes, this guy will be good for a lot of laughs, and we're going to need them on that troop train down to Camp Polk."

Ralph was right about the train ride. The journey took six days, and every other stop we pulled over to a siding and let an express train roar by. We crawled along. Soot poured in from the windows day and night. There were more jolts and bangs than on the Long Island Railroad to Southampton, and not half as much fun. All the greasy food, the jolts, and my endlessly playing court jester to get laughs wore me down. By the time we crawled into the heavy humidity of Camp Polk, Louisiana, angry red dots covered my face. I was fit to be tied. *Me, having pimples!*

After a month in Camp Polk, it was certain I would never follow in the footsteps of Douglas MacArthur. Indeed, there was never a sorrier sight than Pfc. Philip Van Rensselaer. Even my brother told me, later that year when I was out on a pass, that I was the sloppiest looking soldier he'd ever seen.

Most of my military career was spent in the mess hall, serving out a sentence of KP. My hours were spent cleaning out the grease pits under the sink and dismembering capons. Since I'd never been in a kitchen, I was rather curious about how food was prepared. So I guess I did learn something in the army.

In such a manner, my spring and summer passed.

Ironically, Mother, in a July letter, asked me when I was going to get a promotion. Mr. Wanamaker suggested a career in the Officer's Candidate Service, which might lead to the diplomatic service. Mother said she was certain that I was just too perfect for an ambassadorial role. "You know, like dear, attractive Averell Harriman."

One weekend I got a pass, and a buddy and I went to Alexandria to have a long-missed movie orgy. We stumbled in and out of some tawdry cinema palaces, munching popcorn and Hershey's chocolate drops. The highlight of the weekend was seeing *Gilda*, the movie that made Rita Hayworth a superstar and started an army of famous men chasing after her. In *Gilda*, Rita wiggled her snakehips, her lovely breasts practically falling out of her black-satin strapless evening gown. She danced alluringly to South American music, slinking about in her high heels and tight skirts, slit up the side, to reveal her long, beautiful legs. I drooled when La Hayworth crooned "Amore Mio, Love Me Forever" in her sultry fashion, and I shivered all over when she did a wicked striptease in the crowded bar, singing "Put the Blame on Mame, Boys."

It was a horrible letdown to come out into the squalid streets, trudge onto a bus, and return to our concrete bunker of a motel. Lying on my stained mattress and staring at the motel's neon signs flashing red and black and orange, I daydreamed of Rita, the Divine One. How wonderful to ship out to some faraway tropical paradise where no one knew your name and start all over again. There was sure to be a Mr. Lewisohn in the wings, with a Rolls and pince-nez, if you played your cards right. Suddenly I saw myself as a siren doing wild, erotic dances while admirers devoured every inch of my body, the naughty critters!

Another food parcel arrived from Olga: canned pâté and shrimp, which I shared with Ralph, hoping to further endear myself with him and his Brooklyn buddies. But shortly, Ralph announced he was being sent out to California. He also told me that he'd impregnated a dozen girls on his last weekend and, looking at him, I believed it. When he packed his duffel bag and vanished into a truck a few days later, my depression grew. Ralph had always stood by me, taking my side. Now I had no one to defend me.

The next day, during another KP stint, I learned that I was to check into Fort Monmouth, New Jersey, early in August to commence my training in the Signal Corps. Two days later the noisy troop train was crawling through the humid countryside, headed northward, thank God! Plans to go AWOL and escape the army forever were taking shape in my fatigued and confused mind.

I thought of Ralph. Why couldn't I impregnate a dozen females?

New York, September 17th—Three weeks ago, Philip Van Rensselaer, a Private on pass from Fort Monmouth, sat watching the tennis matches at Forest Hills. Midway through the second set, his gaze wandered to the gallery where he caught sight of blond Countess Caja Palffy.

He looked at her, she looked at him, and the score was love, love, love for the rest of the match. In a blitz courtship, Philip, the son of Social Leader Mrs. Brookfield Van Rensselaer, and the Countess decided to get married secretly, sail for Paris on the *Queen Mary*, and honeymoon in style at the Ritz.

The marriage was to have been Sunday and the Countess wrote us a letter a few days before, telling us of their plans. When we called Mrs. Van Rensselaer, however, she said she knew nothing of the marriage plans and explained that since her son is a minor, he would be unable to marry without parental consent.

The windup is that they didn't marry Sunday, and Philip almost got himself in a jam with the Army for being AWOL. As matters stand, their marriage plans have been postponed indefinitely—Philip won't be getting out of uniform for another few months. Then, if Mrs. Van Rensselaer has no objection, they'll be married.

You can see what was on my mind: sailing to Europe on the *Queen Mary* and honeymooning in style at the Ritz. With a countess!

As soon as I arrived at Fort Monmouth with a totally new group to amuse, I grew depressed. I felt exhausted all the time; I could barely drag myself out to drill practice, and marching was torture. My head ached all the time; everything was an effort. I had no energy. I lost things, forgot engagements.

After seeing the movie version of *The Razor's Edge*, I decided I would go to Europe, like Larry, scheme like Isabel, and probably end my days on the Riviera waterfront like Sophie, doped to the gills and picking up God only knows what.

Just after seeing this drama of high and low life, with a bit of spirituality in India thrown in, I went to watch the tennis matches. Suddenly, a hand touched my shoulder. "Where did you get that ring?" cried a wonderfully foreign female accent. "It belongs to Mama!" I turned around and there were a pair of beautiful blue eyes, and a charming, sympathetic face.

"It's the Van Rensselaer crest," I explained, showing my gold seal ring. "I'm Philip Van Rensselaer. Who are you?"

"I'm Caja Palffy," she said with a friendly smile. "Do you, perchance, know anywhere we could get a coffee and an English muffin? I'm starved!"

Presently we were sitting in a coffee shop. Caja, wearing my ring, was examining it. She told me her grandmother had been a flirt of my grandfather's and that she had lots of silver flatware with this same crest.

"We're sort of related," I smiled.

"Yes, we *are* related!" she laughed. She had a wonderful, happy laugh, and I liked her more than anyone else I had ever met. She had a gift for intimacy and made me feel we'd been close friends forever. We telephoned Igor Cassini, who wrote the Cholly column for the *Journal-American*, and he invited us to the Waldorf Towers where he lived. Some photographers took our picture, the next day the scoop was in the paper and we were news! That would show Mother! I could get married, too.

Caja was a fascinating creature. Of course, for me, the main part of her fascination was her story. She was a living, breathing, cinema drama, complete with Max Steiner mood music. Her mother first married the rich Polish Prince Radziwill, and then the rich Hungarian count Paul Palffy. Both these gentlemen had enormous land holdings and castles.

Caja had been brought up in the Castle of Pudmerice, and had fled only a few hours before the Bolsheviks arrived. She'd been in New York only a few months when I met her.

Caja and I had fun together during that summer AWOL time in New York. The automat was our favorite place. We loved putting in dimes, quarters, nickels and getting some English muffins and a steaming cup of fragrant coffee. Caja miraculously lived on coffee and muffins; they were the only thing I ever saw her eat.

For the first time, I realized that the words of that song "The Best Things in Life Are Free" were true. We walked through Central Park, sat in hotel lobbies and people-watched, went to the Frick Museum and gazed at various old masters. Caja would amuse me saying, "Oh, Papa had a Rembrandt like that one!" and so forth. Caja adored her father; he was a famous sportsman, wonderfully handsome and virile, had eight wives and had conceived a son when he was almost eighty.

"That's the kind of man I'd like to be," I said to Caja.

"I don't think it's possible, Philip."

We had many good laughs together, which made it all the harder to return to the isolation I felt at Fort Monmouth. In the late afternoons, we'd wander back to Caja's room at 888 Park Avenue.

It was on the ground floor, far, far removed from the marble lobby, near the noisy boiler room. It must have once served as the janitor's digs. Quite a comedown from the glories of Pudmerice!

But Caja never complained of her shabby, dark hole-in-the-wall. Indeed, she made light of it, and of her financial problems as well. Five days a week, she answered the phone and typed for a nearby doctor, sitting endless hours on a metal chair, but she was always smiling and teasing. She was nineteen, and I thought she was the most gallant creature I'd ever known, a real heroine. She was kind and understanding with me.

One night she went out with her cousins, and I stayed behind and lay on the bed daydreaming of *Gilda*, then restlessly looked through Caja's closets. Quite a tempting wardrobe the countess had. There were some large cartwheel hats like the ones Mother sported, slinky velvet tea gowns, and faded foxes with beady, button eyes and bushy tails.

A little while later, I was standing in front of a wardrobe mirror in this faded finery; I thought I looked a cross between Alexis Smith and Greta Garbo. Not a bad combo!

Suddenly, a contemptuous voice made me turn. "Really, Philip, how could you?" There was Caja, staring at me. Her eyes were so full of disappointment that I blushed with shame. She shook her head. "Really, Philip, you've gone too far! Take off Mama's hat and gloves. Immediately!" Her mother's arrogance was in her tone.

I smiled wanly. "Don't you think I look like Gilda, that cinema siren?"

"I certainly don't!" Caja replied emphatically. "Really, Philip. You look perfectly ridiculous."

I laughed uncomfortably. "I think I'm headed south of the border, Countess, to a little town where no one knows me. Start all over again, you know."

Caja gave me an anxious look. "You don't make much sense, Philip. Perhaps your Aunt Bessie Ellsworth can do something with you. I think we should call her. She'd understand such things, God knows."

Violently I shook my head. I couldn't bear the idea of anyone knowing of my abnormality. "No, no, Caja, please!"

Caja was trying to come up with some solution for me. She did not think I should return to the army in my "disturbed state," as she called it. A profound depression settled over me. I felt Caja no longer cared for me and was eager to have me out of her apartment. "What am I going to do with you?" she kept saying. "Who is going to look after you?"

Presently, we were down on the smoky platform of Penn Station, and Caja was saying good-bye. "I'll call your captain later, if you think that would help." The train was starting to pull out of the dark tunnel.

"Great!" I spoke with false enthusiasm and waved like a madman. Once on board the train, I collapsed in the seat.

I'd told Caja that my captain at Fort Monmouth was sympathetic, but he was damn angry when I shuffled into his office, head bowed, hair falling over my face. He ordered me to sit down and kept staring at me, as if he, too, was wondering what to do with me.

When I looked up at him, his eyes were gentle and understanding. I burst into tears. "I don't know who I am," I said, between painful sobs. Then I covered my face with my hands and slumped deeper in the chair.

After a moment, the captain said, "What's the matter, Philip?" The concern and understanding in his voice caused a fresh wave of tears to stream down my face.

"I feel so ashamed, Captain," I said.

"Why?"

"I've failed as a man."

Later, I managed to tell him that Caja was disappointed in me. Somehow, I had let her down; I could tell she no longer liked me. I'd gone too far. I was over the edge. Soon, I'd be talking to myself on the street, making violent gestures at passers-by, like Crazy Liz Ellsworth, or screaming the house down like her brother, Rensselaer, who was locked away for life at the Katonah madhouse.

Chapter
Fifteen

The captain's concern made life at Fort Monmouth bearable. For a month, I managed to be a model soldier, to prove to him that I was all right. The Caja incident at 888 Park Avenue had frightened me; I tried hard to keep escape and Rita fantasies out of my mind.

Instead, I worked hard to keep the image of General Bill Donovan fresh in my daily thoughts. I concentrated my energies on things military. More than anything I admired the heroism of the RAF pilots, who'd saved England during the Battle of Britain. If only I could do something heroic! My thoughts lingered on Sergeant York and the much-decorated Audie Murphy. How I envied them their honors, bestowed by presidents, kings, and heads of state.

Nevertheless, despite my best intentions, at three in the morning, I'd be wide awake in the barracks. Suddenly, Rita would be beckoning at me suggestively, her large red mouth open and alluring, her mane flying about her face. Then I'd pull my mind back to wireless messages and Morse code . . . momentarily.

One day in early October I called Aunt Bessie and told her I'd been granted a two-week pass for exceptional behavior. Could I house-guest with her, huh?

"Of course, dear," came Aunt Bessie's slow, gentle voice.

Aunt Bessie was born in 1870, in her grandfather's brownstone house on Fourteenth Street and Fifth Avenue. Nearing eighty, she still possessed a quality of purity, freshness, and innocence. Despite everything, her life had followed the ordered routine of her ancestors, who liked to dress stylishly, eat well, and enjoy the social and cultural activities of the metropolis.

There were moments when it was hard for me to fathom the extraordinary changes that Aunt Bessie had witnessed. As a girl she'd seen the great Gothic edifice of St. Patrick's Cathedral completed, strolled through the Venetian arcades of old Madison Square Garden that Stanford White had built at Madison Avenue and Twenty-sixth Street.

As a debutante in the 1890s, she had gone sleighing in Central Park with her handsome suitor from Boston, Mr. Amory, and been married at Grace Church, where her parents, brother, and cousins all had been married. She'd been through the Edwardian splendors of the early 1900s with a devoted millionaire husband, and then gone through the trench slaughters of World War I, the frivolity of the Jazz Age and Cafe Society, the ordeal of the 1929 Crash and the Great Depression. Finally, she'd witnessed the New Deal of Mr. Roosevelt and World War II. She would live on till the end of the 1960s, in the world of Andy Warhol, drugs, and Vietnam, to the ripe old age of ninety-nine.

Since Aunt Bessie Ellsworth had for decades taken in every wounded duck in the family, it would seem natural that I, too, would now be harbored by her. Mr. Lewisohn was tired of paying; it was time now that the Van Rensselaers came forward to take some responsibility for an indigent family member. Especially now, since Adele Van Rensselaer was leaving the protection of Mr. Lewisohn for that of Mr. Wanamaker, who had not come into his hoped-for inheritance.

Aunt Bessie had felt bad about being unable to come to Adele's rescue in 1935. A sense of guilt assailed her. Elizabeth Van Rensselaer Ellsworth had a strong family feeling; she was forever bailing out her daughter, Matilda, called Tillie, and her alcoholic husband, John Morris, who lived far beyond their incomes.

Her sister, Mathilde, had not married the rich man Rhinelander Waldo, whom her parents wished her to, but had married for love, and had been happy in Palm Beach, Florida, all these years. However, after 1929, Mathilde was having financial problems, too, so every month a check was sent to her.

A monthly check was sent, too, to the Katonah Asylum for the bed and board of Stephen Van Rensselaer Ellsworth.

Aunt Bessie also maintained an enormous country house in Bernardsville, New Jersey, full staffed with butlers, maids, gardeners, chauffeur, and guards to ensure the safety of Crazy Liz. Mathilde and her husband spent the summers with her, for Palm Beach was too hot and humid, and Charles A. Van Rensselaer, Jr., came for a weekend and stayed two years. He had never earned a penny.

Aunt Bessie was no businesswoman; she merely sold her stocks and bonds to keep the whole show going in suitable style. She was a member of the Colony and River clubs and the Essex Hounds, and she gave generously to family charities. Her mother's three maids were also on her payroll. Was it any wonder that the Ellsworth fortune dwindled?

During the war years, to stop the flow of capital, Aunt Bessie moved into a small apartment at 145 East Fifty-fourth Street, with two bedrooms and a maid's room. Her staff was cut drastically; only Kathleen, the Irish maid, remained in her employ. And Tillie and her husband were still getting into trouble. Once, Aunt Bessie had to fly down to Bermuda to pay their hotel bill. Likewise, to Palm Beach.

Having been burdened by three children like that, she had to be sure that she would leave enough so they would be looked after when Saint Peter opened the Pearly Gates for her. It was also an expensive task to look after the mausoleum in Brooklyn, where her parents and grandparents were buried.

One day Duncan Ellsworth came to call on her. He was astute in business matters, with his millions safely stored at Fiduciary Trust, and now wanted his beloved aunt to store her fortune at Fiduciary.

Mr. Ellsworth stared at Aunt Bessie's sadly depleted portfolio. "What happened, Aunt Elizabeth?" he said, deeply shocked.

"My poor children," said Aunt Bessie tragically, bowing her white head.

But still, Aunt Bessie took me, too, under her wing, although she seemed rather fatigued.

Aunt Bessie and I had always loved each other. When I was in New York, there was hardly a day I didn't go round and have lunch or tea with her in her cluttered parlor. How I loved that old-fashioned parlor. What feelings of continuity and constancy it gave me! I'm certain it started me on my obsession for auctions and worm-eaten antique furniture. Yes, dead certain that my passion for old masters paintings, cupid clocks, plush curtains quivering with ball fringe and tassels, blood red Bokhara carpets, brilliant blue Loewestoft, the Belle Epoque Carolus Duran paintings, all started with Aunt Bessie.

On the dusty rose-colored walls were some exotic Chinese ladies painted on glass, some prints of old New York when it was still Nieuw Amsterdam under Dutch rule. My favorite print was a Currier and Ives of the uniformed soldiers who guarded the Last Patroon, Stephen. Aunt Bessie was fond of telling me how this famous great-grandfather would drive down to New York in his stately black carriage and four horses, complete with postillions and his English valet sitting across from him, and his own army, on horseback, trotting behind. The Van Rensselaer coat of arms was blazoned in gilt on the carriage doors, and people would line the cobblestoned streets of Manhattan and watch the feudal lord and cavalcade rumble by. Some people would bow low or tip their caps, Aunt Bessie said, because Stephen was known as the Good Patroon.

Aunt Bessie felt sad thinking that all the fine Van Rensselaer furniture was at the Winterthur, having been bought by the Du-Ponts, and that the Gilbert Stuart of Stephen was in the National Gallery in Washington. Another portrait of Stephen by Rembrandt Peale was in the Metropolitan. Also, at the Met was a portrait of Stephen's granddaughter, Euphemia, who started a nursing order at Bellevue for wounded Civil War soldiers.

The only mementos that Aunt Bessie had of the Last Patroon were two side chairs in the Empire style, made in New York in the 1820s by Launier, of mahogany covered in plush.

Her sister, Mathilde, had some of the Patroon's Loewestoft, and her brother, Charles (my grandfather), had a portrait of handsome Henry Bell Van Rensselaer, with impressive side whiskers and a lace jabot. Henry married Elizabeth Ray King.

Her first cousin, Euphemia (Effie), Mrs. Christopher Wyatt, had some portraits of Stephen, the fabled Last Patroon, which she had inherited because she had been living in the West Tenth Street brownstone of Mrs. Henry Bell Van Rensselaer when she died.

Another first cousin and dearest friend, Mrs. Egerton Winthrop, called "Emmie," owned some treasures from the Rufus King house in Jamaica, Long Island.

The most mournful fate belonged to the splendid Van Rensselaer manor house at Albany, overlooking the Hudson River. It had been built on the site of the original manor house inhabited by Jerimias Van Rensselaer, the second patroon, and the first member of the family to come to the New Land. His father, Kiliaen, could not tear himself away from Amsterdam and his pretty stone house overlooking a canal trailing with weeping willows. Holland, at that time, in the early seventeenth century, was enjoying its Golden Age, with Rembrandt and flourishing worldwide colonies. It was Kiliaen who sent over three of his own ships to start a principality in the New World.

Early in the twentieth century, the old Van Rensselaer manor house had been torn down and carted off to Williams College in Massachusetts, where it is now a fraternity house, in a state of decay. The only visible glory remaining today is the hall of this old manor, with its handsome scenic wallpaper imported from France. This hall is preserved in the American Wing of the Metropolitan.

"All these past glories used to mean a great deal to me," Aunt Bessie would say, in her slow, gentle, slightly ironic voice. "But an old family means nothing unless you have the wherewithal behind you to back it up. Mathilde says that money never stays long in our family, that we're the last leaves on the dying family tree."

When she spoke these prophetic words, her heavy-lidded, blue-veined eyelids would droop, and she'd trace a design on the needle-point carpet with her cane. Often, she sighed resignedly. At other times she'd gaze at me from those deep-set, meditative eyes. The only sound was the ticking of the ornate bronze clock from Napoleonic Paris. I felt she understood me, but nevertheless, was disappointed.

After dinner, I'd wander down the narrow hallway to my room and slip between the sheets. I'd turn off the light and stare at the ceiling. The wheels of the grand carriage of the Last Patroon would come to me, as it rumbled through the streets of old New York.

I was glad that Stephen Van Rensselaer had freed his slaves and founded Rensselaer Polytechnic Institute in Troy, New York, in 1824. Aunt Bessie told me Stephen founded this college to train teachers to instruct in the application of chemistry, natural history, and philosophy to agriculture. The Rensselaer Institute was one of the first schools devoted to civilian training in mechanical arts, which later led to the state A & M colleges. (The first school of this type, of course, was West Point, founded to train army engineers.)

Aunt Bessie had a print of Stephen in her hall, with his signature in a bold, commanding, virile hand. His mouth was set in a severe line, but his eyes, under thick, arched brows, looked wise and compassionate, like Aunt Bessie's.

At the peak of his power, he owned a million acres of fertile land. He was the second richest man in America in 1835; John Jacob Astor was the first. Stephen's mother was a Livingston and his wife a Schuyler; his brother-in-law was Alexander Hamilton. He was good-looking when young. He was also gentle, yet manly—he'd sired ten children. Some sixty to a hundred thousand tenant farmers worked his soil and paid him rent.

At the time of Stephen's death in his Hudson River manor house, on January 26, 1839, his uncollected back rents totaled some $400,000. He'd been lax in collecting them, and now his heirs would pay. History books compared his passing to the crashing of a giant oak.

After Stephen's death came the deluge: The tenant farmers refused to pay rent and rose up in rebellion. For years there was a fierce and bloody anti-rent war against the Van Rensselaers and their patroon system. In 1852, New York State's highest court ruled against the Van Rensselaers. After this decision, the Last Patroon's son, Stephen, the eighth Lord of the Manor, sold all his land to farmers. The Patroon's widow was fleeced out of her Albany real estate by an unscrupulous lawyer.

By the mid-nineteenth century all the Van Rensselaers' enormous land holdings were gone. Feudalism was dead and buried in New York State. And, with its death, the end of the Van Rensselaers' power. Subsequent generations thrived on Stephen's prestige, and not a few traded on it.

The fate of the Last Patroon's wife made a strong impression on both my great aunts, Bessie and Mathilde. They always told me to stay away from lawyers, that they'd bleed you white.

Gazing at the Last Patroon's likeness, I often found myself wondering what he'd think of me. Would noble Stephen be understanding and resigned like Aunt Bessie or angry like Aunt Mathilde?

Mathilde had eyes like a fierce eagle, and a nose to match. She terrified me as much as Mr. Lewisohn did. They knew I was a milksop and would never amount to a hill of beans. With me, the blood had run thin.

However, there was brother Charlie. He would save the day, restore the family fortunes, and make a brilliant money marriage. He was also interested in Wall Street and would become a financier like Jules Bache or Frederick Lewisohn. Like Aunt Bessie, I was betting on him to be a winner.

The whole business with Caja Palffy had made me aware of how gone I was. Perhaps, if I could get discharged from the army, things would turn around for me. I could study hard and enroll at the Columbia School of Journalism. I *had* to get out of the damned army! After a shower and a delicious breakfast in the Hepplewhite dining room, I went down to Aunt Bessie's bedroom. She was sitting in a little velvet armchair, sipping her tea. She remarked that I was up early, and I told her I'd made up my mind I was leaving the army.

She gave me an ironic smile, her blue eyes twinkling up at me. "I don't know why they took you in the first place, dear." I laughed wildly and she concluded that she would have a serious talk with my captain at Fort Monmouth.

At that moment Kathleen rushed in and said Olga was on the telephone, that she had some important news for me concerning Mother. I dashed down the long narrow hall, my obsession for Adele in full force again.

"How is the scarlet woman?" I asked, in a breathless tone.

"She's thinking of moving," related Olga. "Things aren't going so well with Mr. Wanamaker. Your mother's in despair. By the way, you're not really going to marry that Hungarian countess, are you, you naughty boy?"

"No money," I replied thoughtfully.

"That's the situation around here, too," said Olga grimly.

My heart dropped; I started to sweat. "I hope she's seeing old Monsieur Lewisohn again," I said with a hard edge.

"She's having a late lunch with him at two o'clock. He hasn't been well, you know."

"It's a pity he doesn't die," I said, meaning it.

"What a terrible thing to say, Mr. Philip!"

"If Mr. Lewisohn died, Mother would be free of bondage, and have her own money again, free to do as she pleased."

"What makes you think so?"

"He's a generous man, my darling," I smiled. "I'm living proof of it, aren't I? If I were Mother, I'd put a pillow over his face. That's what Richard the Third did to the little princes in the tower."

"What are you saying, Mr. Philip?"

"Listen, Olga," I cried impatiently, "when is Mistress Adele returning to the Palazzo Volney?"

"About four," she replied.

"I need some clothes," I lied. "I'll be over soon."

I hung up and sat there at the wobbly veneered telephone table, gnawing my fingers with narrowed eyes. I would rifle Mother's desk, discover mysterious details about her financial state. Bromfield's Edwina had made a list of all the lovers she'd had. I was sure to discover a similar list in Adele's desk drawer. Maybe I'd unearth some delicious emeralds. Then I could hock them and get out of town fast.

First, though, I'd enlist Aunt Bessie to get me out of the army. I had to get an honorable discharge, too, no matter what. I wondered what Fred Beckman would do, under similar circumstances.

There were fleecy white clouds over Central Park. The sun was shining brightly through the greenish trees, giving them a bluish depth beyond. Coppery leaves were beginning to fall. The birds were singing and I watched the squirrels scampering about the wooden benches. A pungent scent rose from the rotting leaves; I breathed the air gratefully, in deep gulps.

My eyes lingered with gentle envy on some young boys in blue blazers and gray flannels being led across Park Avenue at Seventy-second Street, the same way that Charlie and I had been led down the road to St. Phillip's in the Highlands church every Sunday. How long ago my sheltered days at that Hudson River school seemed.

I headed across Fifth Avenue toward Madison, hoping I'd discover some jewels in Mother's desk. Then I'd hurry them over to Provident Loan across from Bloomingdale's and put the money received into a savings account—my mad money to get out of town fast, after my army release. A little nest egg would make me feel safer, more secure.

Perhaps I could get on a freighter and head for Istanbul, or Port Said, or perhaps Alexandria, or even far away across the Indian Ocean to Bombay. I'd be the favorite of a Maharaja, like Bromfield's heroine, Carol, in *Night in Bombay. That* would show Mother! I'd return to Old Gotham with jewels, like Lady Mountbatten, buy a huge town house, be an important host, *my* parties would be noted for *their* splendor.

The Volney lobby depressed me. The dark mahogany paneling and the pink-shaded crystal wall lights burning feebly in the gloom brought the old heaviness down on me. The desk clerk, pale and defeated, nodded at me over a pile of papers. The elevator operator spoke in a dejected manner. He, too, looked wan and listless from the hotel's burning steam heat. (Mother always had the steam heat turned off, for it dried the skin and hair. She'd rather shiver in her sables and pearls and be beautiful. Yes, I reflected, it was worth any price to be beautiful.)

139

It was obvious that Mother had just left Eve Lewisohn's luxurious flat. There was a half-finished rum daiquiri on the piano. In her bedroom a half-smoked Marlboro was crushed in an agate and gold ashtray on the marble top of her chest of drawers. From the bathroom came the scent of her Mary Chess gardenia bath oil, and there was face powder on the curving-legged tulipwood dressing table. Mr. Lewisohn's clever eyes stared at me from the ribbed gold frame.

I thought I heard a sound and dropped the picture frame onto the thick carpeting. What if Mother returned suddenly? What would I say? Knowing me, I'd think of some good lie. Glancing about with a frantic expression, I quickly sat before the red-lacquered kneehole desk, ransacking the drawers from top to bottom. Her Bank of New York checkbook revealed her most recent expenditures. The biggest checks were to Chez Ninon and Knize. Knize was a fine Austrian tailor who made Mother her satin and velvet evening suits and copied her old Molyneux suits in gray flannel and Prince de Galles. Chez Ninon was in Bonwit Teller, and they made suits and dresses for Mother, copied from the French designs.

In the bottom drawer, on the right, I discovered a treasure trove. There were packets of old letters, tied up in ribbons. And there were sachets and pomanders from London that still lingered with a summer garden fragrance. Mother had them in her handkerchiefs and among her pastel blue and pink linen sheets.

In a black velvet box, I found a gleaming pearl necklace and a diamond pin from Paul Flato that Mother never wore. The pearls were from Tiffany. Hidden in the back of the drawer were some men's gold cuff links. Mother had more cuff links than Fred Beckman!

I untied a pink ribbon and started to read a postcard from Istanbul: "Bonge dearest, at this time tomorrow my last Marlboro will be gone," and it was signed, "Paul." Paul Palmer! What did *Bonge* mean? A sort of secret name between them? *Bonge.* What an enticing word!

The next card revealed was a note from André Lord, that *homme fatale* and God's gift to womankind. "Dearest sweet Adele," I read, with a beating heart. "I love you with all my heart and soul. If it were possible, I would spend the rest of my life with you. Always, your André."

The roar of the Madison Avenue bus came to me, and I nervously slammed the drawer shut. I *had* to find some saleable trinkets! Pearls brought nothing in those days; even *I* knew that.

In the second drawer I found two gorgeous blue enamel cases in suede covers. The enamel was translucent and changed color as you turned them in the light. *A. Van R.* in pavé diamonds flashed on the cigarette case and its matching matchbook cover.

I quickly put them into my breast pocket, shooting fearful looks at the door. *Bet I can get a couple of thousand for these*, I thought. I knew they had once belonged to Mr. Lewisohn in the 1920s and came from Cartier, but I had to get more loot!

Mother sure was careless. In the top drawer I found a large spinach-jade-and-gold letter opener and magnifying glass with *R. W.* on them. I studied the marking to be sure it was *14k*, smiling triumphantly when I saw that it was. I stuck them in my pants pocket.

I heard the elevator doors closing shut and almost passed out. Maybe Mother had had a fight with Mr. Lewisohn about Rod Wanamaker and come home early to cry her eyes out on the silken bed pillows?

I listened for a moment, my head cocked fearfully to one side. But, no, the front door didn't open. It was only three-thirty. Still time to get more plunder from that old English desk.

Was it Queen Anne or William and Mary? Weren't William and Mary brother and sister? Or were they married? What had happened to my memory? And history had once been my best subject.

Back to the drawers I went, with a Peter Lorre expression on my face. I imagined I was an Eric Ambler character, looking for top-secret war documents. Then I heard the sinister thud of SS boots in the hall, like that slimy Nazi beast Walter Slezak tracking down John Garfield in *The Fallen Sparrow*. Now, like Garfield's, my face broke out into a chill sweat. There, before my eyes, was the list of lovers, like the one Edwina Esketh had written in *The Rains Came* and which her jealous husband had found. Lord Esketh had tried to put faces to the names, and now I did the same thing. My eyes ran down the list. My throat felt dry, my lips parched. My breath was coming fast. List of infamy!

C.V.R. was the first. Well, that went to prove Mother had been a virgin when she married.

T.C.

J.S.

L.T.

F.B., and here the pencil had underlined *F* in a gesture of fierce passion.

My eyes grew dim. A sharp pain jabbed inside my head. I dropped the list. An army of men had loved Mother, known her in a way I would never know her. She belonged to them. Soon she might belong to Rod Wanamaker, and there would be no place for me in her life. Wanamaker's handsome, sullen face looked out at me from another gold frame. Blind with rage, I swept it off the dressing table.

I stared with hatred at the overlarge bed with its silk-and-lace coverlet and pile of soft, scalloped pillows, all monogrammed *A. Van R.* Suddenly, I remembered the bedroom of Rebecca at the end of that movie, when Mrs. Danvers had set fire to Manderley in a fit of jealous rage. The flames had slowly crept up the enormous bed, consuming the silk coverlet so that only the initial *R* stood out. And finally that, too, was destroyed.

I knew what I must do! I ran into the kitchen, put a pile of greasy bacon on a frying pan and turned on the range. In a moment, the bacon would be burning like hell and the smell would be all over the apartment, ruining the seductive scent of Guerlain perfume, face powder, old rose potpourri that always lingered in every nook and cranny of Mother's apartments. No *cinq-à-sept* interlude at twilight for Rod and Adele!

A bit of paranoia seized me when I stepped from the elevator into the gloomy lobby. The telephone operator usually sat in a little airless space in back of the desk clerk and now she was standing in the dining room doors, staring into space. She was nervously smoking a cigarette, and I could tell by her taut lips and overly frightened eyes that, she, too, was on the verge of a breakdown.

"Hello, Mr. Van Rensselaer," she said, her lips trembling into a little smile. The pasty flesh around her mouth broke into a mass of tiny lines, and I noticed her strange Marlene eyebrows painted up her forehead. She was probably about a thousand, but wanted to look like a debutante. Her scalp showed through the reddish curls.

I felt she wanted to talk to me, so I walked over and shook her hand, suddenly anxious to escape from myself and that list of Mother's lovers.

"You've gained weight," she said, her sensitive lips trembling.

I grinned broadly and said that was due to the army, God bless America, hah-hah.

She asked if I was getting married to that Hungarian countess, and I said I was eating a lot of her Hungarian goulash. Then she blushed and I blushed, too. Suddenly, the telephone operator looked like Margo when she escaped Shangri-La, and I practically ran out of the lobby.

As I hurried into the street, it was almost dark as night. Raindrops splattered the pavement. I stared at the sky with disbelief. What had happened to those fleecy clouds, blue skies, and birds singing?

Wearily, I stepped back into the marble vestibule of the Volney, sank onto a little marble bench, and covered my face with my hands. I stared at the steady downpour, listened to the whoosh of the traffic passing over the wet streets. The sound of the traffic seemed terribly loud, an intrusion, a personal affront. All of a sudden I felt angry. Why did that ambulance have to shriek like that? Really, too appalling!

I was impelled into motion. The doorman was sitting on the bench, watching the people rush by with black umbrellas over their heads, and I said, in a loud, imperious voice, "If it wouldn't pain you too much, would you mind getting me a taxi?"

He looked at me with surprise. I never had talked in such a tone to anyone before. In a blur, I stepped into the taxi, lavishly pushed a wad of crumpled bills I'd found in Mother's jewel case into the doorman's hands, avoided his eyes, and off we went. I felt ashamed of the way I had spoken to him. I would have to be punished for that.

I took out a cigarette from the blue-enamel-and-diamond case, lit up, and inhaled like a dying soldier on his last weed. I puffed away like a madman.

I was above the law. All people who lived as we did were above the law. Louis Bromfield had said that, and his rich heroes and heroines always got away with anything and everything. All you had to do was pay. I'd see to it that I always had plenty of filthy lucre with which to oil the right palms.

Left: Kiliaen Van Rensselaer, 1st Patroon of Rensselaer-wyck, 1595–1646

Below: Elisabeth Van Rensselaer — Aunt Bessie Ellsworth — a debutante at her grandmother's house, 16 West 10th Street, New York City, in 1890

Above: Stephen Van Rensselaer III, "The Good Patroon." His mother was a Livingston, his wife a Schuyler. His brother-in-law was Alexander Hamilton.

Left: Adele Brookfield, graduating from the fashionable Brearley School, New York City, 1923

Below: Mrs. Charles A. Van Rensselaer, Jr., setting fashion on Park Avenue, 1929

THE EVENING WORLD, MONDAY, APRIL 8, 19*

What Society Is Wearing

Coat of Dark Lightweight Fabric for Morning or Afternoon Wear

BY HELEN WORDEN

Copyright Press Publishing Company
(New York World) 1929

One of the most useful of spring wraps, the dark lightweight fabric coat, is worn by Mrs. Charles A. Van Rensselaer Jr. on Park Avenue. The wrap follows the conventional lines—straight side seams, narrow notched collar, plain sleeves and unbuttoned front closing.

It is a type of coat that is quite correct for morning or afternoon wear and is equally smart slipped over a gay printed silk or more formal chiffon afternoon gown.

In this instance, Mrs. Van Rensselaer wears the chic wrap over a brightly patterned crepe dress. For accessories, she has chosen a narrow brimmed dark felt hat, separate scarf of silver fox, la

bag, light suede pull-on gloves, sun burnt tan silk stockings and dark suede kid pumps.

The narrow looped ribbon bows on the felt hat introduce a feminine touch that is exceedingly popular this season. Felt hats have remained untrimmed so long that a bit of ornamentation is a refreshing touch.

Mrs. Charles A. Van Rensselaer Jr., the former Adele Brookfield, is a well known member of the younger set in town and prominent socially.

One of the interesting events of the week is the spring production of the Junior League Theatre School to-morrow evening at the Mansfield Theatre. It goes without saying that the younger group of fashionables will be present.

U. S. CHOIR THAWS

LONDON, April 8 (A.
ton. O., choir now to
gave a recital in Alb
day with a pro
Palestrina and
lean compo
from
It

On Committees for Dance

NEW YOR

Photographed on Park Avenue

Mrs. Charles A. Van Rensselaer Jr.

Mrs. Van Rensselaer, the former Adele Brookfield of New York and Jericho
L. I., was photographed on Park Avenue recently.

Right: Philip Van Rensselaer as a young boy, age 8, in 1936

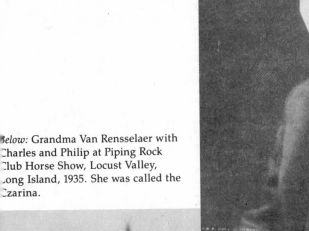

Below: Grandma Van Rensselaer with Charles and Philip at Piping Rock Club Horse Show, Locust Valley, Long Island, 1935. She was called the Czarina.

Law Snarl

Daughter's Divorce Plan Awry†—Husband to Sue—$250,000 Suit Pends.

By ERSKINE GOSLING.

Just as the Charles A. Van Rensselaers, Jr., were about to be divorced, something happened.

The young patrician husband changed his mind, it is believed, and ruined the plans of Maud Adele Brookfield, who married him five years ago, and is now in Reno with their two children.

"Charles decided suddenly that he didn't want a divorce," said Mrs. Florence Q. Bonnell, Mrs. Van Rensselaer's mother, yesterday.

"I'm sure I don't know what they're going to do, but I hear he has changed his mind. Adele hasn't written me in several weeks—and I don't know what to do about it."

Mrs. Bonnell had other legal news. She had just spoken with Max D. Steuer, her attorney, about the report that her estranged third husband, Major Geoffrey Harper Bonnell, was planning a Mexican divorce.

"LET HIM TRY!"

DIVORCE PARTS SOCIETY PAIR IN RENO

Scion of Noted Family Cursed Servants and Guests, Complaint Charges.

RENO, March 4.—Another society marriage went on the rocks here when Adele B. Van Rensselaer, of New York and Long Island, obtained a decree from Charles A. Van Rensselaer.

Extreme cruelty was charged. The scion of the family which has made the name of Van Rensselaer a synonym for social prestige was accused of having an ungovernable temper. He would fly into a rage over trivial matters and cursed guests and servants, the wife charged.

They were married in Oyster Bay in February, 1925. It was supposed to have been a "surprise wedding," although Mrs. Charles A. Van Rensselaer, of Homewood, Syosset, L. I., mother of the bridegroom, proclaimed they had been engaged for some time.

There are two children, Charles 3d, three, and Philip, one. Their sole custody was awarded the mother. She was given complete supervision of their education, Van Rensselaer being permitted to see them twice a week only at specified hours. A property settlement was made out of court.

The bride is the former Maude Adele Brookfield.

Unties Marital Knot

Mrs. Adele B. Van Rensselaer, of New York and Long Island, has won a divorce in Reno from Charles A. Van Rensselaer, whom she accused of extreme cruelty.

Above left, above: Newspaper clippings of Adele's divorce from Charles Van Rensselaer, 1930

Left: Adele Van Rensselaer giving her name to Camels, 1935, at Winifred Rockefeller's Park Avenue apartment

Left: Fred Beckman, handsome playboy, in Monte Carlo, 1940

Above: The Villa Corne D'Or, Frederick Lewisohn's pink marble palace in Cannes, 1935–1939

Right: Charles Van Rensselaer, Philip's older brother, in 1943

Left: Adele Van Rensselaer and Frederick Lewisohn strolling on deck aboard the *Queen Mary* in 1936

Right: Adele and Mr. Lewisohn at Lord Eric Dudley's country house in England, 1937 — Adele dressed by Schiaparelli and jeweled by Cartier to help morale

The stately Rolls-Royce that Philip bought in 1946, cashing in the war bonds that his grandmother had given him. DISASTER!

Adele and Lady Ann Mappin, resting at Versailles before the Riviera

Social Register Blackballs Whitney, Van Rensselaer

By JOSEPH X. DEVER,
World-Telegram Society Editor.

For the first time in its 52-year history, the Social Register has dropped a Whitney and a Van Rensselaer.

The 1959 edition of the social bible, just off the press, also blackballed a few other previous listees, chopping out, among others, a Bostwick and a Chisholm. The Register also listed many names not previously presented within its black covers.

The newly issued copy of Society's Who's Who demonstrated the Register's new open-door policy for "outsiders" of good background and deportment who marry into already registered families. It also underlined its give-"give-'em-the-gate" policy for socialites who divorce too often and too scandalously.

Cornelius Vanderbilt Whitney, whose family has been in Register lists since the first edition in 1886, was given the social heave-ho for divorcing his second wife, Eleanor Searle, to marry a divorced Hollywood actress, Mary Lou Hosford.

Eleanor, daughter of an Ohio country doctor retained her Register listing and will continue as one of New York's leading hostesses.

Banned by the register was Philip Van Rensselaer, much publicized escort of the much-married Barbara Hutton. The two got many headlines, after ~~ed divorce for Miss~~

C. V. (SONNY) WHITNEY.

MARY HOSFORD.

Premice, a featured Negro actress in the Broadway hit "Jamaica."

Mr. Fales and Miss Premice were married last Friday, but the Register has saved itself from making a routine listing of the interracial alliance in its next edition. The Register made such a routine listing when Kip Rhinelander, a member of one of New York's first families, married the daughter of his father's Negro coachman.

Patricia Potter Luce, former daughter-in-law of publisher Henry Luce, brought her new husband, Istvan Botond, into the Register. Sir Winston Churchill's young American cousin, Elizabeth Guest, did likewise for her socially unknown husband, Edward B. Condon.

The new Mrs. John E. Phipps, whose husband has a large slice of the Carnegie steel fortune, is registered although born outside the book as Judith A. Holt. Mr. Phipp's cousin, Andrew Carnegie, introduced his bride, Frances Snead of Chester, Va., to a listing.

John P. Marquand, novelist, lost his listing just a week after losing his second wife by way of a Nevada divorce court.

Philip Van Rensselaer dropped from the Social Register following his much publicized association with heiress Barbara Hutton

Philip Van Rensselaer in Capri, 1964

Above: Barbara Hutton, 45, and Philip Van Rensselaer, 30, arriving aboard the SS *United States* amid rumors of impending marriage

Right: A Faberge box, one of the many gifts from Barbara Hutton to Philip

Left: Philip, acting grandiose, by a signed Louix XV desk under a Boucher

Below: Philip with Tina (Mrs. Aristotle) Onassis (left) at a dinner party with Reinaldo Herrera, 1960. Tina died tragically young, as did her sister, Eugenie Niarchos.

Above: Philip's party for Duchess D'Uzes (the former Margaret Bedford of Standard Oil). Dear friend Ruth Lachman brought butter and Stolichnaya, as always.

Right: Philip aboard the motorboat headed for the Villa —uninvited— 1973

Chapter Sixteen

The next day, at lunchtime, I heard Kathleen open the door, then a raucous voice cried, "Horrible, horrible, horrible trip from Bernardsville!" I knew it was Crazy Liz. She always spoke in this hysterical fashion, habitually repeating words twice, for extra emphasis.

Liz strode into the cluttered Victorian parlor. She had a weather-beaten, red-veined face that matched her legs, with mad blue eyes peering out of thin gray bangs.

She shook my hand like Ralph Lamo and said, "Hello! Hello! Hello!" then bent down and kissed her mother, who was sitting in a red plush chair.

"Hello, dear," said Aunt Bessie, gazing up at her daughter anxiously. "How are you?"

"Ghastly, ghastly, ghastly trip. Too many common people pushing me in the station. Common, common, common!"

She grimaced, then flung herself into a fragile, creaking chair, pulled up her red-and-green plaid skirt, and vigorously fanned her legs. She was dressed like a teenager, with woolen sweater, blouse, and plaid skirt. Glaring at her mother, she pulled out a cigarette and lit it with a defiant gesture, then puffed away, blowing huge clouds of smoke into the parlor.

Aunt Bessie watched her daughter with those sad, resigned eyes. "Dear, must you smoke?"

"I'm nervous, Mother, nervous, nervous, nervous!" Her head began to vibrate, then, in that characteristic manner, she put her fist over her face and ground her teeth, her mouth working in an intense way as if she were having a seizure.

I couldn't take my eyes off her. I watched her with a horrid curiosity and a vague sinking sensation in the pit of my stomach. Then, she fixed those fierce blue eyes on me.

"Hear you're in the army," she said, giving me the once-over.

"Yes," I said, smiling, hoping she'd like me.

"Why don't you get out?" she shouted. "The army doesn't want anyone like you. They wouldn't want anyone like your father, either!"

Her voice had risen alarmingly, and I gripped the arm of my chair. Liz's energy overwhelmed me; I felt my old headache coming on.

"Dear," said Aunt Bessie with her quiet authority, glaring at her daughter, "please calm yourself. And kindly take that dreadful cigarette out of your mouth. It's a vulgar habit."

"I like the habit, Mother," Liz glared back in a defiant manner. "So put that in your pipe and smoke it!" Her stocky body vibrated in the fragile chair, and she did the fist-over-her-mouth routine again.

Thank heavens, Kathleen came out of the pantry with a silver tray of sherry and passed it around. Aunt Bessie adored her Dry Sack sherry and appreciated a couple before lunch every day. Her doctor had prescribed sherry and a brandy before dinner; sometimes, she had a sip of wine at lunchtime.

The doorbell rang and Kathleen's pink-cheeked face grew excited. "That's Mrs. Van Rensselaer!"

My stomach churned as Mother's high heels came into the room, and I felt my face losing color. I smiled faintly at Mother's fashionable silhouette, but she gave me a cold look. She shook my hand in a formal way, then sat down in a Louis XV armchair by the fireplace. A log fire was sputtering in the grate.

What a contrast Liz Ellsworth and Adele made! The two women were a study in opposites, and I forgot my fears as I observed every detail of their faces, figures, voices, complexions. Liz's coarsely veined face had obviously never known powder, mascara, lipstick, or rouge. Her stubby nails had never been lacquered Chinese red, had never known an emery board, or a manicurist.

At the lunch table Liz began to get out of hand, rambling on angrily about this one or that one who had crossed her on her trip from New Jersey. Suddenly, Mother lifted her head and smiled engagingly at Liz across the table.

"Dear Liz, *do* tell me about your summers out West. You know, of course, I *adore* the West. Spent some time there après my divorce."

Liz fell under Mother's spell, and I could see Aunt Bessie sigh with relief.

"Oh, Adele, I just love horses! It's my dream to live out West on a dude ranch and raise horses, horses, horses!" Soon, however, Liz reverted to her ravings, and worked herself up again about our family. "Our family's *finished, finished, finished*. For *centuries* they've been finished!"

The lunch party became a catastrophe. Liz's raging infected me like a disease; always the chameleon, I felt a terrible anger rising up in me.

Finally Liz strode out noisily, muttering obscenities under her breath. Mother and Aunt Bessie looked at each other with sympathy. Then, Aunt Bessie leaned forward and touched Mother's hand.

Mother shook her head mournfully. "I hate and detest ugly things," she said.

Suddenly, my terrible rage burst out. Like Liz, I sprang to my feet, glaring at Mother. "You should face ugly things, *Mistress* Adele!" I shouted. "Ugliness is all around you, you stupid whore!"

Then tearfully, I ran out of the dining room and down the narrow corridor to my Venetian room, brutally slamming the door. I threw myself on the bed and let the tears come in great wracking sobs.

The following morning I slept late. I didn't want to leave the warmth and safety of my painted Venetian bedstead. When I awoke

I recalled with horror what I had said to Mother. My God! She'd never forgive me! What had gotten into me? Crazy Liz, that's what had gotten into me, like an infectious disease. I pulled the covers over my head, feeling very ashamed. How could I face Aunt Bessie and Kathleen?

A little after ten o'clock I was sitting in the Hepplewhite dining room eating poached eggs, crisp bacon, and whole wheat toast. Kathleen served me with a silent, dejected look.

Presently, Aunt Bessie came in, smartly dressed in a violet wool dress with a bowknot on her shoulder. She sat down next to me with a sorrowful look in her deep-set blue eyes. I felt the same sense of feminine disappointment that emanated from Kathleen.

"I see," she observed dryly, "you slept rather late."

"Yes," I said, flushing guiltily as she reflectively studied me.

"I'm sure you feel bad about saying those things to your dear mother, don't you?"

"Yes, I do," I replied, tears coming to the surface. They were always there, near the surface.

"Well, dear," she said putting her blue-veined hand on mine, "I've got rather startling news for you. Your captain from Fort Monmouth called."

I swallowed noisily. I felt horribly frightened.

"The captain is coming in after lunch, with the military police."

The MPs! Suddenly, I broke into loud, embarrassing tears. Aunt Bessie patted my hand and let me sob. After a time she said, "Don't worry, dear, I'll stand by you. Apparently, they're going to take you to some kind of prison, but I'll go with you."

I looked up at her from wet eyes, stark terror written all over me. "You will?"

"Yes," she announced, erect and autocratic. "Now don't be frightened. I won't allow them to put you in any prison. They won't dare." Aunt Bessie's strength and authority began to flow into me, as if by magic; my heart began to beat excitedly. What a drama, seeing Aunt Bessie handle the captain and the MPs!

Gratefully, I put my hand on Aunt Bessie's old, dry one. Her skin felt cold. Suddenly, I was aware of how vastly old she was and remembered what she had been through with her three crazy children. She'd probably had similar incidents with pretty Mathilda, whom she was always bailing out of trouble. I lowered my head, that old sense of guilt swamping me.

"You mustn't be frightened, dear," she told me gently, squeezing my hand. I felt so happy that in my impulsive way, I put my arms around her and clung to her. It was nice to embrace Aunt Bessie. I felt strangely human. I couldn't recall ever hugging Mother like this. Any display of affection like this would make Mother uneasy.

Presently, I heard Aunt Bessie's voice through my reverie. "You've never received any parental guidance, dear. Your mother never received any, either. I feel so sorry for her because she's never had any family behind her. She's the most vulnerable woman I know, and the saddest."

"Saddest?" I echoed.

She nodded sagely. "She should have had much more from life than she has, a woman with all the special gifts she has. Somehow they've all been wasted."

"Yes," I agreed. Aunt Bessie's slow voice trailed away, and she began to trace a design on the needlepoint carpet with her cane.

Before lunch I had a few nips of Dry Sack sherry in the pantry to give me courage for the ordeal ahead. The strong, amber wine hit my stomach, and a friendly warmth buzzed through me that was very sweet indeed. My fears vanished as I brought the bottle to my mouth and poured another swallow down my throat. Drinking up a storm I was! Going to hell like those boozy characters in *The Sun Also Rises*.

True to her word, Aunt Bessie rode downtown with me in the paddy wagon, surrounded by two stalwart MPs. What an incongruous sight Aunt Bessie was in that police van! All of her clothes were cut along simple, severe lines, made of fine materials, and they added to her air of authority. On her white hair, curled weekly at the hairdresser's, sat a pretty toque of deep sapphire blue velvet that brought out the rich, intense hue of her eyes.

I couldn't believe my eyes. Regal Aunt Bessie sitting next to me on the wooden seats, complete with pearls and white gloves, driving downtown to save me from prison. I couldn't believe what I'd heard in her apartment after lunch, either. Aunt Bessie had informed the captain in no uncertain words that she did not wish me to be put in prison.

"My dear Captain," she had said, smiling graciously, "you must see the folly of locking my nephew away somewhere where he would be most wretched and cause you immense grief, not to mention expense. What, pray, would be the point?" She gave him a sharp, intelligent stare.

"Now, kindly release him. I shall take full responsibility for him, have no fear, and see to it that he is put in the *right* place."

Make no mistake, Elizabeth Van Rensselaer Ellsworth was a formidable lady. Her voice and manner had chilling authority; she was obviously used to having her own way. She was also obviously not accustomed to having her word questioned. The captain told her he could not release me, that things were not as simple as that. Why not?, Aunt Bessie demanded. He told her there must be a penalty for my AWOL days.

"Rubbish," snorted Aunt Bessie, and told him to release me there on the spot. "Immediately, Captain!"

The captain said it was impossible, and Aunt Bessie replied that the word *impossible* was unknown to her. The captain, who was getting nervous under her forbidding stare, told her I must be incarcerated at Riker's Island until I could be sent to the Valley Forge Hospital in Phoenixville, Pennsylvania. Aunt Bessie, thereupon, demanded to know what sort of place the Valley Forge Hospital was, and he informed her that many soldiers from the Pacific area were being discharged there and that it was an attractive, well-cared-for place.

But, the captain concluded, first I would have to be sent to Riker's Island, which, he had to admit, was not the sort of place he'd like to see me in.

Aunt Bessie stood up and announced that she was going with me to Riker's Island, and that was that. The captain tried to dissuade her, but she told Kathleen to bring her hat, coat, and gloves. We marched out into the hall and into the elevator, with the captain giving helpless looks to the two MPs, who in turn gazed at Aunt Bessie with some trepidation. Mrs. Thompson was coming in the door as we were going out. "What on earth is going on, Bessie, dear?" she asked, shooting dark, suspicious looks at the military police and the captain.

Aunt Bessie gave a little shrug. "They want to keep my nephew here in the army," she replied with a humorless smile.

Mrs. Thompson gave me a level stare. "I can't imagine why," she mused. Then she gave the captain a look that made him quake in his fatigue boots.

Aunt Bessie introduced Mrs. Thompson to the captain. Mrs. Thompson said, in the grand manner, "Do pay attention to Mrs. Ellsworth, Captain; she knows best. Now, don't be tiresome!" and her imperious figure sailed off toward the elevator.

On the drive downtown, Aunt Bessie won the captain over with her simplicity, force, and directness. Yes, those old girls were unique. How I miss my Aunt Bessie! When she died in March of 1967, the last link with the old days vanished. Today, on my Victorian desk, there is a photo of Aunt Bessie sitting in her cluttered parlor on East Fifty-fourth Street, and another one of her as a debutante of 1890, in a white satin dress with a large stuffed bird on her head.

Chapter
Seventeen

Ward nineteen at the Valley Forge Hospital was nothing but endless metal beds stretching down a long, narrow room. My bed was somewhere in the middle. As I walked down the noisy, crowded space, a sea of eyes watched me—wounded men, bandaged around head or torso.

Then, the kindness of strangers: A tall, thin boy with a prominent Adam's apple and a wild thatch of wiry black hair greeted me.

"Hi, there," he said grinning. "My name's Bob."

"Hi, yourself." I smiled.

"You look all in one piece," Bob observed.

"I don't know about that," I said grimly.

"I mean, you're not missing an arm or a leg."

"No," I replied, "I'm just missing my head."

Bob gave me an intense look. "Psycho discharge?"

"Yup. How about you?"

"Looney Tunes, yeah."

I spent five months at Valley Forge, uneventful but for movie dreams, and waking terrors caused by the shattered bodies and

minds of the convalescing soldiers. At my discharge I was sent back
to Mother.

I sat uneasily on the train, brooding all the way home. Feelings
of love seemed to come naturally for almost everyone. What was
wrong with me? Why was I so different? If only I'd been able to
love Caja Palffy. Recently, she had gotten married; losing her
weighed heavily on me and added to my sense of failure.

I rang the doorbell at Mother's. At first there was not a sound,
but finally, after what seemed like hours, the door opened and
there she was, dressed in a greenish blue herringbone tweed suit,
with a bell-like skirt down to her ankles, 1934 style. Mother caught
my look and said, "Monsieur Dior's new look. Had to alter all my
dresses and suits. Thank the Lord for wonderman Knize!" She had
a tense expression; my stomach turned over. She did not kiss me;
we shook hands, politely, avoiding each other's eyes.

Later, in her bedroom, she lit a cigarette, then ground it out
with an exasperated expression. "What's the matter, Mummy?" I
asked.

"Shouldn't smoke," she replied, with an edge to her voice. "Dr.
Neergaard says I'm anemic."

The phone rang. "Yes . . . Yes . . . You can expect payment in
a few days . . . Yes, I'll see to it right away." She hung up, with a
frozen look. "Swamped with beastly bills!" she cried nervously.
Her gray poodle, Sinner, put his head on her lap and she tenderly
stroked him. "Such a comfort he is, the dear creature. He gives me
so much love, and never disappoints me."

Her remark about being disappointed hit home, and I set about
to win her over. I asked after Mr. Wanamaker, on my best behavior as if I were with a duchess of royal blood. Mother replied that
he was "very well, thank you," in her vague way.

"How is Fred Beckman, Mummy?" Mother sprang to her feet
and started to pack some things in a suitcase. There were trunks of
all shapes and sizes in the room, steamer and wardrobe ones.

"Fred Beckman?" she repeated in a shrill voice. "Poor darling,
he's in terrible shape, drinking badly." She gave a deep sigh.
"Hazel died an agonizing death, bone cancer. Too vile."

"At least he has her money," I said, and then regretted my words. I was unfeeling, crass.

Mother stared in my direction. "Talking about money, Philip," she said rather severely. "I'm going to put you on an allowance. Two hundred and fifty dollars a month, until you get a job and can stand on your own two feet."

"That's awfully generous of you, Mummy," I said with a trembling smile.

She came over to me and gave me a pastel blue check from the Bank of New York, in her pretty slanting writing. Impulsively, I gave her a big kiss and then showed her my wallet, full of the army greenbacks.

"Heavenly days, darling, you're positively Mr. Vincent Astor!"

"I'm loaded, Mummy, loaded!"

"That's nice, dear, but you look rather shabby. Why can't you run down to Rogers Peet? Tubby Clark told me they have divine suits there, for forty dollars, just as good as Brooks or Saks." I blushed at the mention of those two stores, for I had abused her charge accounts only last year at Saks and Brooks.

Rogers Peet! Whenever Mother was strapped, she sent me to Rogers Peet or Roger Kent, and I *loathed* their suits. They had no style, no dash, and they hung on me like a sack. The salesmen were grumpy, too, as they always were in bargain stores. They knew you were a skinflint looking for a bargain. And they knew how inferior their merchandise was.

Suddenly, Jessie came into the room, and we ran into each other's arms. I loved Jessie almost as much as I'd loved Nannie. We kissed, then reminisced for a moment. How happy I was to see her! Now, with a third person in our midst, I knew that Mother could say things she couldn't say to me alone. I felt she wanted to get down to the nitty-gritty. She wanted to get rid of me. The check was the clue—the payoff.

And, then, the terrible news came—but I had expected it. "Philip, dear," Mother began, nervously lighting a cigarette with a gold Dunhill lighter initialed *R.W.*, "I think we are incompatible. Truly, I cannot support your scenes and jealousy. Not to mention the invasion of privacy."

I blushed again, and she went on. "Don't you think it's best that you get a little room nearby? You see, I'm moving downstairs to a tiny little apartment, as I'm terribly hard up, what with all these doctors' bills and all." She looked anxiously at Jessie, who went out and, a few moments later, returned with a frozen daiquiri on a silver tray.

Mother sipped the cocktail gratefully. The scene with me had obviously drained her, she who hated confrontations of any sort. She laughed suddenly, and observed that it was twelve-thirty, and afternoon, praise the Lord, because she had no intention of starting to drink in the morning.

After Mother raced out the door I got to ask Jessie all the usual questions: Why was Mr. Lewisohn still paying thousands of dollars a month into Mother's checking account when she was with Mr. Wanamaker? Why was she suddenly complaining about being hard up? Had Mr. Wanamaker come into his inheritance?

"Your mother has terrible doctor's bills," Jessie said grimly. "That fancy Park Avenue doctor, Arthur Neergaard, charges her ninety dollars a visit, and your mother never questions it."

"She's a soft touch to many friends, too," said Olga, shaking her head.

"What's the matter with Mother?" I asked anxiously.

"She complains of nosebleeds," said Jessie. Then Olga added, "She has attacks of vertigo on the street and sometimes can't remember where she was."

"Probably because Rod Wanamaker's giving her the business morning, noon, and night!" I commented sarcastically.

Jessie and Olga looked shocked.

"Your mother and Mr. Wanamaker are happy together," said Jessie.

"They're going to be married very soon," said Olga.

My old feelings of rage and envy swept over me. I stormed out of the Volney and strode over to Fifth Avenue. It was warmer on the streets than in Mother's apartment because she'd turned off all the steam heat. The idiot woman! No wonder she was sick—too much lovemaking and fiery passion. And she was probably seeing Mr. Lewisohn, too, in the late afternoons, so her allowance wouldn't be cut off.

That very afternoon, I moved into 1081 Fifth Avenue. The room advertised was just my cup of tea—ruined splendor, full of worn, tasseled, red brocade curtains sweeping over French windows, a marble fireplace, and a worm-eaten alcove bed that creaked when I lay on it, and whose foot and headboards were covered in dilapidated Nattier blue velvet. On the pale gray walls were pictures of eighteenth-century men of war blasting each other on a stormy silver-green sea.

The owner of the house looked as if she never saw the light of day. She wore a red wig, and a black lace mantilla over her thin shoulders. She told me that there were six other "desirables" who had seen the room before me but that she would give it to me. My old name helped; she said I was "America's royalty." I gave a courtly bow.

But what *really* got her was when I told her I'd been wounded in the leg at the Battle of Monte Cassino and had gone through fifteen major operations. I noticed on her skimpy breasts a heavy gold cross, so I knew she was Catholic. I gave her a great tale of trying to save all the abbey's works of art before the terrible American bombing.

I returned to the Volney at three to get my duffel bag and some civilian clothes. I decided to steal a little Vuitton suitcase of Mother's—she wouldn't miss it, with her careless nature—and started to throw shirts, ties, gray flannels, and sports coats into it. Olga was also packing some of Mother's objets d'art, and she talked a blue streak. Brother Charlie, apparently, was studying hard at a tutoring school at Princeton to prepare himself for college that fall.

"Isn't it lovely, Mr. Philip?" she said, looking me square in the face. "Isn't it lovely that your brother is keeping Mr. Beckman company? You know, poor soul, he's a widower, and terribly lonely after his loss."

When Olga mentioned Fred Beckman and Charlie teaming up, it was as if the atomic bomb had gone off. Fred Beckman and Charlie! I saw Charlie having maniacal shopping sprees at Brooks, Triplers, Saks, Bonwits, Abercrombies, Cartier, Dunhill, Tiffany— you name it!

Jessie, with her arms full of Mother's fur coats, said she was going down to Mother's new home, and didn't I want to see it. I had a blinding headache but nevertheless went down with her in the elevator. When she opened the door and we stepped into the dreary living room, I said, "Its the black hole of Calcutta!"

She showed me the dismal bedroom facing a gritty air shaft, which prompted me to ask where on earth Charlie would sleep when he came to the big city.

Jessie beamed at me innocently, "Charlie stays at Fred Beckman's. You remember that splendid apartment at 550 Park Avenue, don't you?"

Jessie kept going on about how happy Charlie and Fred were, talking as if they were honeymooners on their way to Niagara. "Your dear mother told me Charlie follows Fred Beckman around like a little puppy dog. Isn't that sweet, Mr. Philip?"

I raced out into the snowstorm like a madman, talking to myself. That stupid Mistress Adele had fed her oldest chick to that hungry satyr, Fred Beckman!

I didn't leave my room for days. I kept the tasseled, red brocade curtains drawn over the tall French windows and stayed under the covers. Olga came by with some clothes, made me some scrambled eggs and bacon, but I wasn't hungry.

Soon I was out in the world, so to speak, taking in endless double features. Every day, there were fresh reports in the newsreels, magazines, and newspapers about Nazi atrocities. I was also reading Hersey's *Hiroshima*.

At the end of March I could stand it no longer. I took a taxi and went downtown. I told the driver to take me to the Broadway district, that I was looking for a flea-trap hotel because I was a failed actor. I'd just returned from Hollywood, that land of dreams, I told him, but I hadn't succeeded. I was defeated; my career was over. It was the end for me.

"You look pretty good," he grinned, turning around to get a better look at me.

"It's only an illusion."

"You must be awfully young, aren't you?"

"Plastic surgery," I told him. "Actually, I'm an old man."

Later, I had a good laugh over that one as I lay in my foul room at the Hotel Normandie. The brown plaster was peeling off the slimy walls. Gritty linoleum in the bathroom was spotty and greasy. The worn brown carpeting looked as if someone had thrown up a good lunch on it. There was an odor of rotting eggs and athlete's foot.

In the middle of the night I awakened with a cry. A large orange cockroach was sitting on my face! And the next morning I itched like the devil. I stared at my reflection in a cracked bathroom mirror. There were ugly red welts on my smooth white chest. Upon closer inspection, I saw the head of a little crab. I pulled him from the wound and burned his body over a flame. He exploded with a pop, full of my blood.

It was an ugly world, to be sure. *Vile.* How and where was I to go to get a gun, would you mind telling me? Would it be painful? Would I go to a better world? Or, would I awaken in Hiroshima? Buchenwald?

On the fifth day of my suicide-starvation, Leonard, the manager, came into my room. He flicked on the bare bulb on the ceiling and stared at me lying on the bed.

"Are you sick or something?" he said. "You've had that Do Not Disturb sign on your door and the maid can't get in your room."

"I'm sorry," I said, uncomfortable under his probing eyes. He was a dignified, middle-aged black man, as run-down as the hotel, but he had a soft voice. "Have you run away from home?" His eyes twinkled with understanding.

"Sort of."

"Aren't you hungry?"

I felt I could take it no longer; I was famished. "Could I order some scrambled eggs and bacon from room service?"

His thin frame shook with laughter. "Room service? You must be joking! The next thing you'll want is a telephone in your room!"

"You're a mind reader, sir," I said with a feeble smile.

He grinned at me. "Shall I call your valet or maid?"

"Actually, I would like to call Olga—that's my mother's maid; she can bring me some breakfast. Or, should I say, lunch?" I'd lost all track of time. Since my room overlooked an air shaft, no daylight came in. The radio sometimes blared next door, but that was the only sound I heard. All at once, I was deeply grateful to this kindly soul for rescuing me. I told him so.

Then I started to get out of bed but felt so dizzy that I keeled over. My new friend took my arm and helped me stand. "Are you drugging or something?" he asked solicitously.

"Heavens, no! I'm only eighteen."

He peered at me suspiciously. "Have you been drinking?" I shook my head, and he continued. "I'm sure you can use a stiff boilermaker. They make a good one at the bar across the way. It's a nice day outside, first day of spring like. And you'll like that bar, full of bad girls trying to sell what everyone's had for centuries."

"Sounds super!" I said, lost in a Eugene O'Neill *Iceman Cometh* fantasy. I'd become a Bowery bum, staggering from one bar to the next. Whores would comfort me. Maybe I'd become religious and see the light?

At the bar I felt so elated that I bought everyone drinks. There was one pale, blond prostitute I couldn't take my eyes from; she seemed to have a halo around her head, and her classical features and delicate nose made me think of Mother. She had beautiful manners, too. After paying my hotel bill, I still had thirty dollars so I pressed twenty into her hand, then told her I had to go to my Wall Street bank, to clip some coupons from my trust fund. We made a date that I knew I would never keep, and out I flew, high as a kite.

Briefly back at Mother's, I was packed off to Eve, Mr. Lewisohn's daughter, and her psychiatrist husband in Topeka. You see, everyone was worried about me, which I liked.

Eve met me at the airport and drove me back to her house. We pulled up before a squat, stucco bungalow in a row of similar houses. My face registered shock. After the Villa Corne D'Or and Eve's country house in Ridgefield, Connecticut, this was hardly what I'd expected.

Eve smiled at my expression. "Irv, my husband, is a poor doctor," she explained. "I want to live as he lives. Plus, I want my children to have a taste of Middle America." The next thing she told me, as we walked up the little path and opened the front door, was that she did all the housework, and would I mind terribly sharing a room in the basement with her son, Michael.

It was a different Eve, all right, full of surprises away from the snobbish confines of the Riviera and the fashionable East Side of New York. I had never seen Eve look so pretty and attractive. She had a lovely trim figure, too, and great legs. *And* a lot of positive energy.

"Whatever do you think your father and mother would think of this ambience, Eve?" I asked.

"They'd think I was crazy," she smiled in her good-natured way. "But, after all, dear boy, I wasn't happy in that social world my parents brought me up in. I always felt it was ridiculous and all the people imbeciles."

For three weeks, I went daily to visit with doctors at Menninger Clinic, a world-famous hospital for nut cases, and there were some familiar-looking faces from the New York social world. They gave me endless Rorschach tests.

It was nice and cozy, living with dear Eve, my longtime savior and redeemer. Predictably, I took on her colors and felt better. But my visit finally came to an end. Eve told me my father was going to harbor me now.

As Eve drove me to the airport, she could sense that I didn't want to leave. "You'll have difficult times ahead," she said, kissing me. "But have *courage*, that's the key word in recovery. And remember, nothing lasts forever."

I smiled. "I hope I don't have to stay with my father forever."

"Your mother has some nice plans for you this summer. We'll keep in touch. You're going to be a winner, but it's going to take a lot of fighting. Life's an endless struggle, you know."

Chapter Eighteen

The phone never rang at C. A. Van Rensselaer's Long Island cottage. Often I picked it up to see if it was out of order. Even the birds didn't sing near this silent house. The house was asleep, and so were its owners. There was no music, no color. The garden was overgrown with weeds, the box hedge ragged.

"I'll call the gardener tomorrow," Vera would say in her monotone. Always she was sitting in the cluttered living room, staring into space.

Shutters hung at a forlorn angle, badly in need of a coat of paint.

"I'll call the handyman tomorrow," she'd say.

One somber day followed the next. I caught the mood of this place. It was difficult to get out of bed in the morning. Vera and my father seemed to have no engagements; the focal point of their days was his going to the antique shop—when he felt like it—and her taking my grandfather for an afternoon drive.

My grandparents lived half a mile away on Cedar Swamp Road. Grandma had bought an eighteenth-century house in Jericho, and she'd restored it with love and taste. It had the same feeling as the Oyster Bay homestead, only there was no life in this house. My grandfather lived in one wing, and she in the other.

The old grandfather clocks still ticked away noisily. An aging butler and maid stumbled about. Grandma was not herself. She seemed childish and empty-headed. She treated me lovingly, but sometimes called me Harold, who was her brother. In his sitting room, Grandpa would chuckle mirthlessly, "Poor old lady, she's lost her mind."

The one bright note in this gloom was going to the Jericho taverns—"dives," my father called them—to shoot the breeze with some of the locals and down a lot of whiskey, which my father labeled "panther piss." It was in this atmosphere that I discovered oblivion drinking, and I couldn't wait till Vera disappeared at three in the afternoon so the old man and I could do some "pub crawling." Pure O'Neill, I felt, and just as despairing.

C. A. Van Rensselaer was paying for the drinks. He liked to play the big shot here and be the big fish in a little pond. I was often amazed by his gift of gab. He liked to give the impression he was God's gift to women, and had as many as Errol Flynn or some of my old playmates from the Riviera.

As we started home at twilight, a mood of respectability would come over him—even a shade of fatherly responsibility. "No wonder you're so mixed-up, Phil, but don't worry, you'll be all right."

"Yeah," I'd say.

"No wonder you don't know right from wrong in that amoral background. What a way to be brought up. Disgraceful! Poor Adele, if I'd only known! Let's hope she's going to be happy at last." But I could tell he wanted her to be miserable. I loathed his guts.

It was pathetic. He still carried a torch for Mother; she remained in his memory the Siren, the Divine One, the Ideal, the Only Woman in the World. In the moments he reminisced about her, I had a dim feeling of affection for him. But I think, in truth, it was pity.

He became quite indiscreet when he was tanked up, to use another of his phrases. Sometimes I urged him to have another, because I knew that then his tongue would loosen up and I'd hear some more sordid details of his married life to Mother.

"What a woman, that Adele," he'd sigh, smoothing his thin eyebrow in a characteristic gesture. "I'll never forget our honeymoon. God, Phil, that poor woman was so damn innocent she thought every time I kissed her she was going to have a baby. Why, you won't believe it, but it took me two months before I could, in fact, call myself her husband."

I muttered something appropriate, and his low voice whined on. "Well, Phil," he said, with a thin smile twisting his lips, "your mother made up for lost time, let me tell you. My, my! What a madwoman! I hardly recognized the girl I'd married." He shook his head mournfully. "I can only tell you, Phil, I loved her, there was never another woman for me. My life's been a misery ever since the divorce." His voice trailed away. I looked at his defeated profile, hunched over the wheel. As we turned into the drive of the cherry orchard, he leaned toward me drunkenly. "Don't mention a thing to Vera. God, she's a spiteful woman; endless criticism. She's frigid, too. What a trial!"

After I'd been in Jericho two weeks, Mother called me. Her vibrant voice was most welcome. I should have been suspicious, but I was so dulled by Vera and CAVR, Jr.

"Sweetheart, you're going to a country club in Connecticut. So *many* glamour boys and girls. Tennis, golf, swimming—pure *Deauville sur la plage!*"

"I can't wait!" I said brightly. "Mañana, I hope!"

"Mañana," cried Mother gaily. "Counting the hours, my treasure. Lucky, lucky Philippe!"

I spun around like a top and danced into the living room. Vera was staring into space and reacted to the news as if she'd been hit over the head.

The blessed day arrived. We got to Hartford at two. At a gas station, CAVR, Jr., asked where Retreat Avenue was. That should have given me a clue about where I was going, but I was so happy sitting next to Mother and drinking her in, that my perceptions deserted me.

Soon gates appeared, and high massive walls. I stared at the large, punishing, institutional type building and the sign that read Hartford Retreat. I still didn't catch on. I noticed some attractive people moving about on the smooth lawn, followed by some men in white uniforms.

"Just like Southampton! What a paradise!" said Mother, watching me uneasily—doctors at Menninger's had told Mother I could be dangerous.

We drew up before a stone building. Breezily, CAVR, Jr., inquired where patients were admitted, and a nice-looking woman said we were in the right place; just go up that flight of steps and a nurse would sign me in. I stared at her hard, and she gave me a nervous smile. *Something's wrong*, I thought, but I was too dazed to take any action. I was apathetic from my weeks at Bleak House, and dulled by a hangover.

Oh, hell, I thought, *what does it matter?* With a stony face, curiously passive, I made my way up the steps and through the door of the famous mental clinic. Mother and her former husband flanked me, both shooting worried looks.

A nurse in a starched white hospital uniform put me at ease. My parents—it gave me an odd feeling to think of them in those terms—vanished into a doctor's office nearby. I was told to sit and wait in the hall. It didn't have that hospital smell, but stern-faced doctors and glassy-eyed patients passed to and fro. Presently, the two Van Rensselaers, together but somehow not connected with each other, appeared. Later, I learned Mother had signed the commitment papers, but she absolutely forbade them to give me electric shock treatments. With some horror, she'd heard the doctor's prognosis: two to three years' incarceration. I was a very disturbed young man. As she gazed at me sorrowfully, her face was tear-stained. CAVR, Jr., looked contrite, as if suddenly aware of the gravity of my case.

A friendly doctor smiled at me. "Everything's settled, my lad, we're going to take care of you now. An aide will take your luggage to your new home."

Mother's lips trembled; she fought back tears. She embraced me and murmured, "We have to leave you, darling. Don't look anxious; everything's going to be fine. Please be a good boy. Promise?"

"Promise," I said.

"We leave you in good hands," muttered CAVR, Jr., with a guilty look. I wanted to hit him. I clung to Mother for a moment, then was led away down the drive and across to a pleasant-looking white cottage. I felt their eyes following me, but I didn't look back. I wanted to show them that I could behave in a manly fashion.

The aide led me into a nice living room, where attractive men and women were playing cards and listening to the radio, then opened a door to my room. I noticed bars on the window. With difficulty, I restrained a surge of violence.

"Why don't you unpack now?" the young aide suggested.

"All right."

"Dinner's in an hour. Your doctor will probably look in on you before." He closed the door and left me alone.

I looked at myself in a mirror; I was white as a sheet, with strangely glittering eyes. I stared out the window. My parents were standing where I had left them. Mother had collapsed; my father was comforting her as best he could. Presently, he opened the door of the car for her and she fell in. Then the Plymouth started down the drive and out the gates. CAVR, Jr., would drop her back at the Volney in New York, where Rod Wanamaker was waiting for her, and then he would return to his wife, Vera. It was the only time I'd ever seen my parents together.

Then the anger hit me hard. It was the bars on the window that did it. And my father, that bastard, looking at me with that guilty expression. All at once, the violence that Mother had been warned about came out in full force, like a destructive Gulf Coast hurricane bending the palms and causing thirty-foot waves to demolish houses along the shore. I started to scream the house down, as Ida Lupino had done in *They Drive by Night,* just before she was led away to an asylum in a straitjacket. Completely over the edge.

Rehabilitation is a slow process, especially if you've been "damaged goods" as long as I had. *Damaged goods* was a favorite expression among the Hartford Retreat inmates to describe the state we were in, and might remain in, if we didn't get well.

The first day in my cottage room, I raged as I had when the policeman stopped me in the Rolls. Only this time, I even delivered the classic line of grandiosity out loud, in plain air: "Don't you know who I am?! I'm Philip Van Rensselaer and my uncle is the president of the United States!"

"Not Napoleon?" said the nurse sweetly, and then I exploded with fury.

"I *demand* that you get my doctor," I shouted. "How dare he lock me in this vile room with bars on the window!"

The nurse made a mock bow. "Your Majesty, I'll get your doctor right away." She started for the door, and I flung my shoe at her. It hit her in the backside, and when she turned around, her face was contorted with an evil smile.

Ten minutes later, two husky men in white uniforms entered my room. Without a word, they lifted me up, carried me through the door, down the hall, and into a waiting wagon.

"Where are you taking me?" I tried to keep the fear out of my voice.

"You'll see," said the driver ominously.

"Some people just don't know when they have it good," the other remarked.

"They have to be given a little lesson," smiled the driver. His smile was as evil as the nurse's.

We arrived at an old and dirty brick building covered with bleak ivy. A century of age and screams, madness and urine, lingered in the murky hallways. Down and down we went. Where were they dragging me? I remembered reading accounts of the Gestapo prisons, and the beatings in the torture room. God, my costly Lewisohn teeth would be demolished.

"Listen, boys," I said, "my mother's rich as Croesus and I'll pay you." They laughed contemptuously.

Finally, we arrived in a huge subterranean chamber with slimy, damp walls. A row of tubs ran the length of this torture room, some with men submerged in the water.

"Undress," commanded the brute, and slowly I started to disrobe.

"Shake a leg, Your Majesty," sneered the other.

I stepped into the water, then sank down with only my head surfacing. The men in white started to strap me down with leather bindings. "Now, just stay here, no violence or acting up, Little Prince, okay?"

"Okay."

This was known as the "tubs treatment." Sometimes you were

submerged in the water for twelve hours. If you were particularly violent, they'd leave you there longer. Some of the men were screaming. I looked at them. What good would that do? I kept silent, as the water gurgled around me.

A few hours later one of the thugs returned and slipped a tray across the tub. "Have some dinner." His voice was gentler, and I smiled up at him.

"What time is it?"

He laughed. "Got a debutante party to go to, m'lord?"

I can't remember how long I stayed in the tubs. This was to be my first glimpse of the strict disciplinary punishment I'd get if I didn't behave. I learned my lesson. I never again raised my voice or threw a shoe at anyone.

It was dark when they led me upstairs. They unlocked a metal door of a sinister-looking ward and turned me over to a grim-faced nurse sitting in an office.

She stared at me and asked, "Have you calmed down?"

"Yes, ma'am," I said meekly.

"Take him to room four," said the nurse. "This one gets special treatment."

My heart sank as I envisioned the Inquisition rack, or solitary confinement in a black cell with rats nibbling away at my flesh. On the contrary, however, I had a large room, with a comfortable bed, all to myself. There were only two private rooms like this in the violent ward. "Dr. Vigue didn't want to be too tough with you right away," said the man in white, locking the door behind him.

The next morning, Dr. Vigue came into my room. He was a shortish, pear-shaped man, with a strong nose and hawk eyes. I liked the look of him. *So would Mother*, I thought. He seemed like a jolly penguin, mixed with a bit of wise old owl. He exuded strength, power—this was a person to look up to. Shyly, I smiled at him.

"Philip, I'm going to be your doctor here," he said quietly, never taking his hawk eyes off me. "I hope you'll cooperate now."

I nodded eagerly. "Oh, yes, Dr. Vigue!"

"No more temper tantrums?"

"No, sir."

"Adults don't behave like that, you know," he told me gruffly.

"Yes, sir."

"You can't always have your own way, you know," he reminded me.

"No, sir."

"Your mother has always given in to you," he said, "but I'm not going to. Do you understand?"

"I'm sorry I caused that disturbance, sir."

He gave me an intense stare. "You want to get well, don't you?"

"I think so . . ."

"All of your adult life you're going to have to take orders, and submit to authority, even if you don't like it sometimes. When you get out of here——"

"How long do you think I'll have to be here, Dr. Vigue?" I interrupted, meek as a mouse.

He smiled. "That depends on how fast you get well, Philip."

I nodded. I got the picture. Boy, would I shape up fast!

"In any case, when you're released, you'll have a good, steady job to go to, and your boss will probably ask you to do many things you don't choose to do. But you'll do them. Understand?"

"Yes, sir."

He consulted his watch, then went to the door. "Discipline, and being able to take discipline, is the key to a harmonious and balanced life," he said. "Your mother told me you want to be a writer. There's no profession in the world that requires more self-discipline."

"Yes, sir."

"All your life, you've been distracted and pulled this way and that way. Now I'm going to make you centered. Whole. No longer fragmented." He looked at me to see if his words had made an impression. They had.

"You mean, I'll know who I am?" I asked.

"You'll know who you are," he replied in his positive way.

"I'll have an identity?"

"You'll have an identity." We smiled at each other. Then he patted my shoulder and told me that I would be allowed out to take my meals; the rest of the time I must remain in my room and think over what he had said to me. I nodded, and he closed the door

behind him, locking the bolt. I sank onto the bed, feeling a comforting relief. There was some hope, after all.

Weeks and months slipped by quickly at the Hartford Retreat,
like boarding school. I followed a structured routine. Therapy
classes in the morning, exercise and meditation in the afternoon.
Three times a week, Dr. Vigue and I had an hour-long session. He
was pleased with my progress. Thoughts of failure and death left me.

I grew to love Dr. Vigue. Probably he was the first man I truly
loved. Respect for him and caring for him went hand in hand. He'd
worked hard and long hours to arrive at his position of importance.
He told me it was gratifying to know that he was able to guide
young people through the labyrinth of their confusion and out into
the mainstream, to begin a new life—no longer self-obsessed and
self-centered, but caring about other human beings. Before Christmas, we had an especially memorable talk.

"You *do* want to be a human being, don't you, Philip?"

"Yes, sir. I do."

"You're acquiring a sense of discipline, my young friend. I'm
pleased you got your high school diploma."

"I've worked hard at it, sir," I returned truthfully. It was good
not to have to lie all the time.

"They tell me that you're good in your typing class, and your
mother was delighted with the leather wallet you sent her."

"I couldn't even concentrate in the beginning," I confessed
sadly.

"You've even learned to cook a good meal," he said, eyes twinkling mischievously.

"Miracle of miracles!"

He put his two hands on my shoulders and gave me a long, level
look.

"You *are* a miracle, Philip."

"I am?" I said, grateful for that word.

"I think you can be released in the spring—May, perhaps."

"That's when Mother wrote me she's going to be married."

"You don't blame her anymore, do you?"

"No, I don't blame her; she did the best she could, under the
circumstances."

"Just remember she's as much a product of her early environment as you are of yours."

I flung back a passionate answer without thinking. "I'm doing everything for her, so she'll be proud of me! She's a heroine."

He stared at me anxiously. "But you're doing all this fine work on yourself to please yourself, too, aren't you, Philip?"

"Yes . . . Yes," I replied slowly. Then burst out with, "It's important that I make it up to Mother! She did everything for me!"

"Yes, she did," said Dr. Vigue. "But keep in mind it was her choice; she *wanted* to do it." Our session was over. Dr. Vigue patted me on the back, congratulated me on my change of attitude, and wished me a Merry Christmas. We'd have another long talk in three days.

Mother and Charlie came up one afternoon after lunch. We exchanged some presents and had a brief visit. Mother seemed like a ghost; I was shocked by her appearance. She spoke little, was withdrawn. Charlie looked handsome and well dressed. I envied him his expensive clothes.

"We have to rush back to New York," Charlie said, somewhat impatiently. "Fred is having a big party at La Rue this evening."

Mother sat strangely still, preoccupied. Suddenly she stood up, and I helped her into her coat. "Thank you," she said softly, her eyes were full of tenderness, but she looked gray. A vague smile flickered on her wan lips. She looked ill. Looking at her, I felt a premonition.

"Is something the matter, Mummy?" I asked with concern.

She laughed, but her laugh had none of its old sparkle. "Just imagine, darling, I'm checking into a hospital after Christmas. Let's hope I get well as quickly as you." Her tone did not carry any conviction that she would.

I watched her gaunt face with trepidation, feeling that old falling sensation.

"What's happened, Mummy?"

"Dr. Neergaard said I'm having a breakdown." She seemed too exhausted to continue, and I was too frightened to inquire further. I looked at Charlie, but he was gazing out the window.

"We'll have to hurry," he said irritably, taking Mother's arm. "Weather report said there's a big snowstorm coming." Charlie led

Mother out into the hall and down the stairs to the front door. It was bitterly cold, and Mother looked far too frail to be out on such a day. It was getting dark already at three o'clock, and I didn't want them to leave.

Mother clung to me, her figure limp as a rag doll. "Good-bye, darling," she said faintly. Then we kissed, and they vanished in the encroaching darkness.

A blackbird screeched. Suddenly, it seemed just like that terrible afternoon she had left us at the Malcolm Gordon School, just twelve years before. How everything had changed. Mother was young and beautiful then. Now she was old, defeated.

In late February the first false days of spring seem as surprising as forsythia in the dead of winter. Birds sing with a fresh energy; people wear an expectant look; hope is in the air. The world is a lovely place and you feel you belong in it. I'd grown strong in the previous ten months. My future was full of bright things. Gratitude for being alive was bursting in me. Some other lost souls had inherited my shroud of gloom and anxiety.

Now and then, a delicious daydream would take shape in my mind: I'd be a highly esteemed doctor—you know, the Brian Aherne–George Brent type—in morning coat and striped pants, and Mother would be my patient. She'd be romantic in silver fox cape and silver fox hat held in place with a mist of veiling. She'd be telling me she was so much in love and I'd be guiding her through her difficulties.

One morning when the landscape was bathed in that false spring radiance, the nurse appeared in my room. "Dr. Vigue wants to see you, Philip." Her normally cheerful face was impassive, and I wondered why the doctor wanted to see me so early. It was not even nine o'clock.

I walked up the path to his office. The snow had melted and the sky was a cloudless aquamarine.

Dr. Vigue gave me a strangely tense greeting. He seemed so solemn that I wondered if I'd disappointed him in some way. He stared at me with unusual gravity.

"You're feeling strong and well, aren't you, Philip?"

"Top of the morning, sir!"

After a thoughtful silence, he said, "I think you're strong enough to deal with this bad news." Then, gently he informed me that Mother had cancer. She was dying, had only a few days to live. The disease had spread too far; it would be pointless to operate.

I cried for five minutes. Mother *dying?* It couldn't be true! Presently, I sat up straight and blew my nose. A dull headache throbbed behind my eyes; the old grayness and despair fell over me.

"You're all right?"

"Yes," I lied.

"Do you want to say good-bye to your mother?"

"Yes."

"This doesn't change anything, you know; your future is secure."

"Yes."

"You can take the train at noon, and a taxi to the hospital." He wrote down the address of the hospital, uptown on the Hudson River, near Columbia University. Louis Bromfield wanted me to go to Columbia School of Journalism, as he had done. Now it didn't seem to matter; nothing seemed to matter. But I wasn't going to tell Dr. Vigue that. The old lies had started again, and with them the old self-disgust. I could never make it up to Mother. All the hard work I had done to get well and find myself was futile. I had done it only for her. Now she would be gone, and nothing mattered.

As I got out of the elevator on Mother's floor, a wild hope seized me. At least I could tell her I was sorry for all the hateful things I had done to her. I remembered with guilt stealing her things at the Volney and calling her a whore at Aunt Bessie's lunch.

Dr. Neergaard, Mother's longtime doctor, stood outside her door. He raised his hand in an offhand greeting and introduced me to the nurse.

"Your mother has been such a perfect patient," the nurse said. "She was in awful pain all the time, but we had no idea."

"Yes, we had no idea," echoed Dr. Neergaard, visibly shattered. His eyes were red at the rims. Stupid bastard! Dumb Park Avenue snob diagnosing Mother as having a breakdown! Perhaps if they'd discovered it earlier, they could have saved her. "I'm sorry, Philip," he said, avoiding my harsh stare.

I blinked my eyes. "Can I go in now? I want to tell Mother how sorry I am."

"I know," said Dr. Neergaard in his high-handed fashion, gazing at me with a patronizing sneer. "But no deathbed confessions. Your dear mother mustn't know. Let her slip away peacefully."

"But it's important I make it up to her," I persisted.

"No deathbed confessions," he repeated with such authority I felt like a child.

Miss Turner, the nurse, looked at me. "Don't be shocked by her appearance, Mr. Van Rensselaer," she said. "When I told her you were coming this afternoon, she asked for her mirror and said, 'Oh, dear, I look so awful it will worry him; my looks are so important to him!' "

I flushed under Dr. Neergaard's eyes. He looked at me with contempt. "Just keep telling your mother that she's going to leave here in May," he went on. "You know she and Wanamaker were planning to get married then."

"Yes."

"She complained this morning of feeling tired, but I reassured her that her weariness was caused by all the new drugs we were giving her."

"We're giving her massive doses of morphine," added Miss Turner.

"She doesn't feel the pain, does she?" I looked searchingly at her face, but she moved away. Dr. Neergaard opened the door, whispering again that she must not know. I nodded and went in.

Mother was lying in bed, her head slightly raised on a pillow. Her eyes were closed and she seemed asleep. She was skin and bone, a skeleton. The stench of decay from her wasted body was powerful. The cancer was eating her insides away; there was nothing anyone could do. She moaned suddenly, as if a sharp pain had pierced her. Her white face was distorted.

"Mummy, I'm here."

She opened her eyes and gazed at me from those soft brown orbs. They were enormous now, in her sunken face. Her bones stood out, like a concentration camp victim's. She couldn't have weighed more than seventy pounds. I took her hand and kissed it.

A ghost of a smile trembled on her pale lips. They must have been dry, for she kept wetting them.

"I'm so ashamed I haven't written you," she whispered.

I nodded, afraid to speak.

"Have you forgiven me?" she said. "Your letters were so dear."

She kept gasping for breath. Every now and then she'd wince as she felt the terrible pain eating her. Her breath was laborious, and the sound of it tore my heart. Mother could not die! Not now, when everything was working out for her. God couldn't be that cruel.

Finally, I got the courage to move to the side of her bed. Her fine, brown hair lay straight back on the pillow. A strand was falling over her forehead. I brushed it back, perhaps the most intimate thing I had ever done to her.

"Aren't I silly, getting sick like this?"

That terrible laborious breathing continued. Panting. Her eyes never left mine.

"Dr. Neergaard just told me you'd be out in May, for your marriage," I said softly.

"For my marriage," she echoed, hanging on to my hand. An ironic smile curved her lips. Then she closed her eyes and moaned as fresh pain came.

I squeezed her hand. "Mummy, please make an effort. You must get well. What will I do without you?"

Her eyes rested on me lovingly. "Darling . . ." Quietly, the tears ran down her sunken cheeks. Then she made a feeble gesture at the towering yellow roses in many baskets. "Mr. Lewisohn sends them every day. . . . Do you remember, like those old days?" She laughed weakly. "And he sends the most sublime meals, from the Colony. Of course I can't eat them . . . I'll get fat as a pig, and that would never do, now, would it?"

"No, Mummy," I said, hoarsely, trying not to break down.

Fortunately, Rodman Wanamaker came into the room. He shook my hand, then stood on the other side of the bed. Mother gazed up at him like a little girl, trusting and sweet. "Do you know something, Rod?" She spoke in her teasing manner. "When I get well, I'm not going to tell you. I'm going to sneak around and surprise you with some pretty girl. What do you think of that?"

"Don't be silly, Adele," Wanamaker said, in a broken voice. "And you better get well fast; I'm counting on you being out of here very soon and joining me in Charleston."

"Charleston? If only I weren't so tired . . ." She drifted away again.

I rushed in, "It's the new drugs, Mummy, that make you feel sleepy."

Mother's eyes went from Wanamaker and then to me. "I know I'm going to die . . ."

Wanamaker and I protested vehemently, but her expression seemed to say, "I know you're lying, but it doesn't matter anymore. Everything is over for me. I'm so tired . . ."

"I must go now, Adele," said Wanamaker. "I'll be back at dinnertime."

"Thank you," said Mother, "You're so kind."

Abruptly, he left the room, a handkerchief covering his eyes. I couldn't stand much more myself.

The sound of a tug came from the river outside. I stood up and went to the window. A few miles down were the piers where the great ocean liners were docked.

Mother laughed feebly. "My traveling days are finished." Her eyes rested on me by the window. She too, must have been thinking of the *Queen Mary, Normandie,* those seemingly endless transatlantic crossings, Mother and Elena, Mr. Lewisohn and Eric, the Waldorf Towers days, the El Morocco dance music, the mammoth trunks being packed for the next voyage.

The nurse came in and said it was time for me to go.

"Must he?" asked Mother, with a protesting frown. "Isn't he handsome?"

Miss Turner gave me a look of frank admiration. "Strikingly handsome." I'd noticed in the station and the lobby downstairs that people seemed hypnotized by my youth.

"Imagine! imagine being nineteen . . . everything ahead . . . all goes so fast you don't know what happens. . . ." She stared at me wistfully. "You must rest now, Mrs. Van Rensselaer," she told Mother.

Mother wet her dry lips. "Remember, dear. You must make something of your life."

"I will, Mummy."

"Wherever I am, I'll be thinking of you."

Numbly, through my tears, I nodded mutely.

"Promise me?" she said, intense.

"Promise." I swiftly put my head down on the pillow beside her, and prayed. Prayed I could leave the room with dignity. I didn't want Dr. Neergaard to see me crying.

As though in a dream, I kissed her a final time, then moved to the door. I found myself waving. "Good-bye, Mummy."

"Good-bye, dearest, lots of love."

In the hall Mr. Lewisohn was talking to some doctors. He looked ashen when he greeted me. Then he introduced me. "These are some new specialists I've called in," he said. "They're going to save my little girl."

"Yes," I said, then started down the long corridor to the elevator. Some doors were open; I could see men and women who looked as bad as Mother—but they were old, sixties, seventies, eighties. Their time was up; they'd lived their lives. Mother hadn't completed hers. From the very beginning she'd always had rotten luck.

Chapter Nineteen

After Mother died, Dr. Vigue told me I could not leave the Hartford Retreat until I was gainfully employed. So Aunt Bessie came up with a job opportunity at McGraw-Hill. In spite of being almost eighty years old, she still kept in touch with corporation presidents, but Charlie's going off to Europe with Fred Beckman was a blow to her. She now knew she could no longer count on him to save the family, and as for me, she was painfully aware that I'd inherited my father's "instability."

Through the *Times* we found a furnished studio, just six blocks downtown from Aunt Bessie's. Eve Lewisohn gave me a gray flannel suit from Rogers Peet, and I was ready to start my business career in New York.

To celebrate, Eve invited me and Charlie to the theater one evening to see the play everyone was talking about, *A Streetcar Named Desire*. It shattered me. At the end when Blanche was led off to the asylum, the tears streamed down my cheeks, as they had at Mother's funeral. It was terrible; I couldn't stop crying. My identification with Blanche was too overwhelming. Years later Tennessee and I would become friends; indeed, in a mad moment, I told Suzy Knickerbocker that Tennessee and I were getting married and going to honeymoon in Key West. Suzy never wrote about my antics again. "Peck's Bad Boy of Society" was all washed up. But I'm getting too far ahead of myself.

After a few weeks of confined boredom, I hated my McGraw-Hill job; hated the sleazy weekends lying in the sun at Rockaway, in the shadow of Coney; hated the subway rides to these places. Abruptly I told my boss I had to go to Europe on urgent business. I didn't dare tell Aunt Bessie that I had quit the job. Fortunately she didn't call me there for a time, so I got away with it.

The studio was at 148 East Forty-eighth Street, an apartment hotel called the Middletowne, a poor man's Hotel Lowell. The rent for a furnished studio was $100 a month, so I'd have $150 left to spend on movies, restaurants, laundry. Right after March 3, the checks from Prudential Insurance arrived; I was to receive from Mother's estate $250 a month for ten years, which didn't exactly fill me with security.

I kept moving the furniture around, to get the most dramatic effect. Mother's forties portrait of the *Laura* school hung in the center of my little room, and Mother's Dutch Louis XVI walnut cabinet and Herring-type horse prints gave a certain personality to the impersonal Grand Rapids decor that I deplored. Luncheons with Aunt Bessie and Mathilde were the high points of my social season until dear Margaret Potter introduced me to Carole Maigret.

At our first meeting at Mr. Lewisohn's, Margaret said in her weary cosmopolitan drawl, "You have the look of someone who'll get to the top at any cost. Have you met Carole Maigret? She's a beautiful model, greedy and narcissistic like all of us, and *determined* to make the big time. You'll love her."

The next Friday evening Margaret Potter opened the front door dramatically and embraced me. "You'll never guess who's here, pet. That divine peacock Carole herself!" Strains of Cole Porter's piano music drifted out from the drawing room, and Margaret added, "That's her husband Jack playing. He's Doris Duke's stockbroker and doing very well as you can imagine, but Carole's after far, far bigger game, like most everyone we know."

"Not me," I said with a cherubic expression.

She burst into throaty, cynical laughter and took another swallow of her whiskey-soda. (She always had a whiskey and soda in her hand.) "Sweetie, you're the oldest young man I've ever met. And after what happened to poor Adele, you must be vengefully dedicated to plundering every palace in Christendom. You're a corsair, my sweet!"

"A pirate? Me?" I was always delighted when people thought I was ruthless.

"With that chin, you're a *determined* pirate," she gurgled wickedly, taking my arm and giving it a good feel. "And *don't* flirt with Carole, I'm warning you. Jack is terribly jealous, he's twenty years older and *insane* about her, like all the gents."

We were standing at the entrance of the drawing room, an attractive well-dressed man in a blue blazer and yellow ascot was playing the piano, and behind him stood the most glorious creature I'd ever seen. My knees buckled. Carole looked like Ingrid Bergman in her *Intermezzo–Rage in Heaven* period—the same freshness, the same radiance. A bit like Joan Fontaine, too, in *Rebecca*—fluffy blond hair, huge innocent eyes, soaring cheekbones, and hollowed cheeks.

Margaret saw the expression on my face and chortled: "I knew I never should have brought you two peacocks together. Why can't I ever learn *not* to introduce people . . . ?" But she was too bored to finish the sentence.

As I stared at this astonishingly lovely creature, Carole's brown eyes were going up and down me. They seemed to say, Does he have any dough? Is he worth knowing? Does he know better people than I do? Is he a waste of time?

That night, over dinner, Carole continued her relentless inspection of me in the formal dining room. From the cream of watercress soup to the raspberry ice and crystal finger bowls she stared at me. I became so unnerved that some lamb spilled on my tie and I could hardly speak. The young goddess herself rarely uttered a sound, and the times she did her husband glared at her and told her to think before she opened her mouth.

"You'll get yours, buster," she muttered under her breath.

As we were leaving the dining room, I caught Carole's eye and smiled at her. She smiled back, and her eyes told me that she was bored to death with her husband and waiting for the right moment to dump him. (My reading proved correct. Less than a year later she divorced Maigret, and two years later she married a multimillionaire by the name of Morton.)

Later that night when I was in bed reading *Père Goriot,* a knock sounded on my door, and Margaret in a pink satin and lace dressing gown slunk in on seductive mules.

"Don't worry," she cooed, "I'm not going to rape you."

"Tell me more about Carole Maigret, she's something! *She* certainly will climb to the top, don't you think?"

"Over a lot of bodies," growled Margaret, sitting on the edge of my bed.

"Is she so hard?" I asked.

"She left behind a lot of bodies in Minneapolis, not to mention a football player husband. But you wait," she continued, tossing back her long, perfumed pageboy. "She'll be operating in Paris very soon, and probably end up a princess. She has all the necessary ingredients to hook a Paul Mellon or a Nelson Rockefeller."

Margaret continued giving me long looks. "Your naked chest is giving me ideas," she purred. "Don't you hate sleeping alone?"

"I'm sort of used to it."

"Well, I'm now returning to my huge double bed. If you're interested, you're quite welcome there."

"What about your husband?"

"He likes you."

Insatiable curiosity was getting the best of me. In a moment I found myself following Margaret's voluptuous figure down the hall and into her bedroom. Tall and good-looking Bo Potter was snoring away on his side of the bed. I stared at him skeptically. He was powerfully built and weighed thirty pounds more than I.

"He who hesitates is lost," said Margaret, and gave me a push into the bed.

The next morning at nine I was having breakfast in the dining room when Carole strode in gracefully, giving me that mad, intense stare. Awkwardly, I sprang to my feet and dropped my apple green Sèvres cup with a loud smash.

"What's making you so nervous, buster?" Humor and madness flashed in those huge brown eyes.

"You, Mrs. Maigret," I gulped.

"Call me Carole, I'm not old Edith Baker's age, you know." Her tone became soft, alluring.

"I know, I know!" I began putting honey on the whole wheat toast, and the sticky stuff started dripping onto the Sheraton mahogany table. Feeling her eyes on me, I tried, unsuccessfully, to get the honey off the polished surface.

"How long has it been since you were sprung from the funny farm?"

"Three months," I replied, meeting her curious gaze.

"That explains it," she grinned good-naturedly. "And how long did you grace the snake pit?"

"A year."

"A year? Gee whiskers, if they ever locked me up, they'd keep me there till the end of time!"

She began combing her marvelous ash-blond hair that curled onto her shoulders like Constance Bennett's in *Topper*. A stylish beige cashmere sweater clung to her girlish bosom, a string of pearls circled her smooth neck, and her flesh looked like Devonshire cream. Everything about her glowed with health. I loved her expressions like "gee whiskers" and "buster" and her devil-may-care attitude. To hell with everyone, her motto seemed to be; she was doing everyone a favor to be in their company. She told me of her "destiny" to end her days as a duchess in Europe, and I told her of my sadness at not being able to apologize to Mother for my awful behavior. Madness ran in her family as well—we were made for each other and were fated to dance together through life.

The Potters made me feel part of their family, inviting me down to Wainscott for long weekends. This Wainscott house was a five-minute walk to the beach, surrounded by flat, fertile farmland, corn and potato fields, red barns and silos. This part of Long Island between South- and Easthampton had a rustic charm that appealed to me, and the peaceful flow of days reminded me of Louis Bromfield's Pleasant Valley.

That summer and various future summers, Margaret fed my

Carole Maigret obsession by giving me the latest details of Carole's meteoric rise in High Society. The Byron Foys had invited her to an elaborate party of the Windsors, then society's favorites, and the ducal pair were much taken with her. Cholly Knickerbocker often wrote of her beauty and charm.

In the afternoons, Margaret and her friend Hope would guzzle, and their scowls would become darker and darker as the whiskeys went down. The summer finally came to an end, and they were tired of me, perversely wanting to gang up on me. They'd made a mess of their lives, had thrown in the towel; I hadn't yet, so resentments were developing. One morning I gave a feeble excuse and took the train back to that sewer, Penn Station.

Chapter
Twenty

As I was unpacking at the Middletowne, the phone rang and Fred Beckman's voice came over the wire.

"Just back from gay Pareee, my heaven child. Schiaparelli gave a swell party for me; the world was there—*divine* woman! We flirted a bit, I don't mind telling you. Noël sat on my knee and Edward Molyneaux as well." He laughed, somewhat tipsily. "The Ritz bar was jumping." Then he let drop about two thousand famous names, including Rita Hayworth and Aly Khan—all chasing Fred, of course.

"Is Charlie with you?" I asked presently.

"Who?" he said, bitchily.

"My brother," I reminded him sharply.

"Must you bring up that depressing and disappointing young man?" I heard the tinkle of ice as he took another sip of his gin and Dubonnet. "So many high hopes dashed, not to mention so much money squandered."

I decided it would be more judicious to change the subject. (I was soon to discover that Fred was a bad drunk.) "Are you at 550 Park Avenue?" I asked.

"In Princeton," Fred replied. "Listen, beauty, why don't I send in the car and chauffeur for you, and then come down for a couple of weeks? It's quiet as a tomb here but we'll find some kind of mischief to get into."

Late that afternoon Fred's Chrysler station wagon with the wooden doors dropped me off at Brook House. It was a Japanese-style playhouse with a tall cathedral roof, a design far before its time. Its enormous plate-glass windows and terraces overlooked the serene waters of a pond. But as I crossed the arched wooden bridge, uneasiness gripped me.

I knocked vigorously on the door for about ten minutes. "Welcome, my handsome child!" came Fred's drunken voice. "Life in the country," he laughed roguishly, throwing out his arms. He reeled over the hardwood floors to the well-stocked bar. I'd never seen so many bottles of liquor. Even rare things like Pernod with absinthe.

"And absinthe caused the downfall of Toulouse-Lautrec, at such a young age!" concluded Fred, beaming in his prima donna way.

"Pernod's for me, then," I said in a falsely bright voice. I needed the most potent brew to knock me out. A little later, evening shadows fell over the pond. It became dark in the Brook House but Fred didn't light any lamps. He sat next to me on the large sofa covered in antelope, and so my Fred Beckman period began.

Soon the days at Fred's artificially simple country compound began to drag. Fred started to drink gin and Dubonnet before noon and by the 3:00 P.M. lunchtime ("Spanish hours, my heaven child") he was three sheets to the wind. Those juniper berries made his slanting blue eyes become slits and sparked a flood of wicked memories of every celebrity and socialite of the twenties, thirties, and forties.

Every now and then he'd stop his reminiscing and fix those evil blue eyes on me. "Don't know why you stay here with a burned-out wreck," he'd sneer. "I bet you want money, don't you?"

"It takes one to know one," I'd reply, and that always gave him a good laugh.

As much as wanting his money, I wanted to hear his steamy reminiscences. My insatiable curiosity kept me there by his side, but sometimes he'd linger too long on his London period where

Tallulah and he had fought over the rich English Lord Alington, and I'd have to drag him back to Mallorca and Mother. I knew he'd used Mother, as he'd used everyone, but I wondered if he had any real feelings for her. I came to the conclusion he must have loved her, for often he'd break down and sob when he was talking about her. "You and Charlie and Adele were my family," he'd blubber.

After lunch, the butler would come out of the pantry and we'd carry Fred upstairs to his blue and white bedroom with the dormer windows. Sometimes he was too far gone, and we'd have to drop him onto the living room sofa.

Fred snored away the afternoons, and I took long walks through the rolling farmland. The sight of homesteads, filled with children, with cows, and horses grazing peacefully in meadows, was a much-needed contrast to Fred.

Many times during those long afternoons, I'd thumb through his photograph albums bound in Florentine leather. The sight of him dancing with Mother at some nightclub or ball gave my heart a terrible twist.

Once Fred staggered into the Brook House and flung out his arms like Sarah Bernhardt. "I never thought it would come to this. My child, I don't know what's happening to me." He fell on the antelope sofa beside me and stared transfixed at the likeness of himself some twenty or thirty years before. Then he began to weep heartrending tears, and I held him in my arms.

Fred responded like a child. On an impulse he decided he wanted some days in New York, to see all the latest theater and "entertain the world."

Charlie returned from Europe, and to get away from Fred, I shared Charlie's rambling duplex at 829 Park Avenue for a month. Charlie could make a dollar go farther than anyone I knew. To augment the rent he took in "paying guests"—socialite fellows who would rather lunch at the Colony and dine at the Stork Club than pay rent. Charlie was gregarious, and nearly every night there were bridge parties, and Mary the Irish maid would stumble out of the enormous kitchen to feed us baked potatoes and hamburgers. Jessie, Mother's maid, had introduced us to Mary; she liked to arrive at twilight for work and spend the evening with us. This annoyed my brother, but it seemed logical to me. Mary was a plump, good-natured woman of about forty, who'd been sent over from the old country as a girl, to help support her enormous family of brothers and sisters.

When I moved to 20 East Sixty-sixth Street, Mary came with me, which delighted me. Twenty-five years later she was still with me; we were still best friends, and she figured out that she'd helped me through some thirty major moves. (I never had to have my apartments painted because I moved every year.) Thus began the period when all my friends complained they had to make a separate address book for me. They all got used to seeing me in the trucks of Day and Meyer, or Santini Brothers, waving cheerily as the huge moving vans carried me, Mary, and my treasures to some new home; sometimes I clutched a big furry dog or marble bust on my lap.

One afternoon Mary and I went over to 550 Park to help Fred get out of those enormous rooms. To have a millionaire's cash flow, Fred unwisely unloaded this magnificent ten-room apartment for $16,000 and some fine old master drawings and paintings for $20,000. In those days such a sum was a small fortune, but Fred was a bigshot, with a reputation for being a big spender, and the money trickled through his fingers. Rarely have I seen anyone go through money as quickly as Fred did, although Carole and Barbara Hutton topped him. (Thirty years later Fred's 550 Park Avenue apartment sold for over $2 million, and one Van Dyke drawing brought half a million. So it goes. Fred always said that terrible sacrifices had to be made when you needed cash.)

While Mary and I were emptying Chippendale chests of drawers in Fred's bedroom, a black-haired, red-lipped man with a huge fat nose and glittering eyes appeared behind us. Mary took one look at him and crossed herself, whispering that it was the devil himself.

"This is Herbert Kende, the auctioneer," said Fred, sweating profusely with his usual hangover. "Herbert is a clever fellow; he disposed of some of William Randolph Hearst's objects at Gimbels during the war, and Mr. Bache's too."

Kende and I looked at each other and smiled. He reminded me of Peter Lorre, oily and obsequious and masochistic. I was to learn many things in Herbert's company.

I'd had my eye on some of Fred's Gainsborough school drawings and some bronze doré figures to put on my fireplace, so after Kende left I said to Fred, "I'll take those English drawings of the park scene and those French chenets. You owe me a housewarming present." I fixed two wild eyes on him as if to hypnotize him. Herbert had just given him a big check, and Fred could be generous when he felt his bank account was bulging.

Mary was rather shocked by my carrying away those Bache treasures. In the elevator she clucked her tongue, but I replied that if I hadn't taken them then Herbert Kende would have.

I never thought I'd see Kende again, but my phone rang one day, and he began in his oily voice, "I was wondering what you're doing, young man."

I replied that I was going to the New School, trying to educate myself.

"How would you like a nine-to-five job at my auction gallery, at 119 West Fifty-seventh Street?"

"What would I do?" I asked cautiously. Fred had paid the rent at 20 East for a year and left me a thousand in the Bank of New York, so I felt flush. Still, working for an auction gallery appealed to me. Herbert cinched it when he added, "Every week we have a new sale, and next week we're selling Renoirs. And the week after, eighteenth-century French furniture. I'll start you out working in the catalog department, so you can educate yourself and learn more. How about it?"

I became madly excited. "Terrific! When do I start?"

"Monday morning, nine-thirty."

My life was exciting and eventful, and working for Kende satisfying. I'd finally found my niche with racy and colorful people. Henry Fonda lived at the top floor of 20 East, and I'd met Marjorie, the Baroness de Jongh, a tall and slinky woman dressed by Jacques Fath and blazing in Harry Winston diamond clips and bracelets. She had dusky skin and claimed to be an Inca princess, but in reality she came from Harlem. Marjorie and I became great pals, and once I gave blood for her when she got sick. A few years later she was thrown off an admirer's yacht in Nassau and devoured by a fleet of sharks. She was drunk on champagne so I prayed she didn't feel too much. People told me a jealous rival did her in.

Then I moved to a splendid red-brick townhouse at 111 East Sixty-fifth Street, just off Park Avenue, and drove a long, yellow Cadillac convertible out to Southampton. My walls at home were red velvet, the fireplace was Empire and white marble, and my curtains crisscrossing over the twelve-foot windows were of filmy gauze like the curtains at Mrs. Byron Foy's at 63 East Ninety-third. I'd become friends with Cinnie Foy, the youngest daughter of the house, and her debut was the most smashing party I'd ever attended. The cast of *South Pacific* performed in the Versailles-type drawing room. I went to this party with Doris and Jules Stein's oldest daughter, Jean. Jules Stein was the founder of Music Corporation of America, and every week Jean would invite me to parties at the MCA offices at Fifty-seventh and Madison. Audrey Hepburn, Henry Fonda—every actor or actress you ever dreamed of was at these galas. Yes, life was worth living.

Early in September 1951, after a mad tour through Europe, I was back in New York working at the Kende Gallery and having daily lunches with Herbert at the Barbizon Plaza or the Café St. Moritz on Central Park South. He could not hear enough details of my triumphant European trip, and suddenly, as I watched his rapt expression, I knew for certain that he wanted to live his life through me. He was married with a wife, child, and mother, living a quiet family existence. On the surface Herbert seemed quite normal, but I knew he was a madman with identity problems. He wanted to be me, and he wanted me to have the very best. He also wanted me to treat him like dirt and seemed amused when I demanded money and presents from him. If I stepped out of character and behaved in my usual well-mannered and good-natured way, then *he* became the sadist and treated me like dirt.

I was brought up to order the cheapest thing on the menu when I was someone's guest, but with Herbert I swilled champagne cocktails, gorged on poached salmon or grilled lobster. One afternoon at the Barbizon Plaza I got carried away and grabbed Herbert's eighteen-karat-gold money clip when he was paying the bill.

"Give it to me!" I said with a brutal voice. "I want it! It's too good for you!" Stunned, meek, humble, he gave it to me. I spied his ruby cuff links and seized them, trying to rip them from his shirt. "I want them! They don't look good on you!"

"What a greedy guy!" he muttered with admiration as we headed back to the gallery on Fifty-seventh Street. Playing a role exhilarated me and I wanted to go on with my performance. Suddenly a devilish idea possessed me. I wasn't quite sure where it would lead, but it would cause some sparks to fly. "You know Mr. Kende," I began—I always called him Mr. Kende because he begged me to call him Herbert—"last night at a terrific party I met Franz-Joseph and he wants to sell me a bed."

Herbert stopped dead in his tracks, transfixed. "Archduke Franz-Joseph Hapsburg?"

I was dying to laugh, but of course I couldn't. "Yes, the dear, sweet archduke himself, and he and his beauty-wife, Marta, heavenly woman, want to decorate 111 East."

"That's an excellent idea," Herbert said in a thoughtful tone. "But your apartment doesn't even have a bedroom."

"Well," I said nastily, "whose fault is that?"

He flushed with a pleasurable guilt. "Tomorrow afternoon we'll go looking for a bigger apartment, in one of those grand limestone mansions off Fifth Avenue in the East Sixties."

"Can you afford it?" I asked coldly.

"I can afford anything you want!" he replied with exultation.

"We'll see about that," I muttered, looking down at him as if he were a bug.

Two weeks later, Mary and I were in the front seat of a moving van and pulling up before the grand limestone facade of 41 East Sixty-seventh Street.

The archduke, whom we all called Putzi, in shirtsleeves, greeted us gaily from a towering stepladder, and Mary glared at his aristocratic face, which seemed too fine for a man's.

"Mary McDonnagh," said I with mock formal manners, "may I present Archduke Franz-Joseph."

Mary gasped and dropped a huge cardboard box full of Baccarat glasses I'd bought on my Paris shopping spree. "The saints preserve us," she muttered and stumbled toward the door, where she collided with three moving men carrying a black and gilt Recamier sofa of Regency design and sweating over the red and white striped satin.

"Never a dull moment around you, Mr. Van Rensselaer," one of them said. "Say, got a beer in the house?"

"Sure, boys." I grinned. "Or would you prefer whiskey or bourbon?"

"Bourbon!" they cried, and soon we were all having a party. Moving days were always traumatic so I tried to make them fun. To make Putzi feel at home, "The Blue Danube" and other old Vienna waltzes were put on. Soon, after a few more drinks, our noble Austrian was telling us how he and Marta had spent the war in Tarrytown on the Hudson with the Duchess de Talleyrand, born Anna Gould, daughter of ruthless robber baron Jay Gould.

"She was a dwarf and a hunchback," our archduke was saying, "and sported a mustache."

Suddenly Princess Marta appeared in the Marie Antoinette drawing room. "Putzi, how could you say such dreadful things about our charming hostess?" She flung some shirred silk Austrian blinds at him and demanded that he hang them up immediately. He obliged meekly, and then statuesque, regal Marta was sipping a spritzer and telling us even worse stories about Duchess Anna.

"And she asked us to leave because she was so jealous of all of our parties for the Palffys and Esterhazys, Apponyis, Lobcowiczs, and Chernins. She said she was tired of paying for our entertainments that didn't entertain her, so I said that common and ugly people had to pay for beautiful and distinguished people."

The moving men got a good laugh out of that one, then tall and queenly Princess Marta added, "And my liebchen Philippe, Putzi and I were just saying that we must organize a little reception here."

At that moment Herbert appeared in the door with some apricot-colored roses. He must have heard everything, but Marta saved the day. She was no fool and quickly got the picture who was paying for all these good times, and she knew he'd overheard her remarks. She suddenly treated Kende as if he were the emperor of the Austro-Hungarian Empire and invited him to a dinner for Queen Marie of Rumania's granddaughter, who happened to be an Austrian archduchess. To make matters even more thrilling for

Herbert, she smiled at him and said in a most confidential tone that she was certain he would know all her guests, who represented the crème of Middle Europe, the Radziwills, Auerspergs, Lubimirskis. Herbert wore such a satisfied and ecstatic expression on his face that I had to escape into the kitchen to have a laugh with Mary.

Presently Princess Marta and Putzi were kissing me farewell, and Marta was gushing on my neck, "Liebchen mine, next week we do give a fabulous reception here. I'll send you my butler and maid and they'll arrange *everything*."

"You won't have to do anything, Philippe, except pay!"

"Ho, ho, ho," laughed the handsome pair, more wet kisses, Mary did an awkward curtsy and almost fell over, and Herbert kissed the queenly Marta's hand with such rapture and bowed so low I thought she'd expire from hysterics. Then they vanished down the stairs.

Chapter Twenty-one

I felt taut the night of my first big party. An avalanche of bills daily fell out of my mailbox from every fashionable antique shop in Manhattan. Was I clever enough to continue playing my role for Herbert Kende? Would he continue to pay?

"You don't look so good, Mr. Van Rensselaer," said Mary, handing me a cup of Irish tea.

To escape my uneasy thoughts, I gave the bushy white azaleas and mauve hydrangeas a long watering, then I checked the smoked salmon from Old Denmark. Later I climbed on a fragile gilt chair covered in Nattier blue damask and lit the oyster white candles in the rock-crystal-and-amethyst chandelier—$950 and still unpaid for. I watched with some irony as the candles started to drip on the rare, circular Aubusson carpet—$1,500 owed to French and Company. Swiftly I strode out into the hall and turned on the Magnavox (unpaid for, $350, Liberty Music Shops), and soon the rhythmic strains of Gershwin rippled out into the drawing room. I swallowed some champagne (unpaid for, Sherry Lehman) and thought, *Oh hell, who cares? I'm living a beautiful life and that's all that matters.*

At six the bell downstairs rang. I swiftly lit the spotlights just installed out in the balustrades, and they cast a daybreak opalescence through the oyster silk Austrian blinds that Mary claimed resembled Queen Marie Antoinette's bloomers.

My first guest was Fred Beckman, stunned to silence by all the splendor. He flung himself onto a low French sofa over which towered an exuberant gilt-framed mirror, courtesy of Putzi.

"Who is paying for all this?" he asked. It was the question on most everyone's lips that evening. "Rothschild or Rockefeller? Oh, my heaven child, I knew you'd follow in my wicked footsteps. I suppose that Herbert has fallen hard for your charms?"

I nodded. "Yes, he wants to be me."

Fred shook his gray-blond head. "Disaster," he said. "Disaster! Get off the sinking ship before it pulls you down with it."

"But how, Fred? *I am* the sinking ship."

Marjorie de Jongh, in an elaborately draped Fath creation, was the next guest. She took one look at silvery Fred Beckman in his tailored English clothes and blood red ruby cuff links and wrongly surmised that he was my golden goose. She grabbed some champagne and wound her sinuous body around Fred. "Always heard you were a great lover, darling. Now when are we going to do something about it?"

"The party's off to a good start," cried society photographer Jerome Zerbe. And indeed it was! Suddenly everyone appeared at the same time. By seven, a hundred people were milling about the Hapsburg rooms, and the noise was terrific. I even forgot my debts.

As luck would have it, Fred became grotesquely drunk, so I asked Marjorie if she would take him back to the Ritz Tower and on the way sober him up on a Pavillon dinner. Diamond clips blazed on either side of her almost-naked breasts, and I remarked on the beauty of the clips and the breasts.

"Darling, I'm having gruesome financial woes."

"Who isn't?"

"Who's paying for this show?" she asked.

"You, Baroness."

"Listen, sweetheart, if you can sell these jewels, I'll give you a twenty percent commission."

"How much do you want?"

"Ten Gs."

Herbert Kende was headed toward us, so I introduced him to the Baroness, told him of her plight. "Fine merchandise," he said, examining the diamonds through a glass.

"Take them!" cried Marjorie, and a moment later they rested in Herbert's breast pocket. Two weeks later Marjorie got her $10,000, I got $2,500, and Herbert pocketed $10,000. The moral of this, I suppose is that one should never worry about money—at least when one is young.

Kende was delighted when the archducal Hapsburgs made their entrance into my drawing room. He clung to their regal presence, salivating over the young archduchess. Later, Herbert talked business with Mr. Lewisohn, name-dropped with Virginia F. Ryan, grinned at Rodman Wanamaker, joked with Freddy Eberstadt.

At the end of the party, the Hapsburgs, Herbert, Mary, and I were sitting in the bedroom, when suddenly Herbert started glowering suspiciously at the Hapsburg heirloom bed, then got on his knees and almost vanished beneath the mattress.

"He's looking for the caviar," giggled Princess Marta, and her mate, Putzi, hastily swallowed the last of the smoked salmon. Doris Stein had brought me some Beluga, but I hid it, wanting to devour it later with scrambled eggs.

Presently Herbert surfaced and said in dark tones, "This bed is stamped Hotel St. Regis!"

"That's pretty good!" laughed the archduke gaily, and clinked glasses with his laughing mate. "After all, the St. Regis *is* the best hotel, ho, ho."

"It cost one thousand dollars," growled Herbert, not amused at all.

"Well, I'll antique it," cried Putzi, crouching under the cream-and-gold fake. He demanded a screwdriver, some nails, and a hammer and was busy for a time. Then he stood up and said he'd improve the wormholes and finish the antiquing the next day.

"Putzi will fix it, and then, liebchen Philippe, you'll have a treasure as fine as any in those antique shops." Marta gave a great bellow.

Then Putzi named three well-known and highly esteemed Fifty-seventh Street dealers who doctored their "antiques," and even baked them in the sun for good measure, and sometimes submerged them in a relentless acid bath.

"As for those Renoirs and Dufys around," said Marta, but she stopped, knew better than to continue, seeing the uncomfortable sweaty flush on Kende's face. (I knew the woman in Passaic, New Jersey, who signed numerous of the Renoirs, Tintorettos, and so on that Herbert placed in fashionable homes.)

Thanks to Marjorie's Winston clips, my bills were paid. And the parties, with the cast of hundreds, continued. During Christmas holidays I threw two enormous and particularly brilliant ones, and on Christmas Eve I drank a toast with Fred. He was rapidly going downhill and several times when we went to the theater he couldn't make it down the aisle. His hair and clothes were beginning to smell of whiskey or gin. If we went to a movie, he snored away through the whole show.

"A beautiful life we're having, my heaven child."

Herbert didn't have his old enthusiasm and eagerness; the names and titles no longer brought that look of ecstasy to his face. Just as well, because soon he was in financial trouble and his gallery surrounded by ugly rumors. He told me in the spring of 1952 over a Plaza lunch that he had decided to give up the auction business. He was also going to move to a smaller apartment in a less expensive neighborhood.

"I'm sorry about your job," he said.

"Don't be, I learned a lot." He gave me a black look, and I could tell he blamed me for his hard times. A short time later he went bankrupt.

My brother, Charlie, had gotten married in Havana, and now he and his bride Yolande, wanted me to accompany them on their belated honeymoon. I managed to sublet my apartment at 41 East, then flew off to Madrid where the young couple met me. Once on foreign soil I felt safer. Herbert had made some vengeful threats; violence was distasteful to me. But I learned my lesson: The next time I'd be more careful whom I became involved with.

In the fall of 1952 I returned to New York and, as a result of Herbert's decline, had to give up 41 East. I did so with a bit of a struggle and some regret. It was too difficult to sublet it when I was away. Despite its beauty and elegance it had a limited appeal, since it had only one bathroom and you had to walk up a flight of stairs, plus there was no doorman to get you a taxi.

My new home was at 25 West Fifty-fourth. Small and practical it was; the bedroom and step-down sitting room had a low-ceilinged 1930s appearance totally different from the Hapsburg glories and Antoinette bloomers. The three Day and Meyer movers drank bourbon while Mary and I sipped spritzers, but the mood of hilarity was gone. In my new home I felt ordinary, run-of-the-mill, middle-American.

"Anyway, Mary, this place is practical," I sighed. "And easy to sublet." I stared at the uninteresting garden below and the brick walls of the apartment house backing up on my building. An aimless feeling settled over me.

A few weeks later, in a panic, I raced back to Europe. At least when I was moving, my life didn't seem so pointless. Besides, something always happened to me in Europe; they understood people like me better. Just before I left there were some ugly messages from Herbert, and once, he was waiting for me in the lobby, glowering, so I felt relieved to get out of town.

In January 1954, Florence Quintard Bonnell died in Bar Harbor, Maine. She was the mother who had abandoned little Adele long ago. I felt nothing when she died, for I'd never known her. But I did feel enormous joy and relief when Charlie told me that he and I were to inherit over $100,000 each. "The end of a Quintard trust," said Charlie, "initiated by her grandfather, the Iron Ore King."

Aunt Bessie, too, was overjoyed with this news and pushed me to see her exemplary nephew, Duncan Ellsworth. Duncan brought me down to Fiduciary Trust on Wall Street, where his and his aunt's funds were invested. Fearful that I might start spending the capital, I prudently placed the money into a trust. My trustee informed me that my portfolio would be in widows and orphans shares (I always got a big kick out of that expression) such as Ma Bell, General Motors, and so forth. My income would be $500 a month, and after a few years of growth they could pay me out some profits.

Me, with a portfolio, of widows and orphans delights! Suddenly, my fears ground to a halt. I had the necessary oil to push forward!

But I seemed to be going nowhere. Friends were marrying, and I felt left behind. After a particularly gloomy day, with lowered eyes, feeling a heavy sense of loss and failure, I shuffled back to 25 West Fifty-fourth Street, where stood Herbert Kende, looking impoverished and glaring at me in my lobby.

"You've been avoiding me!" he cried, seizing my arm roughly.

"You bet!" I flung back, wondering how the hell I was going to deal with this maniac.

"Pay up," he shouted, "I *demand* satisfaction!"

I pushed him into the elevator and gave him a double whiskey in my apartment. "Why are you here?" I asked, falling into my Gestapo-inquisitor role, "What do you want?" Under my fierce eyes he cowered a bit but was relentless about being paid back.

"You're a rich guy now," he pleaded.

"All right," I said, swiftly, and moved to the Louis XVI table desk and wrote out a check. Then I moved to the sofa and handed the blue Bank of New York check to him with a dramatic flourish. "It will take almost everything," I said tragically, "but here you are, Herbert."

He gazed at the check with that old ecstatic expression, then invited me out to dinner. "Anywhere you want! The sky's the limit!"

"Thank you," I replied politely, "but I've had a bad day."

He embraced me, and I caught the odor of box hedge that always emanated from his fat body when he was nervous. "You're not a bad guy, after all. I knew I could rely on you. And wait and see, next year I'll have another gallery and I'll be a millionaire with a villa in Spain. And I'm going straight. No more fakes."

Later as Herbert's bulk and my $10,000 check disappeared into the elevator, I prayed I'd seen the last of him. Ironically, everything he wanted he got, and just three years later he confided that my ten grand was the magic ingredient that caused his turnaround. So all's well that ends well, only Herbert Kende did not go straight; in fact he became more crooked than ever.

In 1954, Paris friends were writing that "the rich Mrs. Morton," as Carole was known in the resorts of Europe, was "cutting quite a swath." She had rented an enormous villa in Biarritz complete with ballroom, for the Marquis de Cuevas costume ball, and though she hadn't made an entrance on an elephant, she'd been escorted by an army of eligible men. At all her receptions and entertainments she served caviar either in crystal swan dishes or in a soft boiled egg, and only champagne, lots of it! Badia Pallido called her the most famous playgirl in all the world, even outshining Linda Christian, who'd made siren history by marrying Tyrone Power.

Carole had caused a sensation in Spain the year before when she danced with gypsies at Pamplona and then ran off to live with them in a cave. I couldn't wait to see her again.

I was always waiting for some excuse to return to Europe. If a man was talking about his impending Cairo-to-Bombay trip at a party, I'd smile and ask, "Do you need a valet to accompany you?" And if it was a woman I'd smile and ask, "Do you need a maid?"

Early in 1955 I did meet at a party a sunbaked soldier of fortune in khaki who looked as if he had thoroughly enjoyed machine-gunning countless Japanese in the Burma jungles. He kept me enthralled, describing his future trip to Tangiers, so I flung out my usual line.

"I *do* need a valet." He grinned. "Can you be packed and ready tomorrow, at daybreak?"

In the blink of an eye I was in Tangiers, where I was left alone a good deal at the Minzah Hotel. Under a whirling ceiling fan, with the scent of jasmine delighting my keen sense of smell, I sung along to Cole Porter's *Silk Stockings* and thanked God I'd brought the album along as the wailing Arab voices in the Medina were monotonous. So was the empty stretch of blue Mediterranean framed by the fronds of palm trees.

Soon we were sailing away from the white houses of Tangiers and back to the Ritz Hotel in Madrid. Once again I was left alone in my gilded room, and once again I sang to *Silk Stockings*. My khaki chum had flown off to Beirut, and I was fancy-free. On an impulse I put through a call to Tony Pawson in Paris.

"What are you doing, you gypsy?" came Tony's melodious voice.

"Listen, Tony, do you think it possible to put me up in your palace?"

"I'm rather pinching pennies at the moment. Can you afford a hundred fifty dollars a month? Breakfast and maid service included."

I agreed, and soon it was Paris in the springtime. It was rainy but that did not stop me from my daily mid-morning walk. My eyes feasted on the seventeenth- and eighteenth-century mansions set behind thick doors and cobblestone courtyards, and I loved strolling down to Boulevard St. Germaine, visiting the oldest church in Paris, which astounded me with its purity. The oldest café in the world, Le Procope, was also a favorite place, and the waiters told me that Victor Hugo, Balzac, and Napoleon had their café and brioches there.

One misty morning under soft rain clouds over the Louvre, I crossed the bridge and started down Avenue Montaigne. I'd left several messages with Carole. Her French maid always said Madame would ring me later, but she never did. Suddenly there was a deluge, and I ran for shelter under the Plaza Athenee awning, my Lobb shoes screaming with fury, for they were not supposed to tread wet pavements. (I was too vain to wear ugly rubbers.)

All at once a classic limousine of the old school pulled up. The Plaza doorman opened the door and out stepped a tall woman, all in black and wearing a large black picture hat. A distinguished-looking man with a hawk nose and mustache was trying to detain her. He seemed quite agitated, as did the woman, but I couldn't see her face, concealed as it was by the marvelous hat. Some Burmese rubies entwined with pearls circled her throat and wrists, and any sophisticate could have told you the black costume was created by the master of couture, the great Dior himself.

Suddenly, the hawklike man in the rear of the limousine uttered an oath, and the mystery lady all in black, who rather resembled Marlene Dietrich in *Desire*, ran toward me on her high heels. There was something familiar about the high cheekbones and wide red lips.

"Carole," I cried. "Carole Morton!" The agitated woman flung me a blank look, and I grinned. "Don't you remember that Syosset weekend at Margaret Potter's and me smearing the honey?"

A light dawned. The taut, lacquered look vanished, and for a moment there were traces of the early Ingrid Bergman. "Darling,

darling, darling!" she cried, in an artificial and peculiar British accent. "Do you have any dough now?"

"Came into a nice legacy; nothing like yours, of course."

"Then *please* take me to lunch," she said with almost hysterical eagerness. "Danny's behaving like such a cad, and I *do* detest having my meals alone, don't you?"

"I don't imagine you suffer from that unpleasantness very much."

"I do, I do! You can't imagine the number of times these bastards here cancel lunch or dinner engagements at the last minute to get even with you! Ohhhh, I'm the most disillusioned girl, *ever!*" To my amazement she burst into a flood of tears, and a dozen people glowered at me as if I were the cause of the weeping.

Carole continued her crying jag. "I'm almost thirty-five; I *can't* keep driving myself from one resort to the next! St. Moritz for a few months, Biarritz for a few months, then London, Paris, Deauville, never alone for a minute, and never getting enough sleep, a heavy, hairy arm or leg thrown over you . . ."

Carole's hysterical voice rose several octaves higher, and my face became redder and redder as the crowd gathered around us. "And," wailed the Morton, naming a famous, highly publicized Golden Greek, "that one gave me a Micky Finn on his yacht and raped me when I was out cold. My God, you don't know what an American girl has to go through in Europe!"

Growing alarmed by her rage, I steered her into the bar, "Come, let's have a little drink in Le Relais."

She clung to me like a little girl. "Darling, so lovely to see a familiar face from back home. Why, oh why, didn't I stay in the good old USA? American men are so sweet and simple, European men so tricky and *evil.*"

The maitre d' bowed us to a corner table where all the action was, treating us like the Rothschilds. "Madame . . . ?" he said respectfully his eyes feasting on the glamour of Madame in Dior.

Carole smiled vividly at me, "You *must* try a Bellini, darling, so mild and utterly harmless, peach juice and a wee drop of champagne, like grape juice and ginger ale."

We began sipping the lethal mixture and soon we were drunk as lords. Many titled men came to our table, hand-kissed like crazy, and gave delicious compliments.

Our talk sparked a host of memories, and she gazed at me wide-eyed. "Hemingway himself came all the way to Pamplona to see me, after my gypsy period, but then by the time he arrived I'd vanished with the bullfighter. That's the way the cookie crumbles, don'tcha know?" It amused me the way the American slang sparkled through her careful Mayfair drawl, and I was touched by the way her face, so expertly made-up, frequently gave hints of an innocent Minneapolis sorority queen.

"Gee whiskers," cried Carole, "here comes José-Luis!"

A tall, thin, fine-looking man, his black hair brushed straight back from his high forehead, was making his way toward us. His progress halted, of course, by numerous hungry-eyed cosmopolitan women, each more gorgeous than the next, whose hands the famous Spanish writer kissed with meaningful stares.

"Heavenly days," I exclaimed, "he's like a leopard stalking."

"Heavenly nights, too, buster!" Then from out of her handbag she pulled a lipstick and drew on the snowy tablecloth. "Longa villa, I call him."

We fell on each other's necks with laughter and were still convulsed when Villalonga stood before us. He gazed at Carole's artwork and she explained, blushing, that she was attempting a Matisse obelisk. "You can add something if you like, José-Luis, amore," she whispered in baby talk.

"I'd rather have lunch—quite famished, you can imagine."

"I can imagine!" She smiled, stood up, and took his arm, and out we went from the fashionable Le Relais. Excited whispers followed our exit.

Lunch was at a Left Bank bistro with the biggest, fattest, whitest pussycat purring in the window and amorous nooks and corners. I don't remember much of our lunch—endless Bellinis and red wine—but some time in the middle of the afternoon a tall and distinguished Englishwoman appeared. She was Villalonga's wife. Carole kicked me under the table and I knew that my role was now the go-between. It turned out to be more fun than my Gestapo role.

Madame Villalonga and I decided to go sightseeing, and we parted with my inviting them all for lunch the next day.

At two o'clock Carole and her Villalonga drifted into the palatial

Pawson house, and we sat on the tapestried gilt armchairs and remarked on the serenity of the garden.

Tony Pawson suddenly burst in with earnest apologies. "Too awful. Barbara just called, is in *wretched* shape at the Ritz."

"How can you be in wretched shape at the Ritz?" said Carole, so marvelously coiffed and groomed that it must have taken her three hours.

"It's Barbara Hutton," explained Tony, gazing at himself in one of the full-length mirrors set into the gray-and-gold paneling. "Her latest marriage has just ended, after two rather costly months."

"Why can't you take sweet Philip along to cure her blues?" said La Morton in honeyed tones.

Tony rolled his splendid Vivien Leigh eyes. "If I take him along, I'd never see Barbara again! By the way, I've got Count de la Rochefoucauld to take my place at your lunch table."

"That's a nice birthday present," said Carole, fussing with her ash-blond tresses under the black cartwheel hat. "Did I tell you, my darlings, tomorrow is my birthday?"

"How about lunch at Maxim's?" suggested José-Luis in his sonorous voice.

"How can you afford Maxim's?" questioned Carole, not too kindly.

It so happened that Hartley Ramsay, my St. Paul's School best friend, was in Paris with his mother and twin. Yes, Hartley would be vastly taken by La Morton and Villalonga. It was quickly arranged.

Hartley and Carole and I were the first to arrive in the Belle Epoque splendor of Maxim's. After a lunch of pâté de foie, chicken with champagne sauce, half a dozen bottles of Mouton Rothschild, and numerous rounds of cocktails, followed by crème brulee and cappuccinos, the bill arrived. Everyone looked vague.

"Do they take American Express checks here?" asked Hartley, catching on and being a good sport.

"Of course!" we all sang.

As we were coming out onto Rue Royale, Hartley said, "I've never seen people vanish so quickly when the bill came!"

"Darling, that's the European way!" said Carole, linking her arm through his.

The culmination of these galas was Cynthia Balfour's dinner for Aly Khan. The hostess, looking like a long-stemmed yellow rose, sat at the head of the long table, and the husky and attractive prince, the love-object of countless women around the world, faced her at the other end. Carole and I sat together at the middle of the table, Carole somewhat drained by the Danny Saint dramas and Villalonga excesses.

When I wasn't making small talk to my female partner on my right, I was listening to Carole's tearful confessions concerning the termination of the Villalonga romance.

During most of the meal I concentrated my attention on the amazingly sensual Aly Khan, then at the zenith of his allure. Women told me he resembled a black puma, but I thought he was more lionlike. Rumor had it that a woman was never the same after a night with Aly. Goddesses like Joan Fontaine and Gene Tierney had been Aly-infatuated, and many people told me Gene had had a series of nervous breakdowns when Aly told her he couldn't marry her. Aly's father, the old Aga, forbade his son to marry another actress after the Rita Hayworth fiasco.

The other great lover in Paris at that time was Rubirosa, the dusky Dominican Republic diplomat. Rubi had bagged both the gold-dust twins, Doris Duke and Barbara Hutton, and had been named countless times as the other man in divorce proceedings. In my next incarnation I was hoping to be Rubi.

Over our finger bowls and dessert, Carole pinched me under the table. "Are you ready?" she asked.

"For what?"

"For a trip to Italy. I want to leave tomorrow at dawn. How about it?"

Dawn! "Sure." I said.

"I'll pick you up at ten, and you better be ready." She gave me a steady look. "Too bad I have a date, otherwise I'd invite you back to the Plaza."

Right on time Carole's smart, bottle-green Jaguar sedan pulled up at Pawson's Rue de Lille mansion. The car was overflowing with expensive luggage, Dior boxes, Paulette hatboxes, and a Skye terrier curled up by the rear window.

A mad dash through France finally brought us to the island of

Capri. We took rooms at the Quisisana Hotel overlooking some pink-and-white oleanders whose sweet odor permeated our dreams. A crescent moon shone through some palm trees, casting reflections onto our bed. Finally Carole consented to surrender, and after a few delirious kisses she was mine. Miracles will never cease. The next morning she gave me an approving look, and I strutted about like Rubi or Aly, barking out orders to maids and valets.

Two nights later, though, we were gliding over the glassy Mediterranean in Piero Mele's yacht. He was Capri's version of Rubirosa, rich and charming, too, so I spent the night with Tussie, the Skye terrier, while sounds of love came from Carole's cabin. My sexual humiliations began. So did our fights, like cat and dog, in fury.

Carole found a suitable villa, and she enjoyed the carefree flow of days on Capri and no longer had any desire to rush off to other resorts, because, as she explained, "Everything happens right on this island and sooner or later *everyone* comes here."

The first "everyone" we met was Joan Crawford, who stayed at Villa Tiberio, and later the Gish sisters, Dorothy and Lillian, accompanied by a rich Texan. I was photographed between these legendary ladies and made a terrible impression on La Crawford because I told her I loved her in *A Woman's Face*. She'd made that in 1941, and quite naturally, she wanted to talk about *Torchsong*, her most recent film in which she had belted out "Tenderly" to a blind pianist. Joan had a striking head of orange hair, cold blue eyes, and a sculptured face that would have stopped a dozen express trains. Everyone on Capri was making fun of her but they were just jealous of her success as a survivor.

As if by divine intervention, a much-needed change came my way. One morning I was strolling through the colorful and crowded piazza when I saw two familiar faces. "Caro Felippo, do join us." This came from Gian Carlo Menotti, and his friend, the young conductor and glory boy, Thomas Schippers, who sprang up warmly and shook my hand.

"Who is that *devastating* blond wildcat you're seen with everywhere?" asked the curious Menotti, his close together, clever brown eyes resting on me.

"That's Carole Morton, a famous siren."

"I want to devour her whole," said Tommy.

"Oh, no, you don't!" I said, so grimly that they sat up in their wicker chairs.

"Does she punish you?" asked the fiendish Gian Carlo, who saw through every situation.

"Yes," I confessed.

"And you like it," said Tommy, who hailed from Kalamazoo, Michigan, and spoke in a more outlandish accent than Carole's.

Soon I began to drop in at their villa at the end of Via Tragara. No cars were allowed here, the peace was God-given. The odor of pines and jasmine blended with that of geraniums. How refreshing to have a drink and talk with Sam Barber and his friend, handsome Chuck Turner, and Maestro Menotti and Tommy. They were all working on various compositions (*Vanessa* was started here), and Tommy was perfecting the score for a Verdi opera to be performed at La Scala later in the year. There was an air of purpose here that kept me returning again and again. The intellectual atmosphere was stimulating, with the exchange of ideas and the insightful dissection of personalities.

The villa's library was plentiful. I borrowed dozens of books and devoured them so quickly that Gian Carlo was as surprised as Malcolm Kenneth Gordon had been in my early boarding-school days.

"You're so well read," observed the maestro in our twilight talks. "Why don't you do something artistic?"

"Perhaps one day I'll write," I confessed, gazing enviously at Tommy Schippers working on a score. "I'd give my soul to have a career."

"And I'd give my soul to pleasure myself around the clock, Philip," grinned the radiant conductor. "But ambition won't let me; music's my life."

I looked at him and I knew he meant it. If only I could believe in something that strongly! Carole and I, indeed the whole Capri crowd, seemed to have given up life's real struggle, surrendered to empty games and parties. Too bad I couldn't tell Tommy the truth about pleasuring oneself. Carole was giving me a hard time, picking on me and criticizing me. Some self-esteem and confidence returned in the music corner.

One midsummer evening in a trattoria overlooking the sparkling, faraway lights of Naples, Carole and I had a disastrous dinner with our usual crowd. She was drinking too much and started shrieking that Verdi wrote the opera *Norma*, and I stupidly piped up and said she was wrong, that it was Bellini.

She flung a glass of wine in my direction. "You stupid baby boy! You don't know your ass from a hole in the ground!"

I stumbled blindly from the restaurant, tears streaming down my face. And I was still tearful when I boarded the early morning boat for Naples. And when I boarded the TWA plane for New York.

Chapter
Twenty-two

An eighteenth-century figurine smashed against the wall of my red toile de Jouy bedroom, narrowly skimming my tanned face.

I had taken on a new role in early 1957—social secretary for Mrs. William C. T. Gaynor of 876 Park Avenue, Montrose, Southampton, and Jamaica, British West Indies. In the latter she was known as the White Witch of Rose Hall, and in the former as the Holy Terror of the Hamptons. Rosie Gaynor, born Warburton, and the stepdaughter of William K. Vanderbilt, sister of Consuelo, duchess of Marlborough and later Madame Jacques Balsam, was obsessed with the Vanderbilts. She told me many times that they were the only family of any social consequence in America.

Montrose, her gigantic, red brick Georgian house, was filled with Vanderbilt mementos. Like all the Vanderbilts, W. K. loved to build spectacular houses—in Northport, Long Island, Fisher's Island, and Florida, to name a few. Rosie, often called Queen Rose because of her imperial ways, believed herself the reigning princess-royal of the Atlantic Seaboard. Biddles, Peabodys, Cabots, Livingstons, were dismissed as "scum." Indeed, there was no one who was Queen Rose's equal in America save Wallis, Her Royal

Highness, the Duchess of Windsor; the Duchess's letters were deeply treasured by Rose, and kept in a secret drawer, tied with pink ribbons, in her signed Louis writing desk.

"The queen's riding for a fall," said the beauty of Southampton, Mrs. Charles Amory, called "the divine Chessie" because of her enormous eyes, classic features, and sense of humor.

All these things made Queen Rose fascinating to me. My curiosity demanded that I discover what living with a monarch of the United States was like. So, as always, I was experimenting, eager for fresh experience. Even if it meant becoming a castrato and going to a plastic surgeon because of all the Sèvres and Meissen treasures hurled at my twenty-nine-year-old face.

"You cretin! You imbecile! You only received a thousand-dollar check from Aunt Consuelo for my pet charity when you should have received five thousand! I thought you charmed her the other night at dinner, what?" This delivered in the most raffiné drawl, from the prettiest Fragonard mouth, under a pompadour of white-gold hair arranged daily by a master hairdresser. And Mummy's twenty-two-carat diamond and collar of pearls flashed on her Mainbocher.

"I'm not taking you to Millicent Hearst's tonight after the catastrophe at Aunt Consuelo's," the petulant and piercing drawl continued.

"Mrs. Hearst sent five hundred," I managed to say.

"Five hundred!" shrieked the queen, her thin, arched brows rushing together. "I daresay that common Mrs. Alfred Corning Morton sent one hundred, what?"

"One thousand," I replied, trying to push Carole's most recent letter under a pile of bills and invitations. I was sitting at a Vanderbilt desk overlooking acres of lawn and, in the distance, a windmill. The air coming in from the open windows was heavy with the perfume of roses from Rosie's famed horticultural specimens. Childish cries came from the swimming pool where her ten-year-old son splashed.

Rosie snorted, her small, upright figure standing on matchstick legs and ankles. She was only a few years old than I, but she seemed older than Aunt Consuelo, who had made her first marriage in 1895. Bills and debts do that to you, and the queen had

plenty of both. It was essential she play in the league of Henry
Ford, Alfred C. Morton, Mrs. William Randolph Hearst. To do so,
she was spending capital and that didn't exactly give one happy
dreams.

"Jean Morton is quite beautiful," I said, without thinking. (One
always had to think before speaking in the queen's presence.)

"Jean Morton is common as dirt," snapped La Rose.

"Aunt Consuelo is very attached to her."

"Jean knows how to charm, as does Carole, who, the Duchess
tells me, is now raising eyebrows."

"Carole *does* lead a colorful life, Rosie," I said, smiling.

"Still mooning over Carole, aren't you?" said Rosie softly, touching my shoulder. She started to go through my papers and caught
sight of Carole's large, sprawling hand from a Roman hotel.

"I daresay you'll soon join Carole in Europe, what?" I nodded,
and she added, "Well, the Duchess tells me Barbara Hutton is in
Venice with her new husband, Gottfried von Cramm, and *suicidal.*
Tony Pawson and her court are with her, all recipients of trust
funds and enormous settlements of money."

"Really?" I said, feeling a surge of excitement.

"Being a courtier might be the job for you, Philip." She smiled
thinly. "You're a rotten secretary. In fact, I don't think you're much
good for anything. You're an amoral beast, but I can't blame you for
that, after the way your doomed mother brought you up. *En plus,*
your writing about your mama is, well, undistinguished."

I hung my head. A butterfly rested on the pink-and-white peonies on my desk.

Rosie rumpled my hair, "Cheer up, now, and get into your black
tie! After all, you *are* decorative, and you have lovely manners, and
that means a lot with Barbara. Can you be ready at seven-thirty?"

We returned to Montrose before eleven, the queen somewhat
depressed. Whenever she went out in public she invariably became disappointed because people never treated her as she thought
she should be treated. Jean Morton always received more attention
than Rosie did, so sometimes the only alternative was to throw a
scene or spill a drink on the hostess's best damask sofa, a calling
card hard to forget.

"I'm going to try my luck in Europe," drawled the queen as we started up the monumental marble staircase.

"I think you'll be happy there, Rosie," I said.

The queen stopped dead in her tracks. "People with our backgrounds can never be happy," she said, staring at me tragically. "I want too much and I'll never be happy until I can have it. And you, charming boy, wouldn't be smiling all the time and making jokes if you knew what lay in store for you."

My eyes clung to hers, dreading what she might see in the future.

"You're going to fail, like your mother. You're not tough enough." She gave me a good-night kiss and wandered down the long corridor to her bedroom, which she shared with her doctor husband, Bill, who was fed up with her scenes and in love with someone else.

The next morning was sparkling, pale blue and green. The sound of the train and the chirping birds and the sight of the gardeners pruning the rose bushes dispelled the fears of the night. Ahead lay Venice and Carole and Barbara Hutton. I would not fail! *I'd show them all.*

Two days later, Carole and I were sitting in our compartment as the express train from Rome raced through Florence and then on to the bell towers and gilded domes of the famed water city.

"What happened to your Jaguar, Carole?"

"Left in some Roman garage, amore, I can't remember which one!" She was painting her eyes, cursing the wild fluctuations of the racing train.

"Carole!" I scolded.

"Actually, point of fact, darling, I had to get papers for it, and it became just too much of a bore!" The train shot to one side and Carole screamed, "Wait till I tell Cecco Pallido about this train. Cecco's the most devastating man in all *Italie,* owns railroads and things, has a sweet, very chic baby sister, Raffinella Maestriossi, in old Venice, gives fab parties in her palazzo." She shot me a tense look from her heavily outlined eyes. "Did I ever tell you about our blissful interlude in St. Moritz? At daybreak I was coming out of Cecco's room at the Palace Hotel and there was Raffinella Maestriossi glaring at me."

"So that means we won't be invited to Raffinella Maestriossi's."
I laughed.

"Well, at least Tony Pawson will introduce you to Barbara Hutton," said Carole, with a weary sigh.

"I wouldn't count on it," I laughed. "He never took me to Barbara in Paris."

"Exhausted," said Carole, with a rude yawn, putting down her giant magnifying mirror. "Oh, darling, I'm thirty-six now, can you believe how quickly the years race by? Everything's such an effort these days, just too much! My best friend Joanne Connelly Ortiz-Patino died of an overdose in Switzerland, aged twenty-seven. Olga Deterding got fed up with all the sex and parties, and now she's working for Dr. Albert Schweitzer in Africa, and lovely Princess Nina, from California, is in India, about to become a Buddhist. Do you think that's the answer for me, Philippo?"

She stared at me with fearful eyes, and I was shocked to see how she had aged. Her marvelous spark was dying out. I had to turn her around, restore the confidence that had been eroded by dozens of European men far more clever than she was in the battle between the sexes.

Once in Venice, we docked at the Gritti Palace Hotel, where Hemingway always stayed, and then followed some porters carrying our luggage through the winding back alleys of Venice.

"Let's rush to Harry's Bar," cried Carole, "and have a real Bellini!"

Half an hour after our Venice arrival, we were pushing open the swinging wooden doors of the famous meeting place. Our eyes were momentarily diverted by the dazzling sight of the yachts of Onassis, Niarchos, and Lopez, brilliantly illuminated from bow to stern to mast.

"The greatest show on earth, Venice in season," said Carole. Then I playfully bowed her through the portals of Harry's, and a madhouse greeted us. People standing at the bar, packed like sardines, tables overflowing with the rich and famous of three continents. Carole pointed out the appetizing Count and Countess Maestro Maestriossi, and Marina Cicogna, whom I had met in New York, talking with Elsa Maxwell, the famed columnist and party giver.

"Hello, my darlings," cried Tony Pawson, embracing us warmly. "Never have I known such a brilliant season in Venice. I *do* hope you're invited to Elsa Maxwell's great Headdress Ball for Maria Callas at the Danielli. Not to mention Countess Cicogna's dinner dance tomorrow evening. And sweet Barbara Hutton's dinner on the isle of Torcello."

"We're just here for a rest, darling," said Carole, trying to look demure.

"To see the Tintorettos and Titians," I said, trying to look monastic.

Tony howled. "You two are here to *climb!*"

Carole and I looked properly appalled. Then Tony flung us against rich Prince Johannes Thurn und Taxis, who promptly invited us to dinner in San Marco Square, and we were off to a good start. After dinner with a cast of hundreds we fell into a sinister dive called Ciro's near our bohemian resting place.

At eleven the next morning we just made the Danielli motorboat to the Lido. We emerged from a dark tunnel and were blinded by the blazing sunlight on the Adriatic. A long line of blue-and-white cabanas stretched down the beach left and right in front of the Hotel Excelsior. The first cabanas on the right as you stepped onto the sizzling yellow sand belonged to Countess Lily Volpi, Count and Countess Maestro Maestriossi, Anna-Maria Cicogna. Now these elegants were changing into their bathing costumes and lying on low canvas beds to perfect their golden color. My heart gave a jump when I spotted the fragile figure of Barbara Hutton reclining in exotic Chinese beach pajamas with wonderful pearls circling her thin neck.

"Now where in hell are we going to change into our bathing suits?" Carole was saying as she stared at the cabanas through dark glasses.

"We'll find some familiar face." We started to trudge down the beach, past endless pleasure pavilions. Carole waved hopefully here and there, but no one rushed out to greet us. Vengefully, Carole muttered under her breath that Countess So-and-so stayed in her Biarritz villa and that Duke Such-and-such had enjoyed her hospitality in Kitzbühl.

"Come and have some white wine, my liebchens," a voice called to us.

"Oh, darling, it's sweeeet Ervine Getcham-Waldek; he's the head of the Corvilia Club at St. Moritz, and a perfect angel."

"An angel I'm not!" cried the Austrian baron, embracing Carole, and then embracing me. I'd always felt an affinity with Austrians since Franz-Joseph. "Now sit down and break bread with me." He handed us some delicious cheese rolls which rapidly vanished, and he gazed at us appreciatively. "Tell me all the hearts you have broken here, and all the grand parties you've been invited to."

"We haven't been invited to any" said Carole darkly and proceeded to tell the jolly baron about our plight.

"Well, get out of this Siberia part of the Lido and show your tempting bodies before the chic cabanas of the Maestriossis, Huttons, and Cicognas." He pulled us to our feet, and pushed us down to the Gold Coast. "There's a wicked story they tell about dear Doris Stein. When she was here a few years ago, not knowing anyone and wanting to be in the right social swim as we all do, she told her little daughters to bounce their balls into the Cicognas' cabana down there, and wouldn't you know, Marina Cicogna and the Stein girls became intimate friends, and soon Doris Stein was friendly with Anna-Maria Cicogna. By the way, Anna-Maria is the true angel of Venice, helping all her poor friends, and many artists, too. Needless to say, Barbara Hutton, the unhappy Lady von Cramm, has been the angel for the whole of Europe. This morning I counted seven men she had made millionaires, and not her husbands either. Now finish your wine and forward to battle."

We both kissed Ervine gratefully and started gingerly across the scorching sands. I turned around and waved at Ervine, and he shouted, "You both look so in love, everyone will want to break you up."

To cool our feet we walked along the shoreline, where wavelets were languidly falling. Anna-Maria Cicogna went out into the sea in a pedalino, to feel the cool breeze, and Carole pinched me and told me to follow her in hot pursuit.

"I think we should stay together," I replied thoughtfully, "and play Romeo and Juliet."

We began to fool around together, splashing each other with

loud screams and shouts, then fell on each other in the water, biting ears and pinching thighs.

All at once Marina Cicogna, nineteen, appeared before us, her intelligent eyes bright with amusement. She was probably the most worldly girl her age. David Selznick was trying desperately to lure her to Hollywood to work for him.

"So what are you two doing?" asked the young and pretty Cicogna, smiling.

Carole sprang to her feet, took the bikini-clad Marina aside, and started whispering in her ear. Marina's eyes grew larger and larger. Finally she moved back to her cabana, giving me odd looks.

I grabbed Carole's arm. "What did you tell her, you fiend?"

"That you made love to me twenty times a day."

"Twenty times? *Dio!*"

When we returned to our rooms at La Fenice, we found a formal invitation from Countess Cicogna asking us if we would care to come in after dinner. After that, all the doors of Venice were open to us.

Carole and I arrived at ten-thirty at Anna-Maria Cicogna's house, which was startlingly modern and a kind of baby palace. We picked out Barbara Hutton all in black lace. Her wonderful pearls and many diamond bracelets, brooches, and rings seeming to be the only sign of life about her.

"Balenciaga," said Carole, staring at Barbara's dress, and she quickly took out a pen and drew its outline. "I'll have my dressmaker in Rome copy it, amore."

"Look at the necklaces on Madame Onassis and Madame Niarchos!" I cried. "Too bad I can't swallow some of those stones."

We grabbed some champagne, and carried on our Tristan-Isolde act. Young Marina, radiant in a beaded white evening dress, was headed in our direction with Aristotle Onassis. He looked marvelously clever and attractive, and I could see why Jeanne-Marie Schley Rhinelander was destroying herself.

"Get him!" I commanded Carole. "Wrap yourself around him, and give him the business."

Carole and the famed Golden Greek vanished onto the dance floor, and Marina gave me a little tour of the mini-palace, all in pastel colors and worked with that stucco design that Venice is famous for. Marina had been a friend of my brother's in New York, and now Marina was very friendly to me. Afdera Franchetti had recently married Henry Fonda, and Marina introduced me to them, Rudi and Consuelo Crespi, and Eugenie Niarchos.

"The huge black schooner, *Creole,* belongs to Stavros Niarchos," explained Marina. "Probably the most beautiful sailing ship in the world. Reinaldo and I are hoping to get invited to Greece with them in two weeks."

"Wish I could get invited to Barbara Hutton's party at Torcello," I said. Then young Reinaldo Herrera danced up, in a smart black dinner jacket with a red carnation in his buttonhole and a corded Faberge cigarette case of ribbed gold in his hand.

"Don't you know Barbara, Philip?" asked the black-haired Reinaldo. I shook my head. "I always visit Barbara at the Ritz when I'm in Paris; I'll bring you the next time," he promised.

"Barbara and I took a trip around the world together last year," said Marina. "Come, I'll introduce you, Philip."

Unfortunately, by the time we reached the courtyard garden, Barbara's enormous black motorboat was pulling away from the entrance.

"Can you come with me to Elsa Maxwell's party tomorrow night?" Marina asked. "Everyone here will be there." She saw my hesitation and added that she could not invite Carole because there were too many women already at the table.

About two in the morning, Carole and I flew into the shabby hall of our pension, rather let down after the Cicogna party. I didn't dare tell Carole about my Maxwell invitation.

Some twelve hours later, Carole and I took Ervine to lunch in a little Lido trattoria under a pergola of grapes. When he asked how we were progressing up the social ladder, I replied that I'd managed to get invited to Elsa's highly publicized gala that night. Carole glared at me across the table and made me pay the bill. From then on our old fights began.

Dozens of photographers swarmed around Marina Cicogna, Tina Onassis, me, and Reinaldo Herrera when we made our entrance into the Danielli rooftop ballroom. Every woman was wearing an elaborate headdress of feathers, jewels, or plumes.

An exquisite creature in a turban with the most perfect figure ever conceived went dancing by, and I asked who she was. "That's Countess Raffinella Maestriossi, the sister of Cecco Pallido, the godfather of everyone in Italy. Raffinella and Maestro are my closest friends here. We see each other every day." This all from Marina.

Half an hour later I was dancing with Countess Raffinella. She asked me where Carole Morton was, and I told her of our fights. I also told her that our rooms at La Fenice were fearfully noisy with opera recitals, and she laughed and said that I'd better move into her palace over the weekend.

Chapter
Twenty-three

The next golden Turneresque morning, Carole and I were entertaining the Gold Coast cabanas, strutting and wiggling. Suddenly, victory! Tony Pawson hailed us, and gave me a conspiratorial wink. "Barbara wants you to come to her Torcello dinner. She said to tell you it's very simple, just forty guests, and no *placement* my dear. Good luck," he added with a somewhat disagreeable chuckle and vanished back to the Hutton cabana. I noticed the husky figure of the former tennis ace, von Cramm, bending down solicitously to better hear his mate on a canvas bed.

Carole did not like my social success at all. She would say, "Don't forget I'm Carole Morton, and you're a pathetic baby boy!" One night she got particularly obnoxious, so I packed my solitary suitcase, hired a gondola, and arrived at the portals of the ancient Maestriossi Palace. I was greeted by a pack of boatmen, liveried footmen, and uniformed maids who helped me into the velvet and gilt elevator, and up I went to the fifth floor. Countess Raffinella's personal maid soon arrived with a note asking me to come down at eight-thirty before dinner in the drawing room. Later there would be a "small" reception, which turned out to be enormous.

Barbara Hutton and her husband arrived at eleven, surrounded by her court, which most people called vultures. These vultures were careful not to let any undesirable come within spitting distance of their golden goose. For a time I was kept away, my advances repulsed by hostile stares and even brute force. Presently, though, the legendary Woolworth heiress managed to join me in the tapestried hall. She was dressed in a splendid Mandarin coat with amazing rubies that Carole said would be more comfortable on an elephant. Believe it or not, we managed to have a nice, cozy talk, and my ability to become intimate right away served me in good stead. A current of sympathy passed between us. Of course I had the advantage, for there was nothing I did not know about her. For decades her life story was blazed across the newspapers of the world, like Greta Garbo's or Rita Hayworth's or John Barrymore's.

"I didn't know Americans like you existed," she said in parting. "If only I had a son like you. Lance and I have little in common, but I feel *we* do. Don't you?" Her enormous, sad, and very lovely blue eyes, fringed with thick, shining black eyelashes, rested hopefully on me. We said good night, her court of vultures glaring at me. "I hope to see you tomorrow at the Lido. Happy dreams."

Happy dreams! I twisted and turned all night in my cream brocade and blue corded bedroom. By the time Count and Countess Maestriossi and their huge house party arrived at the Excelsior Beach Hotel at eleven, my head was spinning and I was nearly delirious. In the Maestriossi cabana I changed into my lean, blue and white striped bathing suit and glanced down at the Baroness von Cramm's. She was lying there looking unusually fatigued; the vultures were trying to entertain her, but she was not amused. A huge diamond flashed on her delicate hand, and she kept staring at it as if hypnotized by its glitter.

I asked Raffinella what she thought about Barbara and she said, "Let's face it, she's a crashing bore, with no energy or enthusiasm, two qualities you have in abundance, Philip, dear."

"Then I'll try to rescue her with them," I smiled, and started down toward the Hutton cabana.

"Be careful, Philip," said Maestro. "She's very corrupting."

"I was born to be corrupt." As I approached the now solitary Barbara, Rosie's words kept going through my head. No. I would not fail! I *was* good for something. After all, hadn't I pumped the divine spark back into Carole? Why couldn't I do the same with Barbara?

I bent down and kissed her on the cheek, and she gave me a glance that told me she had been far away. Right away I set about to cheer her up. So I said, "Carole's going to boil me in oil if I don't get her an invitation to your party."

"Bring her," said Barbara, with a smile. "But I *do* wish you'd tell her not to speak in that dreadful English accent."

"I'd be locked in an iron maiden if I did!"

"I must confess I find her attractive, but she's a trifle conspicuous with all that hair. Is she Swedish?"

"Norwegian."

"How involved are you with her?"

Suddenly I remembered that people always want what someone else has. And my host, Maestro, had told me that Barbara was famous for going after girlfriends' husbands.

"We love each other," I said, with an engaging grin. "But we fight like cat and dog."

"She won't make a scene at my party, will she?" asked Barbara anxiously. "More than anything I appreciate civilized manners in my friends."

Underneath that world-weary facade, I sensed a child, so I boyishly pulled her to her feet. "If she makes a scene, you can iron-maiden me. But first, you have to swim with me." Her eyes sparkled, she seemed alive all of a sudden. She ran into the water, without a bathing cap, her hair streaming down her shoulders. We swam through the water, laughing and flirting like porpoises. For the first time I liked Barbara as a human being, not just as an infamous heiress who could write out checks and display stupendous jewelry.

Later in the afternoon, I was most gratified when Barbara kissed me and said that she had not enjoyed herself so much for ever so long. And at five, when I returned to the Maestriossi Palace, I joined Raffinella and Maestro for a cup of tea. The two older Maestriossi boys, Gia and Lazzillo, aged ten and seven, asked me many questions about Barbara Hutton, and their curiosity and childish cries were pleasing to me. Plus, it was lovely seeing that my new friends had a real life away from the pleasure and parties.

"I was just talking with Eugenie and Stavros," said Raffinella, "and they would be most delighted if you came with us on the *Creole* the day after tomorrow. You'll have a much needed rest," she added, affectionately. "I'm so tired myself that you and Maestro and the others will have to go to Torcello without me. You'll adore Theresina, Maestro's sister; she has the most beautiful eyes and the most beautiful voice imaginable."

"All Maestriossis have beautiful eyes and beautiful voices," said Maestro, and the two boys laughed and shouted, "Oh, Papa!"

"It's why I married your papa," said Raffinella, exchanging a loving look with her husband. The two boys snuggled closer to their mother, and she wrapped her arms tighter around them.

The warm family scene lingered in my mind when I went to bed that night, and I had a fearful dream that the devil had me in his grip, that I was powerless to escape him. The most sinister part of the dream was that the devil resembled Fred Beckman as I'd last seen him, unshaven and disheveled, with three caps missing from his teeth so you could see the jagged points.

So instead of going to the Lido with my host and hostess the next day, I walked to St. Marks Square and entered the great basilica. The hushed interior of the Oriental-style church filled me with awe. I knelt before a golden mosaic of Christ.

At her party the next evening, Barbara, in a simple white dress and country diamonds for this rustic gathering of eighty, stood in a receiving line and greeted her guests. She looked thin, pale, haunted, and my heart went out to her. "You're sitting at my table, Philip, dear," she whispered. "I can't think of my life now without your being in it."

I was deeply touched by this remark and passed it on to Carole, while we were standing at the bar. Over her champagne, she gazed at me sadly. "All I can tell you, my dearest soul mate, is that I've never had a moment's peace since I took my husband's money."

"Then you think it's wrong that I go after Barbara?" I asked.

"It's hard not to think of money when you're with Barbara," said Carole, frowning thoughtfully. "And look at her court of vultures,

racked with greed, thinking only of what they can get out of her.
Do you want to be like them?"

Marina Cicogna and Reinaldo Herrera brushed past us. Marina
said Reinaldo and I were the two best-looking men in Venice that
year, and then Reinaldo laughed and said he was furious that I was
leaving the next day on the *Creole* with the Niarchoses.

Carole's face hardened, and she demanded a martini from the
bartender. She raked me with her savage eyes. "So you're off
tomorrow with those filthy rich Greeks, eh? You have sold yourself
to the devil, Dorian Gray."

Barbara and I had a dance, then we sat down and she said she
was sorry I was sailing off to Greece. "You must come to India with
me this winter," she said in her gentle manner, and I said I would
love to.

"What was your childhood and growing up like?" Barbara asked,
her heavily powdered face lit by the colored lanterns. I told her of
Mother and Mr. Lewisohn, and how generous he was right to the
end, paying for her meals from the Colony Restaurant at the hospital.

"I hope you don't think of me as a kind of Mr. Lewisohn," she
remarked dryly.

"You're prettier, Baroness!" I said, kissing her hand.

"I used to be beautiful," said Barbara in that faraway tone.

"Shall we dance?" I suggested, hoping to change the subject of
herself and her past. The party broke up a little after midnight as
the amazing pink moon was high in the sky. Some curious peasants
stared at us as we stepped into the cabins of our motorboats. I
stared at the illuminated eleventh-century church for a moment,
then we raced back to Venice almost an hour away.

After a magnificent cruise on the *Creole* with the Maestriossis,
and a week at their villa, Rosalia, with them and their children, I
knew I needed to renew my courtship with Barbara and sadly
departed on the night train to Paris. The warm homelife I had
witnessed made me feel more of an alien than ever. Barbara and I
were suited, much as Carole and I were—all displaced and a little
mad. There was nothing mad about the Maestriossis; indeed, over
the next decade they were to be my haven in the storm.

The center of the fashionable world in Paris was, of course, the Ritz. I took a maid's room at the nearby Lotti, on Rue Castiglione, and then raced over to the gilded corridors of the Place Vendôme hotel. The first person I saw in the long corridors that ran the length of the hotel was the queen, Rosie Gaynor, living up to her image, all in rich black, with a collar of pearls, and a veiled hat, tip-tapping along in alligator pumps.

The queen flung me a contemptuous look. "Barbara's been calling every day at the Continental, to find out more about you. What did you do to her in Venice? No, don't tell me any sordid details. Your flame, Carole Morton, is in the bar, angry as a hornet that you ditched her ruthlessly. Are you becoming a relentless social climber like most everyone we know?"

"Uh-huh." I grinned.

"You'll make a mess of everything, I predict," drawled Rose. "Remember, I always defend you."

Her imperious little figure vanished toward the Place Vendôme, and I headed toward the noisy bar overlooking the Rue Cambon.

"You look like an expensive proposition," said Carole, raising her martini glass with an ugly scowl.

"I am." Maestro had given me some Caraceni suits, as we were the same size. Caraceni was a great artist and did for men what Dior did for women. I looked thinner than my 165 pounds, taller than my six feet, broader-shouldered longer-legged, bigger-chested. That day, I even sported a double-breasted vest and some lapis-and-gold cuff links on my pink-and-gray striped Charvet shirt.

"Everyone knows now you're for sale, buster."

"You weren't?"

"Gee whiskers!" cried Carole. "Say a silent prayer we don't end like *her*." There at the entrance of the bar stood Ann Woodward, rather nervous under everyone's stares. This was *the* Mrs. William Woodward, Jr., whom we'd seen all over Venice, pathetically hanging on to people's coattails, begging for any crumbs of attention and affection. In what was called the "Slaying of the Century," Ann had shot and killed her handsome millionaire husband, saying that she thought Bill was a prowler. Rumor had it a lot of money had changed hands, and Ann was off scot-free. Rosie and her group, maintaining that murder was beyond the pale, elaborately cut her and called her The Outcast. Watching her now, a ruined beauty, born a poor girl on a Kansas farm, I felt a wave of sympathy for her.

"If you speak to her," cried Carole, "I'll pull out a shotgun and blast you."

On the way out I spoke to Ann Woodward at the bar, and she said that she looked forward to seeing Carole at the Munich wine festival at Johannes Thurn und Taxis castle the next week.

That afternoon, after a walk through the damp arcades of the Rue de Rivoli, I returned to the Lotti and found a telephone message: Baroness von Cramm requested the pleasure of my company the next day at lunchtime.

"D-day!" said Carole, and her expression was unusually grave.

"Come into the half-light of my bedchamber, dear Philip," came the mournful and weary voice of Barbara Hutton in her opulent Ritz apartment. It was raining, and the immensely tall French windows were flecked with drops. The baroness was reclining on a double bed, attired in a feminine pink satin and lace bed jacket. Around her neck were the famous pearls, and on her wrist an emerald and diamond bracelet of great beauty. On the bedside table were some eighteenth-century gold snuffboxes glittering with jewels. The Ritz itself had once been an eighteenth-century mansion, and the carved woodwork was a splendid reminder of that period.

"Would you care for something to drink?" asked Miss Latimer, the baroness's secretary, who'd been with her for twenty years.

In a moment I was sipping some wine, and Barbara was watching me from those enormous blue eyes under thick black brows. Those brows gave her a look of character, and gazing at her fondly, I concluded she must be strong to have survived all her marriages and illnesses.

"I've been having lovely talks with pretty little Rosie Gaynor," Barbara was saying, lighting a cigarette and blowing the smoke into the hazy room. "I knew Rose in Palm Beach long ago, just before I married Cary Grant. She was living on her stepfather's yacht, and terribly spoiled. What a temper!"

"You're telling *me!*" I gave a playful laugh that sounded quite hysterical to my ears.

Barbara's personal maid entered with a menu, what did Monsieur want for lunch? I looked at Barbara and asked what she was going to order.

She gave an ironic laugh. "I never eat a thing," she smiled. "I shrunk my stomach to the size of a pea after my coffee diet."

Twenty minutes later, room service sent up grilled Dover sole, parsley potatoes, and creamed spinach. She smoked while I ate.

"Rosie feels that people with our backgrounds can never be happy. What do you think, Barbara?"

She sighed and said, "I'm afraid I must agree. My past record certainly is proof."

I recalled that her Woolworth grandparents had died insane, her mother had committed suicide, and her first cousin, Jimmy Donahue, was a madman, especially when he swilled. There was as much insanity in her background as in mine—that was our bond. Suddenly the Ritz apartment seemed a kind of clinic, and Miss Latimer and the personal maid like Hartford Retreat matrons anxiously watching over their patient. I was the gentle, caring doctor, who listened to the life story.

My stint began at the Baroness von Cramm's bedside. I listened and she spoke, sometimes far into the afternoon till a mauve dusk enveloped the Place Vendôme outside her immense windows and the streetlights came on.

There were hilarious outings from the "clinic." Once, Miss Latimer and the French maid got Barbara dressed in a splendid black costume and hat, and we descended into the huge gilt and marble lobby. From the woodwork came every penniless prince, duke, count, and viscount, rushing to Madame La Baronne's white-gloved hand and kissing it with a soulful air.

"People are so sweet to remember me," said Barbara, after an onslaught of flattery.

The chauffeur and I helped the delicate Barbara into the rear of her Rolls-Royce. "How shall we kill this rainy afternoon?" she asked.

"Mad Hatter tea party at Versailles," I suggested.

She wrinkled her pretty nose.

"Monsieur Cartier might have some new things to show us."

Right around the corner was the famed jeweler, and Barbara's entrance into the shop provided another stampede to her white-

gloved hand. After more flattery and hand-kissing from sleek salesmen, Mr. Cartier appeared, treating Barbara like a little child who
was naughty, but who might be rewarded.

"I do hope you have *something* to cheer us up, Monsieur Cartier," said Barbara, and soon we were ushered into a private chamber that was oval in shape. Cartier was as clever as Dr. Freud,
tempting and teasing her, saving the prize piece till the very end.
For an hour he'd been telling us of the rare emeralds that had come
into his hands from a great estate belonging to a woman of great
nobility who'd come upon hard times, and on and on.

"You're driving me quite mad," said Barbara. "Do kindly show
me these emeralds."

The emeralds were brought out in a leather-and-gilt-splashed
box that looked as if it had survived the Russian and even the
French revolution. The necklace was astounding, huge blue-green
eggs, surrounded by diamonds. I'd never seen Barbara become so
animated. "Tell me the bad news, M. Cartier," she said gaily.

"Since you're such a good customer, Baroness," he said, bending
low, "a million dollars."

Barbara frowned delicately at me, and then at the jeweler-
doctor. "Well," she sighed, "Barbara needs to have a little treat."

Soon M. Cartier was accompanying his good client to her shining
Rolls. "This will be the crowning achievement of your collection,
dear Baroness," he said silkily.

"Can you send them around to the Ritz, C.O.D., M. Cartier?"
asked Barbara, now sitting in the rear of the grand car.

"Of course, dear friend."

We rolled off toward the stately outline of the Ritz. "At least now
I'll have emeralds as large as Sita Baroda's. Don't forget, Philip
dear, that we're dining at Maxim's with her this evening."

I'd met the Maharani of Baroda on the Lopez yacht in Venice,
and had recently seen her white Rolls-Royce parading through the
boulevards, flying the Baroda flags. She always wore saris and was
covered from bow to stern with elephantine jewelry.

"How did she ever get that loot out of India?" I asked.

"She stole it," said Barbara, somewhat spitefully. "She's as
greedy as Wallis Windsor."

"The Duchess? Greedy?" I asked, astonished.

"Who do you think paid for all the presents my cousin Jimmy Donahue gave her? Little Barbara, that's who. It's not a pretty world we live in, sweetheart."

Melancholy settled over me. The doorman and I helped Barbara out of the Rolls, and I gave her my arm to the revolving door, then dropped her off at her door on the second floor. A dozen Vuitton trunks stood in the corridor, stamped von Cramm, Grant, Reventlow.

"Rather sad, isn't it?" said Barbara, catching my eye.

"Yes."

"Are you feeling all right?"

"Yes," I lied, giving her a kiss. "Thank you for the watch and the cuff links."

"Don't thank me, thank Grandpa Woolworth."

"Thank you, Grandpa Woolworth."

Barbara vanished into her dimly lit and loveless apartment, and I went back to my garret in the eaves of the Lotti. I opened the Cartier boxes and stared at my tank watch and my gold and sapphire links. They didn't seem to be worth anything. Next to Barbara's million-dollar emeralds, they *were* nothing. And let's hear it for Grandpa Woolworth.

I flung myself on my narrow bed, drew the pillow to my side, and cried. I was surrounded by greed, and greed had infected me.

Fortunately, Raffinella Maestriossi arrived at the Ritz, and two days later I returned to Rosalia with her. She and Maestro tried to keep me there in the country with them, but I felt a violent need to finish my Hutton experiment. Greed was now my master. How far would it carry me?

Barbara telephoned me one evening, and I told her I was returning to Paris in a few days. "I'll reserve rooms for you at the Hotel Vendôme," she said. "And would you care to return to New York with me November tenth?"

Opera arias playing in the Rosalia drawing room echoed in my mind as I boarded the night train for Paris. Underneath, the wheels seemed to say, "Failure, Failure, Failure." The next morning when I arrived at the Ritz for lunch, the same look of failure was in Barbara's eyes. Yes, Barbara and I belonged together.

"Do you think you could be ready to sail on the *United States* in ten days?" Barbara asked.

"Silly question." I smiled, beaming like a clown.

"I've been lying here in bed thinking of you, sweet Philip," said Barbara, with a mysterious half smile on her thin face.

"Adoption?" I asked.

"No, you silly thing," she replied meeting my gaze. "What you need is three hundred fifty thousand dollars to round out your social personality."

"You mind reader!" I laughed.

"Shall we have a tiny drink to celebrate?" All Barbara's gin bottles were watered by Miss Latimer, so I went into the drawing room and made her a gin on the rocks while I had a double. I looked at myself in the tall mirror set in the Louis XVI paneling above the fireplace.

A few evenings before we sailed to America, I took Barbara to a large reception at the British Embassy. A fleet of butlers were passing trays of gin cocktails and champagne, and Barbara took one before I could stop her. She downed it, and clutched her stomach. "I've been poisoned!" She collapsed and I led her behind a column under a potted palm.

"Is anything the matter?" asked the queenly Lady Jebb.

"It's bad gin," gasped Barbara.

"My dear woman, that's quite impossible," said Lady Jebb, giving the poisoned one a scorching look. Barbara insisted in a hostile fashion, but fortunately Tony Pawson and I managed to get Barbara outside into her Rolls.

At the time, the *United States* was the fastest ship on the transatlantic route, and Barbara told me that her old Hollywood friend, Merle Oberon, and her Mexican husband, Bruno Pagliai, would be on board. Also Mrs. George Baker—much excitement! Plus Barbara told me to prepare myself for publicity and headline news when we docked in New York.

Once on board the American ship, Barbara had her pretty cabin, and I mine. While Miss Latimer looked after the ailing baroness, I resumed my role of the listener by the bedside. When Barbara needed sleep, I went to the bar and stared at myself in the mirror above the bottles. A stranger looked back at me. What was happening to me? Could it be possible I was drinking at high noon? Well, never mind, $350,000 would soon be in the Bank of New York. Then people wouldn't think of me as a failure.

Chapter
Twenty-four

Time magazine, the *Daily News, Daily Mirror,* and *Journal-American* all interviewed us in the lounge of the *United States.* Merle Oberon glared at us; we were stealing all her thunder. A limousine took Barbara out to Syosset, Long Island, to Broadhollow, the red brick Georgian house of Cousin Jimmy Donahue, and I checked into the Plaza. The next morning when I awakened, my face was on the front page of three daily tabloids—headline news! Nancy Randolph, from the *News,* telephoned me to get a scoop.

"Are you and Miss Hutton going to marry?" she asked.

"Sure thing," I replied. "Barbara will soon be Barbara Mdivani Reventlow Grant Troubetzkoy Rubirosa von Cramm Van Rensselaer."

"Can I print that?" she asked.

"Why not?" I said, high as a kite.

Aunt Bessie seemed quite overjoyed by the news. "You'll have a home at last, Philip. When can I meet her?"

A week later, Aunt Bessie invited us to dinner at the River Club. It was a family gathering, brother Charles, Uncle Steve and Aunt Lily, and *moi.* Barbara looked quite ravishing in a black suit with white mink collar and white mink hat, and a few of those sapphires and diamonds that I'd always wanted to swallow.

Aunt Bessie, too, seemed to lose her heart to frail, sad-looking Barbara, and after dinner Barbara whispered in my ear that Aunt Bessie was quite like her Aunt Jessie Donahue—the same sweet character, the same supportive manner.

Discreetly, I dropped Barbara back at the Pierre Hotel, then went for a little talk with Aunt Bessie.

"I'm quite captivated by the dear girl," began Aunt Bessie. "But tell me, dear, has she really been married and divorced twice?"

I gulped. "Well, Aunt Bessie, actually, Barbara has had six marriages and five divorces."

Aunt Bessie looked faint. "Six marriages? I've never heard of such a thing! What will I tell Duncan Ellsworth and Mathilde?"

"I'm sure they know," I replied.

"Six marriages," repeated Aunt Bessie, staring down at the flowered needlepoint carpet in a tragic way. She never brought up the subject of Barbara again.

The next day, my St. Paul's School friend Scotty and I went to a Billy Graham revival meeting at Madison Square Garden. The evangelist was compelling, and the enthusiasm of the crowds gave me goose flesh. Come to me and start a new life. Repent! Rejoice!

"Scotty, there's hope for this sinner!"

"For both sinners, amigo."

At the conclusion of this powerful meeting, Billy Graham stood at the center of the stage and urged all of us to join him and become one with God. Scotty and I looked at each other. We'd been brought up in church schools and believed in God, yet we seemed paralyzed to make the move down to the stage. More than half the audience kneeled by Graham and received a blessing, like Holy Communion. It had been more than ten years since I had knelt at an altar and taken wine and the wafer of our Lord.

Presently, Scotty and I were in a taxi going uptown. We sat in silence. I dropped him at his Seventy-eighth Street brownstone.

"I guess we're not ready," he said glumly.

"No, not ready," I said.

I walked back to the St. Regis Hotel (I'd moved), a growing

sense of defeat slowing my steps. When I opened the door, the phone on my bedside table was ringing.

"I'm missing my fox," said Barbara. "Can he play with his friend tonight at the Colony?"

Both rooms and the vestibule of the famed restaurant were packed to capacity with the glitter, the gold, and the tarnished. Gene Cavallero, Sr., and Gene, Jr., the owners of New York's most glamorous luncheon and dinner boîte, were two old friends, and I was pleased to see them. Barbara had become something of a recluse these years of her forties, so now people strained their necks to get a better glimpse of her.

We sat on a red plush banquette under some pink-shaded wall lights and looked happily at each other. Barbara was living out at Cousin Jimmy's house in Syosset, and she was urging me to join her there, but I had misgivings. Jimmy's tongue could be vicious. His evil temper was something I did not relish.

"It would help me so much, beloved, if you kept me company," Barbara was saying. "Grandpa Woolworth would make it worth your while."

I gulped my champagne cocktail and stared down at the white tablecloth and vase of red roses. This was V-day. But, strange to relate, I felt no exultation. My failure to join Billy Graham weighed heavily on me.

So began my six-week stay at Broadhollow. Alfred Gwynne Vanderbilt had built a beautiful house, on grounds that were suitably romantic and rustic. Billy Baldwin had decorated the rooms to give the illusion of a grand English country gentleman's home. Every room was carpeted wall to wall, and the carpets were so thick you sank in them. Yet the whole place lacked the warmth and dignity of Rosalia. Like Barbara's apartment at the Ritz, Broadhollow was loveless. I felt I was in prison and counted the days before we'd be released for the Mexican trip Barbara was planning.

"It's enchanting, isn't it, Foxy?" said Barbara, lying in bed.

"Enchanting, my angel."

"You're not bored, are you, beloved?"

"I'm never bored, Baroness."

"My lawyer of twenty years, Graham Mattison, is coming down for a Christmas visit, Foxy. He only allows me to write out checks to the tune of ten thousand dollars. He's quite furious with me about those emeralds in Paris. Did I ever tell you how we met? Well, to make a long story short, I was living in London at Winfield House, the house I gave to the American Embassy in Regent's Park. Reventlow, the greediest and cruelest of my husbands, was squeezing money out of me right and left, and Graham, bless his heart, warned me that I wouldn't have a penny left if I continued such spending."

My days here followed the same pattern as the Ritz days. Barbara told her life story and I listened. The rock crystal boudoir clock with the diamond numerals told the hour; sometimes time jumped, but usually it dragged. Often Barbara dozed off and I would wander through the large morguelike house. Nobody awakened till mid-afternoon. I had my breakfast and lunch in the dimly lit dining room, eating my scrambled eggs or lamb chops. Barbara and Jimmy ate little (Barbara sometimes indulged in some vanilla ice cream), so the chef was happy to produce his masterpieces for me. Barbara gave me silk dressing gowns and brocade lounge jackets to wear by the bedside, but I had no intention of wearing pajamas all day long like Jimmy. Desperately, I thought that I must keep to some routine. I would not allow myself to slip into despair and madness. In the afternoons I dashed about the grounds, the blackbirds making terrifying screeching noises as I approached.

The feared father figure, Graham Mattison, made his entrance like an iron horse a few days before Christmas. His eyes were like Carborundum and gave me shivers down my spine. Barbara greeted him girlishly from her bower of silk and lace plumped-up pillows, her long black lashes shining with the pomade that Cary Grant had gotten her in the habit of using before facing the cameras.

"Are you an invalid, Barbara?" asked the good-looking and stony-faced financier-lawyer standing by the bedside.

"I haven't been well," said Barbara, with a deep sigh.

"You might get well if you got up," the lawyer flung back.

"Sweet Philip here, my darling fox, is such a comfort."

This was the cue for Graham to produce my bonus and overtime check. He gave me a sarcastic glance and took my arm in a viselike grip. "Your darling fox and I will have a brief talk now, Barbara."

We vanished through the bathroom and into my luxurious little bedroom. Sweat was trickling down my armpits.

Mattison surveyed me with scorn. Then he produced a check from his breast pocket. "Do you feel anything about taking money from a woman?"

I said nothing, lowering my eyes.

"It's pretty disgusting from my point of view. My God, if I caught one of my sons working over a sick woman, I'd thrash him within an inch of his life."

He flung the check at me and seemed amused when I bent down to pick it up. My humiliation was complete. I vowed I would never again take money from anyone.

On Christmas Eve I sat beside Barbara on her bed, wearing the newest Chinese red dressing gown from Sulka. A pile of presents was on my lap. I'd gasped over the large and splendid bishop's cross studded with large stones, made by Faberge.

"Oh, Barbara, I've never seen anything so beautiful."

She cast me a mournful look. "If one gives one's heart, all else are trifles."

"Gee whiskers, what a gold box!"

"Eighteenth century," sighed Barbara. "I wouldn't mind having it for my collection."

"And these diamond and sapphire cuff links must be one carat each!" I almost shouted.

"One and a half carats, beloved," said Barbara with a wistful smile, watching me tear open the lavish presents.

"Do you think I can wear them in Mexico, Barbara?" I asked.

"I'm giving a little party to open my new house in Cuernavaca, sweetheart. Graham Mattison is livid that my Japanese-style pavilion is costing six million." She raised her thin arms and studied her new diamond bracelets. "He'll punish me, somehow, I'm sure."

Years later I read that Graham Mattison had annexed all of Barbara's Woolworth fortune, and that Perla, his second wife, a Brazilian, was wearing all of Barbara's jewelry. Many of the Mattisons' friends expressed surprise, but it didn't surprise me.

One day at lunchtime, a little before New Year's, Jimmy Donahue joined me at the Chippendale dining table. He was a year or so younger than Barbara but looked twenty years older. His face and body were puffy, overweight, and soft, and his blue eyes, bright with malice and disappointment, had almost disappeared in the unhealthy, bloated flesh. Red veins stood out on his thick nose. It was amazing to think that this had once been the favorite of the Duchess of Windsor.

"When you were in New York, young man," he began, "your devoted Barbara was on the phone to Paris, calling Jimmy Douglas, who I hear is even handsomer than you, pretty face."

"Really?" I said, trying to keep the shock from my voice.

"Barbara always gives a cross to her beloved when he's on his way out. It's curtains for you," he added, with a high giggle.

"So it's all over," I said, feeling some sadness and yet, at the same time, relief. I was beginning to drink too much and take sleeping medicine.

"The gravy train is all over, pretty face," Jimmy taunted.

"I guess love never lasts, does it, Jimmy?"

"Hasn't for me," he replied, bitterly. "And a lot of money has changed hands, too."

Feeling soiled and sordid, I picked up Jimmy's crystal decanter and poured myself a generous Scotch.

He watched me with a knowing smile and started to laugh. I had to get out of that house.

A few weeks later Barbara and her entourage left for Mexico City. Said entourage consisted of Barbara and her fox, Miss Latimer, Jimmy Douglas, and his friend Rod Coupe. Barbara's south-of-the-border court met us at the airport, Señor and Señora de Landa, from an old Mexican landed family. Señor Natcho had been the favorite court jester of Hazel and Fred Beckman some fifteen years before. And believe it or not, we all stayed in the very same Cuernavaca house that the Fred Beckmans had lived in.

Our days in Cuernavaca followed the same routine as those at the Villa Corne D'Or in Cannes. Life centered around the large swimming pool where we met for noon drinks and oiled our bodies with Bain de Soleil. In the afternoons Barbara and Jimmy Douglas would vanish to her bedroom, and *he* would listen to her life story.

We took a flying trip down to Acapulco and stayed in Las Brisas, complete with pink jeeps and mini pools. My last days with Barbara were spent here. With gardenias in her hair, next to Jimmy, who resembled an Arrow-collar college boy, she seemed a tragic Ophelia.

"You'll never again meet a woman like Barbara" were her last words to me.

Then I flew off to New York. Dorothy Kilgallen, Earl Wilson, and Knickerbocker reported that there had been a feud down Mexico way. But there had been no feud. Love had died, and that was that. I was so exhausted that I slept at the St. Regis for two weeks; long periods of sleep always worked miracles. I went on the wagon and stopped taking Barbara's Seconals.

Chapter
Twenty-five

Early in February 1958, I leased a mansion apartment at 39 East
Sixty-seventh Street, next door to the infamous Hapsburg one.
This one was even larger and more grandiose. I hired a valet to
press my thirty new suits. Barbara had said a great gentleman
always had a valet; indeed, all her husbands had had one.

One morning James, the valet, announced a telephone call from
Countess Maestriossi. She was in town for a few days with Maestro,
and she wanted to know if I would go with them to Palm Beach for
a visit with the Charlie Wrightsmans. I told her I was worn out,
and she laughed and asked if I would join them at Mrs. Thomas
Bancroft's at 740 Park Avenue that evening. Peggy Bancroft was
written about as the "new Mrs. Cornelius Vanderbilt," the queen
of New York, and I was quite enthusiastic about meeting her.
Reinaldo Herrera told me Peggy had a flower bill of $60,000 a year
and, to make her library look attractive, had ordered leather-bound
volumes from French & Co. to the tune of $30,000. Nearly every
day she had open house, with champagne, caviar, and a new chiffon dress from Bergdorf.

"You must get invited, Philip," said Reinaldo. So now I was, courtesy of the Maestros, as they were known in the fashionable world. Reinaldo's gorgeous parents—from Caracas, Venezuela—had five Rolls-Royces and were bigshots on the international scene. Papa Reinaldo spent his time romancing Park Avenue matrons.

That evening at Peggy Bancroft's mob scene in her 740 duplex (decor by French & Co.), Raffinella asked me why I had left Barbara.

"Survival," I replied, giving her a long look. "I couldn't take the Seconals and gin. I have a strong constitution, but not that strong!"

"But you never drink to excess, Philip."

"I did with Barbara." I gave a sigh like the Baroness's. "It was all too much. You can't have any dignity with Barbara."

"Well, we'll have fun in Yucatán seeing the Mayan temples. You *are* coming with us, aren't you, Philip?" I nodded, then we were swallowed up by the celebrities and high-society luminaries.

A little later I was sitting on an antique French sofa with Peggy Scott-Duff, a delicate blonde who had even more energy and enthusiasm than our hostess. Maestro was talking with Jackie Kennedy, but after a time he joined us. Peggy Scott-Duff was grabbed by one of her admirers, and Maestro confessed gloomily that Mrs. Kennedy did not flirt. Maestro loved to play the flirtation game to amuse himself, and he could tell you who liked to flirt and who didn't. All parties were a challenge for him, and he always enjoyed himself for this reason.

"What was it like with Barbara?" Maestro asked, giving my arm a pinch for extra emphasis. He was full of Italian drama, and I liked him for it.

"I'm not tough enough, Maestro," I revealed pensively. "Her lawyer made me bend down and pick up a check, made some odious remarks that had a ring of truth. That humiliation and her cousin Jimmy Donahue were my downfall."

"Well, darling Philip," said Maestro, patting my cheek, "you have a home with us, don't worry. We expect you to spend the whole summer with us in Venice. And don't forget to bring old clothes for our Yucatán adventure."

"I don't have any old clothes," I laughed.

And so my suitcases were packed again, and again I returned south of the border, this time trudging up and down the snake-infested Mayan temples at Uxmal. A lively piece about this journey even appeared in Doris Lilly's "Inside Society" column.

I'd just returned to 37 East Sixty-seventh early in April when the phone rang and Fred Beckman's voice drifted over the wire. He asked me to please come out and visit him. His house in Scottsdale, Arizona, had just burned down, and his little dog had perished in the flames. His speech was slurred and there was the sound of weeping after he mentioned the dog's death.

"I'll come out tomorrow, Fred," I said with a false energetic voice. "And I'll help you find a new house."

"*Have* a new house, baby," he said drunkenly. "Right in the middle of the desert. You'll adore it, my heaven child, and do bring some old clothes for old Uncle Fred."

Old Uncle Fred met me at the airport, embraced me theatrically, and fell down. He was almost sixty by then, and in very sad shape. At least he'd shaved, and some of the capped teeth had been replaced so he didn't look so much like the Phantom of the Opera. But his legs had given out; he weaved and stumbled.

Fred drove me to an isolated place surrounded by cactus and windswept sage which was quite Brontë in feeling.

"Don't take any walks, my child," said Fred, falling out of the car. "Lots of rattlesnakes."

I smiled, and felt my knees buckle. Just what I needed after the scourge of coral snakes in the Mayan temples.

"Isn't this a heaven house, my child?" said Fred, stumbling toward the entrance. Heaven house? It was a *dump!* If only I could have spoken the words as tellingly as Bette in *Beyond the Forest.*

When I came back to the living room in suitable rags, Fred had passed out on the couch, and some chicken was burning in the oven. Friends have always said that I was a menace in the kitchen, but I pulled myself together, made a ham-and-bacon sandwich, and felt quite good about myself playing the doctor-in-the-house role.

I managed to haul Fred to the kitchen table and then got some food into him—spoon-fed him like a child. What would Mother and Hazel have said seeing this miserable wreck? And the shack itself was forlorn. The wind howled about us, and Fred told me we were five miles from the nearest village.

"Why did you pick this isolated place?" I asked gently.

"It was the cheapest," he replied.

"Are you okay financially, Fred?"

"My brother sends me two hundred dollars a month," he said, staring at me from his empty and watery blue eyes. "That's what I used to live on in Paris, in the twenties, when Louis Bromfield and I went out to wild parties. Everyone was chasing me then; the phone never stopped ringing. Now I don't even have one."

He fell into a deep sleep almost immediately after lunch, snoring away loudly, his mouth hanging open.

At twilight I laboriously got Fred's big frame into some country Caraceni clothes that Maestro had given me—corduroys, tweeds, and cashmere. Fred was delighted as a child with his new image. "Feel like a new man, my heaven child, but I do miss my little dog." Tears streamed down his face.

"Let me buy you a new dog," I said. "You need one to keep you company."

"Yes, I do need one to keep me company," he repeated in a simpleminded way. With horror I realized he had wet brain. He'd been in the ring too long, been knocked about brutally by all the parties, affairs, and selling himself out to the highest bidders.

After the purchase of a Lhasa terrier, Fred was shot into a gleeful state, but a few days later he plunged into more heartrending gloom. When I told him I could stay through the weekend, he slapped me on the back and worked his old charm on me.

"Your heaven mother was always changing her mind with me," he grinned.

I was becoming an emotional wreck as the days dragged by. I'd been brought up not to reveal too many strong feelings and of course to be polite and well-mannered at all costs. With stiff upper lip I raced through the snake-ridden sage, not even caring if a hellish rattler or scorpion delivered the coup de grace.

Fortunately when I returned from one walk down Wuthering Heights, a middle-aged policeman was drinking with Fred.

"This is Ron Baby," said Fred. "He gives me a mother's care, bless him!"

"I'm a neighbor, Phil," said the burly cop. "Live down the road a piece. Whenever we can, we tie a good one on." His voice sounded like two cannons had gone off.

"Isn't he the most fascinating creature you've ever known!" cried Fred, throwing out his arms, thus displacing poor Miew-Miew off his lap, causing great hilarity.

"I hear you've been leading quite a life, Phil," said Ron Baby, moving his eyebrows up and down suggestively. "Can you tell us about it?"

"Actually, I can't, Ron."

I made some more drinks in a manic state, seeing that Ron Baby was my avenue of escape, my savior! Over our fresh cocktails I spun out some zany tales. Ron was an appreciative audience and I really got into amusing him.

"Gee, look at Fred," said Ron. We'd been entertaining each other so well that we'd quite forgotten about our host. He was out cold. The bleak look on his face was fearful.

I led Ron into the kitchen and dumped my situation on him. "So Ron, I can see that you give Uncle Fred a mother's care, and I don't feel so bad about leaving him."

"Just keep writing him, Phil. He told me you and your brother were the only real family he has left."

The next day before noon, a stony-faced Fred drove me to the airport. I kept a vigorous running commentary on Ron and how lucky Fred was to have such a caring neighbor and friend. Fred was sporting his new Caraceni duds, and I told him he couldn't hold a candle to his look-alike, Joseph Cotten. As for his Gary Cooper shoulders——

As I rambled on, a terrible weariness permeated me. I prayed I could get through the farewell ordeal. In my heart I knew I would never see Fred again; it was like saying good-bye to Mother at St. James all over again.

When my flight to New York was announced, Fred broke down and wept. I gave him a big hug, and he clung to me. I bent down and kissed the little fluffy white dog and told her to look after Fred like a good girl.

I started into the plane and didn't dare look back. Dear old Fred, the outcome of a big moneyed life. Yesterday's glamour boy. If I wasn't careful, the same fate lay in store for me.

*   *   *

Back in my drawing room at 37 East Sixty-seventh there were some telephone messages from Peggy Bancroft and the Maestros. James said that I must move, the owner wanted his $1000-a-month apartment back. I sat at my expansive, gilt-encrusted table desk and tried to balance my checkbook. I'd thought I had saved some money living quietly with Fred, but James had to be paid his salary, and I'd promised Gian Carlo Menotti some money for his Spoleto festival, opening that year for the first time. Money was going out like crazy. I was powerless to stop it.

Must stop spending, I told myself, looking into the mirror above the fireplace. *A fool and his money are soon parted company. Must not end like Fred Beckman.*

Charlie and Aunt Bessie called to wish me a happy thirtieth birthday. Thirty! My God, the dreaded age had been reached.

Raffinella and Maestro wanted me to come in the middle of May, when Venice was its loveliest. Maestro would be taking his annual cure at Cian Ciano, near Rome, and Raffinella would be lolling at the great villa at Beaulieu. The villa, perhaps the most splendid house in the south of France, was built by the king of the Belgians during the Belle Epoque, and now belonged to Cecco Pallido, Raffinella's brother. Certainly it would be a change from Fred's isolated desert shack . . . and Ron Baby.

"I'll forward your mail to the Maestriossi Palace in Venice," cried Mary when the limousine buzzed downstairs. I told her I hoped she'd enjoy my apartment for the summer and was off to the airport with four suitcases of new summer duds.

Settled in briefly at the Excelsior in Rome, I called Carole Morton in Capri where she'd just bought a villa overlooking the red Fariglioni rocks.

We danced everywhere to "Volare," swore eternal love, and felt some kind of contentment. The fountains of Rome splashed exuberantly. We took long walks in the Borghese gardens and visited some favorite churches.

"We'll probably end our sinning days together," said Carole, still teary-eyed after my telling her about Fred Beckman in Arizona.

"Probably," I said. The next day I was off to visit Maestro and his sister, Theresina Coraggioso, at their cure.

"Why don't you go and stay with Raffinella at Cecco's villa?" said Maestro, thinner and leaner than ever. He weighed himself even more often than Mother had, and insisted on extreme thinness from all his friends.

"Why don't you go and stay with Maestro at Cian Ciano?" said Raffinella, in her magnificent bedroom at the villa. The night I arrived, the fountains were playing in the stone basins and the lights of Monte Carlo glittered on the dark waters of the Mediterranean. It was pure palace, and the gilded rooms were very formal with Jacob furniture of the early Empire. One hundred marble steps led down to the sea.

Before I returned to Maestro taking the waters, Cecco Pallido took me to Monte Carlo in his Chris-Craft. We all dined several times at famous restaurants in Cannes and even gambled at the Palm Beach Casino where Mother and Mr. Lewisohn had once gambled, flirted, and danced. The Villa Corne D'Or looked just the same as I remembered it, only the blue-tiled pool and rose gardens were gone, destroyed by the Germans, who had occupied the house during the war.

Cecco Pallido was a few years older than Raffinella, and when he wasn't working in Turin, he was playing in some resort. And play Cecco did—better than anyone. His great love had been the siren Pamela Churchill, but he was now married and happy with his wife Badia, from a princely Neopolitan family. And Badia's mother had been a Miss Morton from Boston.

Badia with her famed swan neck and regal appearance was a beauty without equal. Her voice was so melodious that I hoped she would never stop talking (unlike most people!).

Two days later Maestro and I arrived in one of those dreamlike evenings Venice is famous for. Venice is still cool in early June, and a fresh sea breeze, full of fish and brine, brushed my face as I stood outside next to Maestro's boatmen. The sleek brown motorboat grunted and gurgled through various side canals; we almost collided with several gondolas and barges, and fierce Latin fights broke out. Maestro, lounging in the cabin, impeccably dressed as always in brown Prince de Galles, smoked his cigarette in its customary holder.

Suddenly we burst out into the wide spaces of the Grand Canal, the long line of palaces glittering and sparkling against a purple sky. I'd often hear tourists complain of the smell of the canals, and others groused it was only a decayed museum. But it was precisely the decay of the ancient water city that appealed to me, and the odor of the canals was like the perfume of a garden.

As the boatmen were slowing down before the fragile Gothic facade of the Maestriossi palazzo, Maestro joined me outside.

"That's the Rezzonico Palace," said Maestro, pointing to an immense stone pile nearby. "Browning died there, and Cole Porter rented it in the twenties. My father almost bought it, but thought this was more cozy. Fifteenth-century Gothic is more cozy and livable, don't you think, than seventeenth-century Renaissance?"

"I'd have to think a lot about that," I said with a hearty laugh.

Sometimes Maestro didn't feel like taking the plush and gilt elevator, so tonight we walked up the formal red-carpeted staircase that made one feel one was at least Prince Rainier. He asked me if I'd seen the large gardens of the Palazzo Papadopoli and the Tiepolo ceiling in sister Theresina's dressing room. The Papadopoli belonged to Theresina's husband Count Coraggioso and was just as grand as the Rezzonico.

A footman with white gloves and gold braid on his shoulders and cuffs opened a monumental door. Maestro vanished down an acre of corridor, through rosy, tapestried gloom, and I went upstairs to my rooms. We all met a little before nine in the drawing room overlooking the Grand Canal. Raffinella and Maestro's rooms faced the garden in the rear.

Angello, the head footman, announced dinner, and we walked down an endless corridor of polished antique wood flooring to the dining room. Perfume from the garden below drifted in through the open windows. Two more footmen in white livery and gold braid served us a meal in that stupendous green velvet room. So swiftly did they follow one on the other that I hardly had time to take a mouthful of eggs in mayonnaise before the fish and meat courses were raced by my nose. Very quickly I learned to say not a word, masticate like a madman, and smile at my host and hostess gratefully as I wiped my lips with a heavy damask napkin.

Raffinella was not a reader, but she was highly intuitive. "You need us, Philip, need our family life."

"Yes, yes. I do need you, Raffinella."

"You weren't really happy with Barbara, were you?"

"I can breathe now." I smiled at her gratefully. We were rocking on the express train to Rome, and soon we were in the square at Spoleto talking with Gian Carlo Menotti and Tommy Schippers. That evening we went to see *Moon for the Misbegotten,* and I was entranced by Colleen Dewhurst. My friend José Quintero directed the O'Neill piece, and later he introduced me to the actress. She was my age, and she was the most radiant creature I'd ever seen and had the most delightful laugh I'd ever heard.

José, a real O'Neill character, was in the good graces of the widow Carlotta Monterrey O'Neill, who had lived at the Lowell in New York and then gone mad. José had visited the widow in the asylum, and that further endeared him to me. He was as thin and sensitive-looking as most rich women would like to be, and he'd had a success with his Circle in the Square theater company in Greenwich Village. Recognition came his way also with the O'Neill plays. Unfortunately he got so caught up in the tragic mood of the master's works that he lived on whiskey and little else, deep into his image of the doomed poet.

I saw a lot of Dick Evans that year at Spoleto. He'd graduated from the post of Menotti's secretary to that of stage manager of the local productions. Jerome Robbins liked him so much that Dick switched allegiances, mainly because Gian Carlo was famous for underpaying his talent.

"Got to think of my future, Philip," said Dick one afternoon when I visited him on a stage set. His handsome face was haggard; I was worried about him and he was worried about me, too. Whenever we were together we fell into soul searching, and we'd both play Freud.

A few weeks later Dick went off on the round-the-world tour with Jerome Robbins. How I envied him! He'd worked on getting his life and career going in the right direction, whereas Carole and I had remained lost in our dreams. The rest of the summer, indeed the rest of the year, sped by as if I were on a train with the scenery racing by my window.

That was also the year Nancy Mitford gave us nursery names. Raffinella was Naughtiness, I was Prettikins, Rosie Gaynor was the

Sewer, and so forth. Nancy loathed most Americans but the former queen of the Hamptons offended her sensibilities the most.

It was a gross mistake for Rosie to try to take on Venice. It was also a gross mistake to take on Hugh Chisholm as her second consort. Hugh thought that Rosie was a great heiress; Rosie thought that Hugh was a great heir. Both were dismally disappointed, and *furious*.

For the summer, Rosie Chisholm had rented the vast and ornate Papadopoli Palace, one of the famous landmarks on the Grand Canal. She came once to the Maestros for dinner, absurdly over-dressed and trotting out French phrases from her Fragonard mouth, but Miss Mitford took an instant and total dislike to her. Maestro was highly amused by her, even flirted with her, which delighted the queen since she was getting no action from her poetic mate.

Rose couldn't get a motorboat on credit as she did her food and wine, so she started to arrive at the Lido in a gondola. The gondola ride took about two hours in the blazing heat, and she would arrive damp and foul-tempered, in a picture hat secured under the chin by chiffon scarves. Pearls and diamonds, too. Raffinella and a cousin of Maestro's and the Cicognas all shrieked with laughter. And the former queen was forced to change her bathing costume at the farther end of the Excelsior cabanas, banished into Siberia.

The most dreadful incident of the summer was Rosie's great dinner. The Maestros and I, Anna-Maria Cicogna, Nancy Mitford, and Patrick O'Higgins, all arrived and were ushered into the Grand Salon under a gorgeous painted ceiling by "Tintoret," as the queen called the great painter.

In the damp heat, we sighed and moaned, sitting on gilt chairs, as liveried footmen (on credit) passed warm cocktails. Nancy and Raffinella, in simple summer dresses of cotton and no jewelry, fanned themselves with peevish expressions. A grand clock chimed seven, then eight, but still no queen. The baby countess started to leave.

"Pardon," cried Rose making a dramatic entrance in bouffant white net, looking like Empress Elizabeth by Winterhalter—sash and all, and *beaucoup* diamonds. On her tiny high heels Queen

Rose spun about from one guest to another, saying that the duchess had detained her, wasn't that too perfectly awful?

I thought from their expressions, that Raffinella and Nancy would beat Rosie to a pulp but no such luck. As it was, Raffinella would never have her at the house again, and Rose had to make do with a series of house guests from New York, Paris, and Rome. At the end of the summer, Rosie and Maestro both celebrated their birthdays on September 11, and then the former queen left with her consort and tons of Vuitton baggage. Actually, she fled, leaving behind enormous bills.

The season ending, I kissed Raffinella good-bye in her mile-long bedroom of sapphire damask and cream silk Austrian blinds, surrounded by her children, then gave Maestro a hug in his lofty, emerald green damask bedroom with matching curtains over the balconied windows.

"Must you leave, Prettikins?" said Maestro, his enormous eyes resting on me affectionately. "We'll miss you. Come back anytime, and remember it doesn't matter to us if you work. We love you just as you are."

High praise. I felt my eyes misting, and swiftly, abruptly, I vanished down the endless corridor and downstairs to the grand motorboat by the striped wooden poles.

Chapter
Twenty-six

My friends were soon complaining again about having to add yet another new address and phone number in their address books. My new home was at 131 East Seventieth, a block known as the prettiest on the East Side, between Park and Lexington. The house was ancient by New York standards, built around 1870, and decayed in feeling, which of course appealed to me. The front of the house bulged with bay windows, and my sitting room jutted out so far I had a glimpse of Central Park and the Frick Museum. Alas, none of the furniture looked right so I had to rush to Parke Bernet and buy a whole new lot of antique daybeds, gilded consoles, and gondola-shaped chaise longues. Diana Barrymore said it looked like Venice.

What an exciting autumn! Marina Cicogna arrived and took me to a dinner for the duke and duchess of Alba given by Elsa Maxwell; Gian Carlo Menotti and Sam Barber took me to the opening of the opera *Vanessa* at the old Met, resplendent in gilt, crystal, and red plush. Then, after the gala opening, I was off on a weekend at Capricorn, the Barber-Menotti country house in Mount Kisco. Diana Barrymore took me to the opening of *Roots of Heaven* at the old Roxy, a 1920s cinema palace that had featured Gloria Swanson epics.

Diana Barrymore and I had become inseparable; she was my new obsession. She called me Dorian and seemed to understand me better than Aunt Bessie—my self-destructive side, anyway.

"If you can overcome your background, Dorian, you can overcome anything," she was fond of saying.

When the *Daily News* reported WHITNEY AND VAN RENSSELAER BLACKBALLED FROM SOCIAL REGISTER, she clapped her hands happily, "Now you've become a human being, Philip."

Diana had gone to school at Miss Hewitt's classes, with Rosie Gaynor Chisholm, not to mention super-debs Cobina Wright and Brenda Frazier. Then she'd gone to Hollywood and starred in some B movies, and, after that, returned to the stage. Failure greeted her everywhere she turned, and she picked the wrong husbands. Like her father, John Barrymore, the handsomest man ever seen on the silver screen, Diana liked her booze, and, also like her father, she soon went into a long, destructive spiral that ended at AA.

"I'll just have a Coca-Cola, Dorian," she'd say wherever we went. She lived in a brownstone across from the Colony Restaurant, and sometimes we lunched in the blue-and-white-striped bar. Once my curiosity got the better of me, and I begged her to let me accompany her to an AA meeting (on Park Avenue at Sixtieth Street).

"You'll probably hear the truth spoken for the first time, Dorian," she said, in her New York–debutante drawl.

"What do you mean?" I asked.

"You're so frightfully polite and well-mannered, Dorian, and people like you never speak the truth. Maybe now that you're kicked out of that ridiculous blue book, you'll let down your facade, and let the veils unfasten. Philip, you're like a mummy!"

She was right, and I responded strongly to the middle-aged man who spoke in the church basement. His descriptions of escaping responsibility, blind and willful behavior, grandiosity to the extreme, and narcissism struck home. I went back to Seventieth Street with his words still going through my head and wrote in my engagement book that I must call Dick Evans's psychiatrist. Of course the next day was ice blue and wintry, and Countess Marina asked me to be her escort to Jacques Sarlie's dinner party for the Bernadottes of Sweden. . . .

The pages on my calendar fluttered by. Early in June 1959, I arrived at the Palazzo Maestriossi for my second Venetian summer. The sight of black-robed priests, the sound of church bells tolling, and the smell of incense were all comforting, and I wondered why I wasn't Catholic. Also comforting was Maestro in his emerald green chamber having a pedicure and reading a Russian novel. And Raffinella, also reclining on her bed, surrounded by her four children and listening to their confidences—a happy image.

"Think I shall have another child," said Raffinella, looking at me dreamily. "I'm only truly content when I'm carrying a child."

Maestro came into the room, dressed for the Lido in striped cotton pants and a shirt of Mediterranean blue. "I'll think about it," said Maestro, and the four children clapped and cried, "Papa, Papa!"

Maestro and Raffinella rarely raised their voices at each other, and then only when the baby countess would suggest her husband might feel more purposeful if he became a museum curator and made use of his knowledge. Maestro did not wish to work part-time, full-time, *anytime*. He was joyfully alive doing his Venetian routine.

And what a routine it was!

The motorboat ride to the Lido, alone, half an hour away, was something I looked forward to every day. And the rougher it was, the better I enjoyed it. What a panorama went by—columns and gilded domes of Palladio, and Longhena, the astonishing spectacle of the pink Doge's Palace, the green gardens where the Bienale was held, the British and American warships in the harbor, the big white boat that went to Athens, the barges full of coal, lumber, and fruit.

The Lido itself was something to look forward to as well. Maestro would lie down on a blue canvas bed, close his eyes, and luxuriate like an animal. He was always brown, for he found great pleasure in taking the sun, loving the feel of the warmth seeping through his lean, long body. Raffinella, on the other hand, found baking in the sun utterly pointless.

"Come, Prettikins," said the little countess. "Come, we have a long walk."

"Yes, *do* walk, Prettikins," said Maestro, sleepily. "Your buttocks."

A shriek of ironic humor came from Anna-Maria Cicogna's cabana next door. "Prettikins's buttocks!" cried Nancy Mitford, handsome and slender in her bathing dress. Then Gia and Lazzillo got into the act and shouted, "Buttocks, buttocks." They were entranced by certain English words.

At one-thirty, Maestro's boatmen served lunch right on the scorching sand. We sat on little canvas pillows and ate on a low wooden table. Veal with tuna sauce was my favorite, with iced white wine, followed by cheese and a pear or apple. Another favorite lunch was thin slices of ham and juicy slices of cantaloupe. And the conversation was just as delicious, with Nancy, Maestro, and Anna-Maria, all well-read people, gabbing about this and that. And their minds had not been dulled by endless television. In fact, Maestro had never even *seen* a TV set.

After lunch we all fell into a coma. The lapping waves on the sand, the cries of children, and the oily perfume of Bain de Soleil gave us pleasant dreams. When we awakened, the heat had died away. We then vanished through the long, dark tunnel that ran under the Excelsior and emerged at the dock where the motorboat lay waiting and the boatmen would stagger under the weight of our picnic hampers.

In the rear cabin, I'd sit next to Raffinella on soft-cushioned armchairs as we raced back to the palace. The light was lavender now, and Venice in the distance seemed a mirage of bell towers, domes, and orange-tiled rooftops. The little countess wanted to know if people had more fun in Monte Carlo or in Biarritz. Raffinella always imagined that there were far more interesting things going on away from Venice. She felt she was missing something locked away in this ancient backwater.

During that summer I took a little trip to Carole's Capri villa. She had written me that it was a stupendous mansion, so when we got there I just stared at the sitting room and bedroom with shock. It looked like Hansel and Gretel's gingerbread house! There was always a distortion of reality in what Carole wrote.

She threw her arms around me, gazed at me intently, and said that I must have had work done on my face. "Give me the doctor's name, buster!"

"I sleep all the time."

"A sleep cure?" she cried excitedly. Then she told me of some princess who'd been packed in ice, knocked out with a needle, slept for about six years, and came out of it thin as a razor with a face like a baby's.

"In my Venice cure I sleep five hours in the daytime, twelve at night, so I'm awake very little. But of course I'm much more clever and pretty as a result."

Carole burst into laughter and kissed me again.

It was a seductive summer evening as she and I walked down to the Quisisana Hotel. The pink and white oleanders struck me with their loveliness. The vineyards gave forth an earthy fragrance, and there was a fresh breeze from the sea. The peacocks lounging on the terrace of the creamy hotel, drinking and flirting, came as something of a jolt. In the center of the orgy was the bejeweled and voluptuous figure of the Maharani of Baroda, the infamous Sita, surrounded by hand-kissing playboys of every nationality.

Carole presented me to her current amour, Fred, who was the Count Chandon, and his wife, who was the Countess Francesca, and to Adine Stern, who was married to Francesca's cousin Jacques. I kissed the hand of the maharani, licking her with oily compliments, then withdrew from her pink-saried figure and positively obscene egg-sized rubies. Her jasmine perfume lingered on my hand for days.

Like Carole, Adine had a bevy of young men dogging her footsteps. These boys, from good families, lit Madame's cigarette, stared at her face, her cleavage, her legs, and threw out compliments and flattery. They were radiant and I often wondered what the reward was for these baby boys. Always they offered me endless diversion; their eyes bulged like spaniels', and their tongues hung out of their mouths, salivating. Sometimes, they even ordered and paid for a round of drinks but their habit was to take scraps from the table.

I decided to leave all the lovers alone, so I checked into the Quisisana at daybreak. The phone buzzed at nine.

"Fling open your shutters, amore. You've never seen such a brilliant blue sea! Wasn't Fred too divine?"

"His wife is divine, too."

"Listen, buster, you're going to get a bottle broken over your head."

"Be sure it's Chandon champagne."

The mad whirl continued: briefly back to Venice, then on to meet Carole again, this time in Monte Carlo at the Hotel de Paris. It was exhilarating walking through the Belle-Epoque corridors of this famous sin-spot, two bellboys following me, carrying eight Vuitton suitcases (I didn't travel light in those days). My room looked like something from *The Merry Widow*, and I was immediately shot into the delirium of arrival in Monte Carlo.

"In a few months, amore mio," cried Carole, embracing me with frenzied cries, "I'll be Countess Chandon, one of the queens of Paris!"

"What about Francesca?" I asked.

"Don't be so middle class, darling!" She was lost in her unrealistic dreams.

I gave her the album of *Gigi*, and soon she was twisting and turning before me in a daring, red chiffon evening dress. Long, trailing wings were attached to the shoulders and she swept these wings about my face, pirouetting on red high-heeled sandals.

"How do you think I look?" she cried ecstatically, butterflying about the lofty room.

"Everyone will be mad with desire when they see you *ce soir*, Countess."

With a delighted shriek she flung herself on a fragile, caned dressing table stool and started to work on her love-goddess face. She tossed her head at me, reflecting in the oval mirror. "Do you think these emerald-and-diamond earclips are too much, amore?"

"Not as long as you didn't pay for them." I'd taken my customary position by the dressing table.

A defiant look flashed in her brown eyes as she glared at me. "Darling, I know you'll scold me, but I've broken my trust fund and sold all my shares."

"And now your fate is in the hands of Count Chandon." My high spirits were suddenly deflated. I had a fearful glimpse of what lay ahead for Carole—and for me.

Her vibrant voice rolled on, vying with the *Gigi* overture. She was aware that I was angry about her trust fund and childishly set about winning me over. "I've taken one of the *largest* tables downstairs for the gala tonight, Philippo."

"Why didn't the champagne king take a table?" Again my voice was sharp.

"Well, sweetie," she said, brushing her hair up into a more bouffant mass, "you've got to spend money to attract money."

"You mean all this is to dazzle Fred Chandon?"

She nodded her gold head vigorously. "New Balenciaga dress, new emerald-and-diamond earclips. The gala dinner; he's so impressed you wouldn't believe it!"

"But how could someone with two hundred million be impressed?" I said trying to be logical.

She tapped her temple meaningfully. "Darling, when I gave him the beautiful Cartier watch this afternoon he almost had an attack." Her voice went on as the vodkas went down.

Hopeless, hopeless, hopeless, I thought.

Days drifted by under the poisonous green sky of Monaco. Despite my warning lectures, Carole showered Fred Chandon and her new favorite, Jacques, with some delightful baubles from "good old Carts," as she called the jeweler. Jacques was rich and attractive, and most taken with La Morton. A Harvard graduate, he was sick to death of his hysterical beauty-wife, Adine. Carole was hedging her bets. If Fred didn't make her an honest woman, then Big Jacques would. Jacques actually was a small fellow but he was reputedly well endowed.

One day we saw Jessie Donahue, Barbara Hutton's Woolworth aunt, driving off in a Rolls-Royce of stunning proportions, followed a little later by the famous New York–London hostess Mrs. Gilbert Miller, nee Kitty Bache, the sister of Hazel Beckman. Fred had died that year, and Frederick Lewisohn had died the year before, right upstairs in a room facing the sea.

Eve Lewisohn had told me that her father was in very bad shape financially, couldn't even afford his car and chauffeur the last two years. I suddenly remembered how Mr. Lewisohn had spanked me one evening in 1936 when I had been howling out the car window as he and Mother were about to step into their Rolls. Charlie and I often stuck nails in the tires of the grand cars and had often been spanked by the chauffeurs as well.

Carole became even more erratic than before, and the unreality of Europe descended on me. I decided to return to New York and work.

Twenty years later Carole was living in a maid's room at the Barbizon Hotel for Women and working nine-to-five at Gucci on Fifth Avenue. One night we dined in a little coffee shop and she said, "What happened to Carole Morton?"

"Remember Monte Carlo, 1959?" That was all I said.

She stared at me and nodded. She remembered.

I felt horribly tired, unbalanced, when I stepped into Raffinella's bedchamber to say good-bye. Her two youngest children were curled up by her side, and she was smoothing their hair. We made conversation for a while and then she fixed her intelligent blue eyes on me.

"You know, Philip, you can stay here as long as you want, but I'm wondering if it is right for you to live with us in this very rich way. The only reason I can is because my father and mother died young and I'm free to do as I choose."

"I understand," I said quietly.

"I think you'd feel happier, more complete, if you had a life of your own. And a job."

"I think you're right, Raffinella," I said smiling back at her.

"When I come to New York later, I shall take you down to Lehman Brothers to meet Mr. Mannheim, who handles my account. I'm certain he will like you; you'd be superb as a stockbroker, with your looks and charm."

It was hard, also, to say good-bye to the count. Maestro was having his usual pedicure, lying on his emerald-green moiré daybed, his back against a pile of white-linen pillows. The linen was heavily coronetted and initialed.

"You don't look well, Prettikins," said the Count.

Domenico came in and announced that the boat was ready to take me to the station.

"Good-bye, darling," said Maestro, turning his brown cheek so I could plant a kiss on it. "Come back anytime; you always have a home with us. Don't worry, we'll look after old Philip." And he handed me a fat envelope stuffed with lire, francs, and dollars.

I walked down the tapestried hall, past marble busts and gilded throne chairs. Angello opened some monumental doors for me with his white-gloved hands, bowing respectfully when I handed him an envelope stuffed with lire notes. I overtipped all the servants, hoping they'd love me, just as Mother hungered for people's love and approval. Maestro was a trifle disturbed about the way I made friends with his servants, asked me what on earth I talked to them about. "I'm curious," I'd reply. "I like people."

Maestro frowned at me; this did not go with his code. Raffinella and I were often told there were only eight people with whom we could speak in Venice; Paris and New York the same.

Chapter
Twenty-seven

Raffinella arrived in New York a few months later and, good as
her word, made the Lehman connection for me. In the meantime
I was taking an economics course at the New School, plus a writing
course. I was determined to make it on my own—no more exper-
iments with the high life. After all, I had the nice trust fund at
Fiduciary, which I had added to with Barbara's money. I had
experimented selling myself here and there and I did not like the
feeling of self-hatred that went with it. By the time Raffinella arrived in November, I was eager for a job interview.

"I've arranged an appointment for you to meet Mr. Mannheim
next Monday at eleven o'clock," she said. For good measure she
took me to lunch with Robert Lehman, who showed us his fine
collection of religious paintings at his West Fifties townhouse.
Bobby Lehman was quite amused when I told him I was Adele Van
Rensselaer's son; he had given her a Scottie in Mallorca.

Raffinella brought me to interesting parties whenever she came
to Gotham, taking care to introduce me to people she thought
might be useful. Jean Stein, Jules Stein's daughter, did the same
for me. She set up an appointment with Ben Sonnenberg, the

famous PR man, who lived in an equally famous house on Gramercy Park, once the residence of Mrs. Stuyvesant Fish. I thought if one didn't like me, the other would. It turned out that neither did.

Mr. Mannheim at Lehman Brothers was agreeable; we chatted about this and that, and I left his office thinking I had made a favorable impression.

A few days later I received a letter from Lehman Brothers stating that they did not think I would be quite right in their firm. A terrible sense of defeat came over me.

My interview with Ben Sonnenberg was even worse. He was a fat, jolly man with hard eyes. His luxurious wood-paneled office was filled with unusual and rare paintings and furniture. I often saw him at auction rooms, so I remarked to him that Parke Bernet was having a staggering French sale that weekend. I showed all my teeth, but he didn't smile back. He gazed at me as if I were a foul-smelling cheese. His stare began to unnerve me; I fidgeted in the Adam armchair, and sweat trickled down my back.

"What does a playboy want in a serious enterprise like this?" he asked from behind his enormous desk.

"I'm not a playboy," I said, politely.

"You *were* with Barbara Hutton, weren't you?" He sneered. "And handsomely subsidized by her, I've been told. And now you're the companion of Count and Countess Maestriossi, who are even richer, rumor has it. You're doing rather well, I'd say, young man. You *are* young, aren't you, although I'm certain there's nothing young about you."

Somehow I managed to get out of his house and stumble into the little private park. As I sat on a bench, my eyes must have had the same blank stare as Carole's and Fred Beckman's.

I was still living at the old, crumbling corner house covered with ivy at 131 East Seventieth Street, but by the beginning of 1960 my rooms were more cluttered than any auction room. My auction mania had become so intense I was wretched if I could not buy something beautiful at every sale. To deal with all my new treasures, I took two little tenement apartments, at 312 and 314 East Sixty-second Street.

I attempted another novel, and on weekends I rushed to the

auction rooms. Often I neglected to examine items at the exhibition, so when the movers brought them home, often as not they fell to pieces, or were as fake as Franz-Joseph's bed. My place became so crowded that I decided on an impulse to move to an apartment at the Lowell, which had always been a haven for me.

Finally my novel was finished, and I sent it to Viking. A week later it was returned, rejected, with a sticker on the envelope that read, "Highly Dangerous!" Carole Morton had written me that Capri was divinely peaceful—why didn't I come and keep her company? By then, I was waking up in the mornings with evil headaches, and the slightest decision exhausted me. Somehow I managed to book passage on an American ship going to Gibraltar, Cannes, and Naples.

Sometimes the top of my head felt as if it might explode. During the day I felt dizzy, sometimes faint, and the anxiety sweat would pour down my body. I had to down a few shots before I boarded the ship, then I lay down on my berth and slept for ten days. The steward brought me meals regularly, and he was tipped like Barbara Hutton's steward on the *United States*. Anyway *he* liked me, and that made me feel better about myself.

In the past, sleep therapy had been my savior, but when I arrived on the pleasure isle, my equilibrium was poor. Capri was anything but divinely peaceful, and after a few hectic days and nights at La Morton's, I moved into the Quisisana. I tried to stay by myself but that is impossible in Capri. I smoked some marijuana with Carole and slowed down a bit, but then the next morning the evil headache was back.

Some new "baby boys" were trailing Carole, teenage Brazilian giants. Their energy was an insult to my weary state. I had words with Carole, and my anger worried me; I seemed to have no control over it anymore.

Carole's best friend, Carlotta, was a Neopolitan duchess about my age. She had recently gotten married, and Carole and I joined the couple in Rome. We tried to save money, staying at the Ambassador near the Excelsior, but hundreds of dollars a day slipped through our hands. In the evenings we dined and danced in dolce vita clubs, surrounded by popping balloons, titled satyrs, and sinister middle-aged women. I never learned whether it was me or Carole they craved.

"Probably both, amore!" screamed Carole, who'd been drinking and smoking marijuana most of the day. The sixties were in full swing, and drugs and booze were to be her downfall.

We were all dining together at some club one evening when suddenly there was a commotion. Carlotta's husband had gone to the bathroom for a fix and he'd had a fatal heart attack. Carole and I couldn't believe our ears. Just a minute before he'd been sitting there with us at our table, and then he was gone.

Panic broke out; Carole and I were advised to get out before the police arrived.

"I'm staying," said Carole, suddenly sober.

"I am, too." It would be too horrible to run out on Carlotta and leave her alone with the dead body. Carole's loyalty made me love her deeply at that moment, but her manic, self-destructive life was taking its toll on her—and on me. I had to leave Europe. I was in such a depressed state I even turned down an invitation to the Maestriossis' Rosalia. After a dreadful week in Paris, I returned to New York.

Although I was staying with brother Charlie at 16 Sutton Place South, I felt frightened and alone. I could see that my strange state worried Charlie, so I moved back to the haven of the Lowell. Mother had lived there longer than anywhere else; her spirit might still be there to give me solace. I now began my investigation into New York's finest psychiatrists.

The first was a smooth Park Avenue Daddy who told me how he loved the squash courts at the Racquet Club, and did I know . . . ?

After trying various others who charged me hefty consultation fees, I spilled my story to Dr. Dave, on Central Park South. He was thin, nervous, highly agitated, and crazier than I was, so I loved him on first sight.

Richie Berlin, a pretty and clever debutante of this period, told me that her Dr. Feelgood gave her a painful injection, making her pass out. She awoke to find the fellow on top of her, still in his white jacket. That never quite happened to me, although Dr. Dave did attempt some peculiar therapies on me. Late in the sixties he committed suicide, which didn't surprise me at all.

Every time I saw Diana Vreeland on Park Avenue she'd say, in her outlandish drawl, "Isn't this the most thrilling period?"

"Yeah, Diana," I'd say, although I was yearning to scream, "NO!" Of course, I was always far too polite to tell people the truth.

After an expensive month at the Lowell, Dr. Dave reserved a room for me at Columbia Presbyterian Hospital, way up on the Hudson River overlooking the George Washington Bridge. He told me that many famous socialites and celebrities were gracing the country club halls. "In a few weeks you'll feel like new, Phil," he assured me, his drugged eyes resting on mine.

A river-view hospital room was being prepared for me for the July Fourth weekend, which suited me fine since I dreaded long holiday weekends. I was all dressed and packed by July 1, rather nervous, and taking a few nips to give me courage. The phone buzzed, announcing that the limo was waiting outside.

As I was floating out the Lowell entrance, Anne Domville, Charlie's ex-mother-in-law was coming in.

"Darling, where are you going? Southampton?"

"The funny farm," I said, and she looked confused.

"The nut house!" I hollered so loudly that everyone in the art-deco lobby turned around.

Mrs. Domville lived in a world of polite society and had often remarked on my old-world manners. She knew there was something really wrong when I raised my voice and showed emotion. She decided to ride up to the hospital with me, to see what I was getting into. She hinted darkly that they might be locking me up to get control of my money.

I panicked when I saw the long institutional halls, the white-coated orderlies, and the nurses. And when a sweet-talking doctor led me into a room with bars on the windows, I shouted at Anne that I'd kill myself here. I broke down and started to cry, Anne comforting me as best she could.

"You don't have to stay, Philip," she kept saying. "They can't keep you here against your will."

"Those bars on the windows. My God!"

Finally my doctor appeared, looking at me sternly. He told me I was not well and needed a few months inside so that they could do tests. Check on Dr. Dave's diagnosis.

"I'm sorry, Doctor, I just don't have the courage to stay here. Can't bear to be locked up."

The doctor tried to talk me out of leaving, but I was firm. And Anne—tall and imperious with Greta Garbo features—backed me up.

"I'll take care of him," she said in her high-handed and autocratic tone. So he shrugged sadly and we left. Years later I bitterly regretted this. The Maestriossi scandal and all the other horrors would have been averted.

"I'll take you down to Point of Woods on Fire Island, darling," said Anne. "You won't know a soul, you can lie on the beach and have proper meals. You've been moving around far too much, now you must stay put." Anne treated me like an imbecilic child, which I needed. I clung to her all summer long and deep into the autumn.

Two years—1961 and 1962—went by. I went to Dr. Dave and other doctors. Doctors were the only people I saw besides Joe Pilates, a ninety-year-old Tarzan who ran a gym on Ninth Avenue. My energy and enthusiasm began to return.

My apartments at the Lowell and 131 East Seventieth had been given up, dismantled. To preserve my waning capital I was living in the ground-floor apartment I called the Slug at 314 East Sixty-second.

Carole, who—surprise, surprise—had not become Countess Chandon or married Jacques (she'd turned on both of them), arrived at the St. Regis for a month or so in the winter. I was in Carole's spacious Louis room at Mr. Astor's hotel, sitting, naturally, by the dressing table as she did Operation Face. The years had treated Carole well. A good body like Carole's lasts forever, and good bones in the face help you from developing the chipmunk look with sagging cheeks and double chins.

"Darling, you're going to adore my lawyer," she was saying. "A sweet little pussycat." A vodka tonic rested on the table, and in an ashtray were two joints.

We piled into a taxi and rocketed across town to the lawyer. I was telling Carole of Dr. Dave, and she laughed hysterically.

"Darling you always do terrible, *terrible* things to me."

The lawyer, of course, was not a sweet little pussycat. Nevertheless, I, too, fell under his spell. He took us out to dinner in a smart Italian restaurant that resembled a Capri trattoria.

"Well, Carole," he said, his red, Cupid's-bow lips curving up his round face in a deceptively childlike manner, "Well, Carole, you're now the proud owner of this here restaurant."

"Huh?" said Carole, zonked, and he repeated the news.

"And, my dear Mrs. Morton, you are also the owner of two large apartment houses in Greenwich Village, which, I hasten to add, will give you twice the income your stocks generated."

Carole flung her arms around his bull neck like Minnie Mouse. "Oh, amore, tesoro, you are splendido! How am I going to pay you back?"

"We'll talk about that when we return to my apartment, dear."

I didn't see them again for a week. Then Carole asked me to take her to the airport. In the taxi to Kennedy she claimed the Almighty had sent her this lawyer who was going to make her a rich woman again. The lawyer had promised to send her a big income in Europe. Then she said something that floored me.

"Darling, that sweet pussycat now has my power of attorney."

"He has your power of attorney?" I gulped.

She nodded and lit up another joint. "He's *mad* for me, of course."

"Of course," I echoed, uneasily.

"He inspires confidence, doesn't he? I suppose because he's so big." She inhaled deeply and started to laugh hysterically, and was then off to Europe.

Chapter
Twenty-eight

My trust was now down to $115,000, the principal having been invaded upon several occasions. However, I still had the nifty portfolio of Aunt Bessie–style stocks, most of them growth-oriented, so they gave off some income. I called Carole's pussycat and he told me over a Laurent lunch that he could get me $20,000 a year from such a sum.

"I'll just charge you five grand to break the trust, Phil," he said, "and then we'll get you into some offshore oil companies that pay sixteen to eighteen percent return. I'm on the board of directors of most of these companies, so I have the inside story."

The lawyer broke the trust, but thank heavens, I thought twice about those offshore oil babies. Instead, I put the stocks at Merrill Lynch, then promptly spent $15,000 on the decorator Keith and new antiques. At Savoy Auction Gallery next to Saks Fifth, I saw an Elizabethan tester bed and decided that was the period I must have at 166 East Sixty-first, my latest home.

So thrilled was I with my new home that I threw an enormous party. Brother Charles had told me somewhat angrily that I must be more social, pull my weight in the boat, so I'd given two big lunch parties at the Colony Restaurant. Each party was a mob scene of fifty, and the two cost over a thousand with tips included.

Bill Blass brought me the 1935 Camel ad picture of Mother that had been on the back of *Vogue*. Bill was a handsome, relaxed fellow with a marvelous smile and lots of energy. He was good to his old friends; Carole had been his favorite model in the forties, and she spoke well of him.

That September I arrived once more at the Maestriossis' Gothic palace in Venice. There I found Yul Brynner and his pretty new wife, Doris. Yul was a pleasant fellow with no social graces, and like all actors, he loved to talk of himself. People always sense I'm interested in hearing the nitty-gritty, so Yul spilled his saga to me in the motorboat, in palace corridors, on the Lido. I was surprised when he told me the big love of his life had been Ingrid Bergman. They'd fallen for each other when they were filming *Anastasia*, but both were already married.

"What on earth are you talking about with Yul?" asked Raffinella.

"Yul," I replied. "And more Yul."

"Philip," said Maestro, "be so kind and meet Audrey Hepburn and her husband, Mel Ferrer, at the station tomorrow, then show them their apartment—the new one which we've just redecorated."

Audrey Hepburn was as winning in person as she was on the screen. She exuded warmth and charm, had the same well-bred quality of Raffinella Maestriossi. Mel Ferrer was a tall, engaging fellow. Audrey and Mel were hardly Hollywood types. As soon as I'd deposited them in their splendid stuccoed rooms facing the Grand Canal, we went to the Lido, Yul's voice droning in my ear.

We met for evening drinks in a huge, beamed chamber that had been decorated with Indian batik on the walls and sofas. Formerly it had been a guest room for very important personages such as Madame Pallido. I'd even lived there in 1958, tickled pink by sleeping in a double bed held up by gilt porpoises! Every summer I noticed that the palace and Rosalia were constantly being redecorated by the master, Renzo, who even had his own apartment at Rosalia. I wasn't rich, but I enjoyed constantly redecorating, which makes you think something is happening to you.

As I was packing to return to New York, the Maestros made me promise I'd meet them in Hollywood in November. Cecil Beaton

was doing the decor and costumes for *My Fair Lady*, and Audrey
Hepburn had the part that Julie Andrews had made famous in New
York. Cecil, who was called Cecilio by the Maestros, was an inti-
mate friend who knew how to make them giggle.

On the TWA plane back to New York I dreamed of Carole
Morton. Oddly enough, as the taxi was dropping me home to 166,
there was Carole striding up Park Avenue in her yellow Chanel.
She was talking to herself, making violent gestures. People turned
around and stared at her.

I called the St. Regis and asked her how she was. It came as no
surprise when she told me her income had abruptly stopped, that
the lawyer said he was terribly sorry but all the Manhattan prop-
erties were worthless.

"What are you going to do?" I asked.

"Sue!" replied Carole. "I've hired a tough lawyer, and we're
going to break his balls, buster. He'll be sorry he crossed Carole
Morton, you better believe it."

Every day until I left for Hollywood, we had lunch and dinner
together. She was not drinking or taking drugs and so made sense.
She even convinced me she was going to have millions after the
case was brought to court. And her old arrogance had gone; I'd
never seen her so full of humility.

On the way from the airport into Los Angeles and to the Bel Air
Hotel, the palm trees, fragrant eucalyptus trees, brilliant fuchsia,
and gold bougainvillea struck a Mediterranean note. How could I
have resisted La La Land for so long? Birds were singing in the
gardens surrounding the Bel Air hotel, surely a paradise on earth.
I arrived at four o'clock, a little after the Maestros, Princess Irenee
Galitzine, a Russian beauty who had once been engaged to Maestro, and Baroness Lena Rothschild, a Bulgarian beauty.

"You look awfully shabby, Prettikins," observed the little countess.

"I'm trying to pinch pennies, Naughtiness."

"Don't!" cried Maestro, a lean and elegant fashion plate as always, even without his valet.

"I won't!" I laughed. And I didn't. The hell with trying to econ-
omize. I was with the richest, most successful people in the world.

Soon my book would be published and sold to the movies. Raffinella said she'd introduce me to Swifty Lazar.

Every grand house we visited in the Hollywood–Bel Air area had a history. Merle Oberon, a Eurasian siren, certainly did. She was described as a slut who'd worked in a Bombay bordello, and so forth and so on.

At Merle Oberon's I sat next to the hostess, gleaming in white satin and diamonds, and Raffinella sat next to George Hamilton. Across from me was Natalie Wood, and we kept smiling sympathetically at each other. She was the gentlest person I met in Hollywood. George was a tanned Beau Brummel, the image of his mother, Anne Hamilton Spalding. Anne had black hair parted in the middle, classic features, and a great sense of humor. George had all these assets, plus kindness of heart. He always looked after his mama and saw to it that she had the best.

The daughter of Fanny Brice, Mrs. Ray Stark, gave a dinner for us, too, and Frank Sinatra came on strong with the little countess.

"It's a compliment," I told her.

Sinatra sent us all to Las Vegas in his private jet. We stayed at his hotel, and the sight of the highly civilized Maestros walking through gambling rooms and attempting slot machines was something I never thought I'd see.

"Who *are* all these people, Prettikins?" Maestro kept asking.

"Rochefoucaulds and Somersets."

He was completely lost, and to use his words, not amused at all. Raffinella was, vaguely, although I could tell she was eager to return to Paris and the house she'd bought there. Marie-Helene Rothschild was her new best friend. The Rothschild receptions were more to her taste than Las Vegas slot machines and poker players.

As 1964 dawned, my mania had become worse. I gave up 166 and moved into 48 East Sixty-eighth, a limestone townhouse of French style. My Tudor decor and tester bed did not go in the Louis XVI decor, so the Tudor treasures were auctioned off at a loss, and the more stylish eighteenth-century Marie Antoinette took over.

I spent the winter and spring typing *The House with the Golden Door*, my novel about life in Venice with the jet set. I was a recluse again, going out only to see Aunt Bessie, who had moved to the Lowell, and Anne Domville, who also made it her home when she wasn't in Paris or Lourdes working with the sick.

My novel was sold, and in my new literary persona I met John Dodds, a big shot at Putnam.

"Don't you have any new ideas for a book, Phil?"

"The Count Rasponi story," I replied. Then I explained that Lanfranco Rasponi had a stable of anonymous women who wanted to be known. So he cut off their noses, starved them into skeletons, and told them to throw out their elaborate "gowns" and dress only in simple rags. They got rid of their Bronx whines or Brooklyn snarls at elocution school so that they talked like Gloria and Consuelo. Some even developed a French or Italian accent.

Dodds sent me to the McDowell Colony for Writers, up in Peterboro, New Hampshire, and gave me a nice advance on the book's outline.

The greatest moment of achievement came at my publication party in spring 1965. My new obsession, Leila von Saher, hung on one of my arms and Tennessee Williams on the other. Tennessee, my idol, often told me I was a male Blanche DuBois. Madame von Saher had a salon, with the stars being Tenn, Jerzy Kosinski, who'd just written *The Painted Bird,* and James Leo Herlihy, who'd just published *Midnight Cowboy.*

"Stay by my side, Tennessee," I kept saying. "You'll bring me luck."

"I'm afraid I'm jinxed, baby," he'd say sadly. Tenn was fascinated by pale-faced, childlike Andy Warhol and his entourage of Edie Sedgewick and Gerald Malanga. Edie was a glorious young creature, speeding on God only knew what, with glittering earrings about two feet long. She danced like a wildwoman, and I soon joined her on the dance floor. One manic recognizes another. The next day the *Herald Tribune* gave me a disastrous write up.

One afternoon I was making tea for Madame von Saher and our god, Tennessee. "Stick a little bourbon in it, baby," cried Tenn and swallowed a few pills. Leila was in great form, utterly in a state of unreal delirium, describing the baby she'd just had. She even described how she'd been to Saks and bought the infant baby clothes.

"When can we see this blessed event?" asked Tenn.

"He's now with his father, in the pram."

In the midst of this Mad Hatter tea party, John Dodds buzzed and appeared in my Louis XVI drawing room. Later after my guests had gone, Dodds said I must return to the McDowell Colony and not be distracted by such fascinating company. So back I went, to my solitary writer's cabin in the woods.

One day Mary called me, her voice urgent. "Mr. Van Rensselaer, Count and Countess Maestriossi are here, and want to see you very much. When are you coming back?"

"Tonight," I replied. "And get my party list, and make a few calls, please, my Irish imp."

The next week found me gnawing the flesh about my fingers, waiting for my hundred carefully chosen guests to arrive. To create a suitable setting for the Maestros, I'd rushed up to Parke Bernet and bought ten lots from the estate of Robert Goelet, a multimillionaire connoisseur from Newport and 4 East Sixty-sixth. Anything from his houses must be special, so I didn't even bother to examine any of the chairs, tables, screens, and chests.

The Goelet treasures transformed my apartment into a living, breathing Trianon. The gold damask screen matched the fringed curtains that swooped over the French windows. And a richly veined rock crystal chandelier and wall lights reflected in the tall arched mirrors. I was standing on a ladder lighting ivory candles when Pyrma and John Pell arrived. They were a distinguished couple who lived around the corner on Fifth Avenue, and their houses at Fort Ticonderoga and Center Island were weekend retreats from the storm.

"It's magnificent," cried the blond Mrs. Pell. "Are they family pieces?"

"Courtesy of Robert Goelet, Esquire," said I, and explained the auction the day before.

"Yesterday?" screamed Lady Jeannie Campbell, the Duke of Argyl's daughter who had recently divorced Carolen Mailer.

"Things happen very quickly around here, Milady," I said. Jeannie nodded. She moved around almost as much as I did.

All at once everyone arrived. The Count and Countess were thrilled to meet Andy Warhol, and he them. Baby Jane Holzer, another rage of society, had warned me to put away all my little silver and gold snuffboxes because Andy's entourage had loose fingers. Unfortunately, with all the last-minute preparations, I forgot, and I was cleaned out of every small object in both the drawing room and the bedroom, including my gold hairbrushes. Gone, too, were Valium from the bathroom—even my vitamin E pills from the kitchen!

Chapter
Twenty-nine

In November 1966, I had some crushing news. John Dodds told me that Putnam had decided not to publish my book.

I flung a vase of flowers at him, and went berserk. I shouted all the foul language I knew. When he left, I was appalled by the violence of my words. I'd always kept my rage in check. To calm myself and forget my sense of failure, I sank onto the canopied Goelet bed and broke some poppers under my nose.

When I came to, Dick Evans was standing over me. "What's the matter, baby?" he asked. "Tell Uncle Dick."

"I'm not going to be a failure!"

"Failure. Success. What does it matter? I drove myself to a breakdown, during *Funny Girl*. Now, I'm a success, painting in Greece."

"Do you think I'd like Greece?"

"Greece is the only place for you, baby," Dick replied. "It's a great place when your finances are shaky. How are yours?"

"Shaky." I laughed. "Been gambling on Wall Street to try and recoup my capital. *Disaster*. Down to fifty thousand dollars."

He whistled. "I thought you had ten times that." He glanced

around at the Goelet glory. "I thought you were a millionaire."

"In my head."

"In Greece, especially in the Greek islands, you can act out your fantasy. Every expatriate does."

On January 18, 1967, Athens was in the midst of a bitter snow-storm when my American cruise ship arrived. Dick Evans was standing at the pier with some Greek friends. In the customs shed Dick asked how much luggage I'd brought.

"Twenty trunks," I answered. Dick and his friends broke up. The customs officers were somewhat amused, too, by the size of the wardrobe and the steamers, and by their content. I'd emptied my Day and Meyer storage rooms, given up the two Slug apart-ments, and auctioned off my Goelet treasures at a loss at Savoy Galleries. Without the Goelet name they weren't eighteenth-century, but turn of the century.

Early in the evening I stepped out of the taxi and registered in the modern lobby of the Electra Hotel. The manager asked me how long I intended to stay. I reflected. I was anxious to get to Hydra, where there was a mansion owned by a former husband of one of Maestro's cousins. "I'll be staying one night." As I spoke the words, my twenty trunks came into the lobby with Dick and his friends who'd brought them up from Piraeus in two vans.

"That's your luggage, Mr. Van Rensselaer, and you're just stay-ing one night?" We all laughed. Then we all went into the hotel's bar and had some ouzo. Ouzo is a lethal drink that is off limits to the U.S. armed forces. The effect of two ouzos is like a few pop-pers. It twists your head around. It didn't bode well for my Greek experience.

The next morning I sailed off to the isle of Hydra, three hours away.

Everyone on the island had bought mansions for three to five thousand dollars, and they had two or three hundred a month to live on. Some survived on less than that, eating the leftovers from people's plates at the port's restaurants.

I paid a quick visit to the Maestros in Venice, then took the large white tourist boat back to Athens. Back to my island home. I planned to spend the rest of my life on Hydra. Unfortunately I got a telegram from Herbert Kende: "Newhouses need columnist to write for their newspapers. Call if you are interested."

I rushed back to Athens, to Dick Evan's neoclassic brownstone at Lykabettos to discuss the turn of events with him. He had six rooms and a roof garden for fifty dollars a month, danced in the Plaka clubs every night, and had enjoyed two shows of his paintings.

"Philip, you're just going back to those materialistic values that made you sick. Why don't you buy that house you were looking at for sixteen thousand and then you have three hundred a month to live on? Don't go back to greed and auctions and all that social stuff, it'll destroy you."

I nodded my head, and said he was right, but greed and the desire to be famous swept me back to Manhattan.

I wrote a column called "Van Rensselaer's World" for the Newhouses three times a week. I enjoyed doing profiles on Gloria Vanderbilt, Tennessee Williams, Mart Crowley, Truman Capote, and other luminaries of the day.

The *Long Island Press* paid me $1,000 a month. My rent at 100 West Fifty-seventh was $375 so that didn't give me much pocket money. Kende now had a gallery at Sixtieth and Madison and was flourishing. One day he invited me to lunch at the Polo Bar of the Westbury. He had achieved his dream of taking Greta Garbo to dinner and had a large villa in Marbella; the crème of Middle Europe were his guests, and he lingered proudly on their names.

"You're not still selling fakes, are you, Herbert?" I said, giving his expensive Savile Row suit a suspicious look.

"Are you mad, young man?" he shouted, shooting some saliva in my face.

"I'm forty years old now," I said calmly, "and I'm broke." I told him my predicament, and that very afternoon he sent me up to my old stamping grounds, Parke Bernet. He wrote the numbers of the paintings he wanted me to buy and the prices he wished to pay. Three I got for under his price, questionable old masters they were, but soon, after a bogus provenance, they became worthy of a museum. And that's where they ended their days, with a terrific profit for Kende.

It was swell having two thousand a month coming in—cash, too. Kende's secretary suggested that I start buying objects at auction and selling them from my apartment.

"I don't have the right apartment."

"Moving shouldn't be any problem for you, Philip!"

Early in 1969 the famous decorator Michael Greer told me there was a marvelous apartment at 525 Park Avenue, at Sixty-first Street, where he lived. I rushed over to the old-world building, fell in love with 12B, and signed the lease then and there.

The rooms were large with high ceilings, a perfect setting for the auction treasures I would dispose of. The drawing room was thirty feet long, the bedroom twenty by twenty, and the bathroom even larger. A woman had just died there, and I bought the silver-blue Scalamandre silk curtains from the estate for next to nothing. They also sold me a chaise longue of carved walnut, a trumeau with a Hubert Robert painting, and a Queen Anne drop-front desk. They didn't know what they had, but I did.

That weekend Herbert brought a rich woman to my new apartment and the following week her movers took everything out. I'd tripled what I'd paid and started rushing to every auction room in town. Suddenly I had a new business, and for two years I flourished like Kende.

By February 1969, I even managed to throw a birthday party for my new obsession, Miss Gloria Vanderbilt. My usual cast of celebrities cavorted in my regal rooms—Ruth Ford, Kevin McCarthy, Marion Javits. Lady Jeannie Campbell promised to bring Carolen Mailer and she did. Kende promised to bring Miss G., but no such luck. Suzy Knickerbocker and Earl Blackwell came at midnight, and the next day in Suzy's column I read I was the new Elsa Maxwell.

So the late sixties went by. I spent my time writing my column, selling antiques and paintings on the weekends, and rushing to the Bank of New York on Monday mornings to cover the auction checks I'd written to pay for "my inherited pieces."

Early in 1970 I flew to Athens. On the way, I stopped off in London to see Carole, who had opened an art gallery bearing her name.

At the Heathrow Airport I saw a strange, turbaned woman rushing toward me, screaming. She had taut skin, slanting eyes, and was wearing a dramatic gray coat bordered all in gray fox. The daughter of the Orient flung her arms around me.

"Don't you recognize me, buster?" She giggled.

"Carole! My God, I thought you were Merle Oberon!"

"The doctors said with my bone structure I can be lifted forever, time and time again. And isn't it thrilling I'm to be the new Lord Duveen!"

We had a few oyster lunches at Claridges, waved at friends like Sunny and Claus von Búlow, and Carole's flame, the Duke of Marlborough. She was soon to be his duchess, she informed me, and was spending nearly every weekend at Blenheim. I told her I'd just bought a Hydra hideaway, formerly a ruin but I had a dear friend there, Yioulie, who was dealing with the workers.

"Imagine," I said, "I made so much money in my estate sales that I could purchase this Greek Blenheim."

"Darling, let's face it, we're brilliant, *brilliant!*"

"Let's have another vodka," I cried gaily. Vodka and Claridges Bar always made me feel I was a success.

Yioulie met me on the Hydra dock a few afternoons later. She was twenty-five, was called the Greek Sophia Loren, and she had the reputation for being Hydra's Barbara Hutton because of her spending sprees and generosity in the bars. A sadistic Chinese millionaire had been the source of her riches. When I met her she was tired of endlessly packing her bags and boarding planes, and she couldn't stand being humiliated by the Chinese brute any longer. Yioulie and I enjoyed being together; we liked talking about our corruption by the very rich. And we liked the idea of sharing a house, and making it a home.

Half an hour after the boat docked and the donkey train delivered my baggage, Yioulie and I were standing by the wrought-iron gate, peering into my garden. The ruin had been transformed into a mansion! There were yellow shutters on the windows, and balustrades on the terraces. Tubs of gardenias everywhere, and fine marble balustrades.

"Where did you find those, Yioulie?"

"A Plaka house was being torn down," she explained.

"And the marble fountain and terra cotta statues of Minerva?"

"From the same neoclassic house, Philippe." She called me Philippe and spoke six languages superbly. She also could write like Françoise Sagan, and I was helping her develop her talent. She had no confidence in herself at all. Despite my self-destructive ways I learned, with some surprise, that I could be a constructive influence on others. My happiest spring and summer on Hydra began, with Yioulie by my side.

Late in August I flew back to New York. My apartment at 525 had been sublet for the summer months at a small profit. After I paid a few bills, my account at the Bank of New York was empty. I put an estate sale ad in the *Times*, but no luck, not one call. My column came to an end; the Newhouses, Caroline and Ted, said it hadn't been a success. I kept calling my agent, Roz Cole, at the Waldorf Towers to find out news about my new book. Nothing but rejections.

The manic high that had fueled my energy abruptly died. Looking into the bathroom mirror I thought, *You're forty-three, the same age as Mother when she died. You've failed, too, it's time to go.*"

I went to several Dr. Feelgoods, complaining of insomnia. By the middle of September I had a large bottle full of Seconals. I looked at them and thought, *That will do the trick, buster.*

I called Ted Peckham, told him I wanted to return to Greece. Could he dispose of my estate?

"I've disposed of Diana Barrymore's and Jeanne de Rothschilds, why not yours?" He said. He carefully examined everything in the bathroom, bedroom, kitchen and drawing room.

"Would ten grand help you out?" he said. I nodded and he sat down and wrote me out a check.

"The movers will be here tomorrow, bright and early."

So, my last rude awakening. In my pajamas I stood in the drawing room and watched my best treasures going out the door. Felt a terrible sense of loss. Why did I always leave a Scorched Earth treatment behind me—burning everything behind me so nothing I cherished would remain? Standing there by the door I watched my possessions vanish, powerless under my destructive impulses.

Christmas Eve 1971 found me in my large studio room on top of

the balconied Hydra house. I had told Yioulie that I had important
business to attend to, so she had gone to a holiday party. My
important business was to end my life. The bottle of Seconal pills
and the bottle of vodka lay on a silver tray on an Egyptian Louis
desk. (My last few thousands had been spent in the Athens flea
market.)

It takes courage to kill yourself, especially if you've never done
it before. The vodka helped. Glass after glass of the burning liquid
went down.

I kept wandering from one end of the long, narrow room to the
other. Some windows faced the garden, and the terra-cotta Athe-
nas stared at me coldly. They knew what I was planning. The other
windows faced the sea, and I stood there a moment watching the
moon make a silvery path over the dark waters. The fragrance of
jasmine drifted through the open window, and I breathed deeply.
Life was sweet, after all.

I turned and saw the Seconal bottle. The zither music from *The
Third Man* came to me, and I remembered Orson Welles's funeral.
He'd played a rotten character named Harry Lime; they'd finally
killed him in the sewers of Vienna.

Suddenly I found myself standing by the desk, emptying the
Seconal bottle, tossing back my head, and swallowing. The pills
tasted bitter, dry. I had no control over my actions . . .

There, I've done it, I thought. Then I went over to the windows
facing the sea, hypnotically drawn to the moonlight on the dark
waters. The moon seemed to be coming right into my studio!

All at once I didn't want to die. Something good was just around
the corner for me. I started toward the stairs and cried for help.

"Yioulie, Yioulie. . . ."

I fell onto the floor.

Three days later, I was brought back to life. A doctor was sticking
a horse needle into my backside. I heard someone screaming, and
then with horror I realized that I was hearing myself! Every nerve
in my body was on fire. Jumping! Mercifully, a final injection
blacked me out.

Yioulie shared a room with me in the gloomy asylum. The doctors wanted her to leave but she refused. We were in a large,

monastic room with vaulted stone ceilings. Icons of a suffering Christ stared down at us.

One morning I did not receive breakfast. Instead, two white-coated orderlies appeared like the Gestapo. Yioulie tried to keep them away from me, but they dragged me out of the room and down some stone stairs to the subterranean chamber where the mad doctor had revived me. They flung me onto a wooden table, tied me down with leather straps, stuck a gag in my mouth. Looming over me was a cruel doctor who resembled George Zucco in those 1940s horror movies. He pulled a switch. I went into violent convulsions and soon lost consciousness.

The dreaded electric shock treatments had begun. I awakened a few hours later and couldn't remember where I was. When Dick Evans came to visit, I was mute.

Some evenings Yioulie read passages out loud from *Vanity Fair* or *The Idiot*. Other evenings we joined an army of living dead walking around and around a confined space, shadowed by a thick stone wall. I could almost see the Nazi storm troopers standing above the barbed wire fence, holding machine guns. For hours we marched round and round—tormented souls, heads bowed, eyes haggard and darkly circled—like Van Gogh's horrific vision of doom.

The winter months went by. One March day I was led into a truck, and we started down past the long avenue of cypress trees. "The final solution," I said, horrible images of death trucks crossing my mind.

"No," said Yioulie, laughing. "We're going to a private clinic in Glyfada. You can leave for New York in a few weeks. The doctors say you're quite well."

"And what do you think, Yioulie?"

"You must work to get well."

Aunt Mathilde wrote me a letter from Palm Beach, saying the same thing.

> You must fight to restore your health. You have many assets, and must make use of them. Enclosed please find a check which might be useful. Remember, I love you and stand behind you, no matter what. I've inherited you from Bessie.

The letter fluttered to the floor. Aunt Bessie had died in March 1967, the same time her favorite nephew, Duncan Ellsworth, had died. The world was a sadder place without them.

The day of departure came. Yioulie accompanied me to the airport. It was painful parting. My flight to New York was announced, we embraced and clung to each other, lost children who had taken the wrong path. I waved, fighting back the tears. She followed me right to the departure gate.

Chapter Thirty

Back in New York I paid attention to what Aunt Mathilde had said: I made use of my assets. Roz Cole introduced me to Frank Zachary at *Town and Country*, I bought antiques at auction and sold them to various friends who were doing apartments. I wrote many interesting articles and was paid well by Frank.

In the summer of 1973 I was living at 55 West Fifty-fifth, and speeding at a dangerous pace. Doctors had warned me not to drive myself, but it seemed I was doing ten different jobs to survive. To come down from my high, I drank vast quantities of vodka and swallowed ten-grain Valium pills. I abused both.

I was typing a *Town and Country* article on the men's clubs of New York when brother Charles came in. We were very close, even though he'd moved down to Palm Beach. He said he had a rich friend, who would pay me $10,000 to get her invited to the Maestriossi Palace. The Venice season was coming up, and she wanted to be with the cream.

I quickly telephoned Venice and told Maestro the plan. He laughed, and said that it sounded like a pleasant way to make some money. "Come immediately, darling," he concluded. "Raffinella's in Paris but will be back in a few days. It's been so long. How are you?"

As soon as I stepped into the tapestried halls of the Maestriossi Palace, I knew I should not be there. It was bad enough to have invited myself, even worse judgment to show myself in my manic state. I knew the Maestros insisted their guests be well dressed, so I'd charged a blue blazer and cream flannels at Jaeger and was relieved to observe that other males like handsome André Oliver, and handsome Kim d'Estainville, the favorite of Madame Rochas, were both similarly attired at the evening parties. Madame Rochas herself, labeled "La Belle Helene," and "Queen of Paris" by the press, was an ice goddess with the hardest blue eyes I'd ever seen. She was a good ten years older than I and looked ten years younger. I loathed her and her dark, muscular favorite, Kim, and my feelings were returned. This was really a Paris house party. Raffinella spent most of her time there now, and I did not fit in. I had not been to their parties, did not know their scandals. I was a bore!

Maestro himself seemed glad to see me. But after studying my bloated outline on the Lido, he kept saying, "Poor old Philip." This hardly helped my already shaky self-confidence. My charm and enthusiasm, as forced as a hothouse flower, fell on barren soil. As the days dragged by, I felt more and more as if I were standing outside, looking through a window at the goings-on.

I was dreading the little countess. And indeed! She arrived in a nervous state, her lips tight, her eyes glittering. Most of her footmen and maids had gone to work in factories, and her French chef was being temperamental. Gasoline and oil prices had skyrocketed, so her motorboat cost three hundred dollars a day to maintain.

Presently, in the privacy of her bedchamber, she fixed those fearful eyes on me, and I noisily swallowed. "Maestro tells me you expect me to receive that dreadful swine. Have you gone mad?"

"Ten thousand would be nice to have, Raffinella," I said, with a big smile.

She did not smile back. "Remember, Philip, I owe you nothing."

"I know, Raffinella." The sweat was trickling down the back of my neck. I felt an anxiety attack coming.

"Have you sunk so low, Philip? Have you any idea the reputation of that swine in Paris?" The phone by her side buzzed—hideous problems with the French chef.

I left Raffinella; our intimacy was now a thing of the past. Another defeat. I should have gone then. But I stayed on—an unwanted and uninvited guest. In the back of my mind I was hoping desperately to have my position restored as the Golden Boy of Venice. I had forgotten I was forty-five years old and over the hill. Shock treatments and Seconal overdoses were hardly beauty aids.

The Rochas gave a large dinner party at Harry's Bar that evening. Andy Warhol was holding court, accepting homage like the pop monarch he was. I didn't think highly of his silk screens of Jackie and Marilyn, but he'd handled himself cleverly, licked and oiled the right people. Unlike me.

Maestro pinched my arm and whispered, "Imagine, Philip, he has over ten million dollars, and that's more than Helene received from the sale of her perfume franchise."

I felt that sick sense of failure again, but I fought the panic.

Maestro went on and told me that Gia, his elder son, was about to marry the daughter of a prince who had more money than even Raffinella.

"I'm glad, Maestro," I said quietly, downing a goblet of vodka and wishing there were Seconals in it. Across the table the young blond German actor Helmut Berger gave me a glassy eye. He'd just had a big success with the Luchino Visconti movie *The Damned*. The corrupt atmosphere of that movie seemed to permeate Harry's. Silver-wigged millionaire prince Andy, with his white clown face, was a constant reminder of how I had mismanaged my life.

The Maestros gave several dinner parties for their Paris contingent. One morning on the Lido Raffinella told me that this was her way of paying back all the people who'd been kind to her. Suddenly she stopped and fixed those blue eyes on me. "Really, Philip, last night when I watched you sitting at my dinner table, I begrudged you every bit of food you put in your mouth."

I winced.

"And what are those red marks on your face, Philip?"

I flushed. A friend had given me some makeup he said would

eradicate the sickly Warhol look. Of course I'd rubbed on too much. Nothing I did was right.

That afternoon I went to the piazza and made a reservation on the white boat that was leaving for Athens the following day. Then I returned to the palace, packed, and said good-bye to Raffinella and Maestro.

"Where are you going, old Philip?" said Maestro, having the eternal manicure.

"Off to the isle of Hydra," I replied as brightly as possible. "One can live there for next to nothing."

"Why don't you go and visit your old friend Rafaello de Banfield?" suggested Raffinella, her face and eyes as soft as they had been when I'd first met her. The chef had calmed down, and she felt more relaxed.

No, I said, I needed to return to Greece. So the next morning the Maestros' motorboat carried me away from the striped wooden poles. The count waved cheerily. "Come and stay with us next month in Rosalia, good old Philip."

I fell in love with Hydra once again. I had just received a letter from Carole with the sad news that the Duke of Marlborough had tired of her.

Bill Cunliffe, the owner of Bill's Bar—Hydra's answer to Harry's Bar—showed me a house overlooking the port, a splendid view. My spirits soared. The Maestros would give me the money for the house, I knew. I put a call through to the count in Venice.

"When are you coming, darling?" he said. The "darling" gave me some hope.

"Tomorrow," I replied, and quickly made a reservation on the white boat to Venice.

We docked early at Athens, so I had a quick visit with Dick Evans. In his green roof garden we sipped ouzo and stared at the columns of the Parthenon, gleaming in the lavender haze.

"I've been in Greece almost ten years," said Dick, sadly bloated and tired. "The bloom is off the rose. Know what I mean, baby?"

"Sure do." I told him some details of the Maestros' house party, and Andy Warhol.

"We stayed too long at the party, Philip," he sighed. "Do you know I'm not even painting anymore? And I don't give a damn about being a success. Worthless American values." He smoked three packs a day and kept inhaling. "Back to the good old USA for Uncle Dick. The Greek dream has turned sour. I guess paradise always does."

The Maestros' motorboat met me; then we went to the station, switched to a car, and soon we were driving through the gates of Rosalia. Off the drawing room was a spectacular new space called the Garden Room, full of rare trees and plants.

"Renzo has done a superb job, hasn't he, darling?" said Maestro, pinching my arm.

"It must have cost a pretty penny," I remarked rather nastily.

"You're jealous that we have so much money and you have none, aren't you?" Maestro had stopped and was staring at me coldly.

"Yes, I think I am, Maestro," I said angrily.

We stared at each other. Under the circumstances, I couldn't ask for a loan. At lunch with Raffinella, Maestro, and Maestro's sister Theresina, Raffinella told me that they had to take a trip to Russia that evening—business, you know—but would return in a few days. Theresina, who had a castle nearby, said she would look after me.

Suddenly there was a silence in the dining room as they all looked at me, expecting me to be amusing and clever. I'd had two vodka-and-Camparis before lunch and drunk two glasses of white and two glasses of red wine during lunch. I felt drunk and confused, my head racing alarmingly. In a crazed voice I told of my party on Hydra and of the artists there and how they survived. I talked in a crude and vulgar fashion, wanting to shock them. The two women looked at me with pity, but Maestro was furious. He glared at me.

"Philip, how dare you talk in such a way before my wife and sister! What has happened to you?" His brown eyes were raging. I'd never seen him angry before.

After lunch Raffinella took my arm and told me to take a little rest, then we'd all meet in the drawing room, have tea, and go for a drive to see some churches.

That evening after dinner they took off on their Russian trip.

Theresina kissed me good night, and left. I was alone in the silence, with only my thoughts.

Rosalia and the Maestriossi Palace were filled with exquisite objets d'art, most of them museum quality and known to dealers and collectors. Such was my madness, and my cleverness, that as I systematically looted their house, I chose only small, easily carried treasures. Faberge pieces, eggs, boxes, statues, and figurines, all were packed into my suitcases.

There was no thought of right or wrong; no thought of stealing. I had earned these things; I was entitled to them. If the Maestros had been nicer to me, had given me more, had not grown tired of me, I would not be forced into teaching them they couldn't dismiss me as they would an unsatisfactory servant. I'd been their friend, their family. How dare they disown me!

As I ran from room to room, gathering up the precious bibelots, the sheer rush of acting on my own, of "showing them," carried me beyond any kind of rational behavior. *They'd* find out. Fueled by rage and vodka I filled twelve suitcases, and left for the airport.

The flight back was surreal. The enormity of my act, the finality of it, began to creep through the alcoholic fog, so I made sure the fog didn't lift. Incredibly, my bags cleared U.S. Customs unopened. But it wasn't incredible to me at the time—after all, I'd just been visiting my cousin Jackie Onassis and was on my way to visit the President. The customs inspector didn't have a chance against the whirlwind of fantasy I unleashed. He obviously wanted to get rid of this crazy man, but to me he was one of my friends, someone who understood me, liked me and wanted to help me, as he should, as everyone should, as the Maestros should have.

The pills, the booze, and the anger may have explained my thievery, but it was simply the cunning Philip who decided to sell the things. I had them, they were mine. Why shouldn't I sell them as I had sold so many other things "given" to me? Still fortified by a sense of justice, and more vodka, I brought some of the Faberge items to Vieille Russe on Fifth Avenue. They knew at once the provenance of the Maestro pieces and suggested I leave them until a check could be cut the following day.

When I returned to the store, I was returned to reality. To the knowledgeable, the objects were as well known as the Mona Lisa, and any attempt to sell them was an act of incredible naivete or arrogance born out of the strange flowers that grew wild in my head.

There would be no scandal, no publicity. Philip would return the pieces, and no legal steps would be taken. But word of my action swept across the Maestriossi world, and if my reputation was suspect before, it was irreparably and irretrievably damaged now. For I had done the unforgiveable: in getting caught, I had brought rich and powerful people to the edge of notoriety. My brazen act came close to turning the Maestros into tabloid personalities. For people of their standing, that act was beyond redemption.

Epilogue

Today, I think often of that morning I left Rosalia. *Turn back the clock*, I pray.

I'm sixty-one now and have a small income thanks to my beloved aunts, Bessie and Mathilde. My physical health is good, thanks to Corgard, which keeps my heartbeats under control. In 1975, Alison Gold, a dear friend from Hydra days, took me to AA, and this time I took to it like a duck to water and made many new friends there. My new doctor put me on Lithium, a nonbarbiturate pill that keeps my bipolar disease (formerly known as manic depression) on a more or less even keel.

At sixty-one I no longer play different roles to please people. I don't have as many friends as I used to—honesty somehow doesn't make for popularity—but the chameleon process of taking the colors of the people I'm with has gone. My courtly, old-world manners have been discarded, too; they kept people at a distance, and I no longer wish that distance.

My new home is an 1870 brownstone that for me resembles a bombed-out wreck of 1945 Berlin. Heaven only knows what holds up this ruin. When a heavy truck or bus rumbles by, the whole house shakes. The subway, too, causes a violent fit of trembling. In any case, its fall-from-grace atmosphere rather suits me, and the whole place does have *character,* a word often on my great aunts' lips but rarely heard today.

Most of my old support system has gone. Aunt Mathilde died in 1978, aged ninety-nine, with all her teeth and a good heart. Mary McDonnagh died in 1980, and life has never been the same without her. Dick Evans died in 1988 and Anne Domville in 1989.

Joan Watson Maule is my best friend today, my neighbor and confidante. God always gives you what you need, I believe. Joan is endlessly curious about the Maestriossi scandal and Carole Morton.

"What happened after you stole everything, Philip?"

"My life was finished."

"But you returned everything, didn't you?"

"Yes, but I was ruined anyway. People who hated me and envied my friendship with the Maestros spread such horrible tales, you wouldn't believe—that I was locked up in a dank prison in Venice, that I'd tried to extort money from them, and so on and so forth. I became an outcast."

"And what happened after 1973?"

"More suicide attempts, more hospitals, more shock treatments. More adventures—exotic and bizarre ones, of course!"

"Of course!"

Nearly every day Joan and I have lunch together at neighborhood places like the Lowell. (It has been renovated and is no longer art deco but Louis-Ritz). Gino's is another favorite, and it still has the red zebra wallpaper from the 1950s. Mulholland Drive has a fresh California accent and Los Angeles murals that remind me of my amazing six-year Hollywood period. Talk about playing roles and living in fantasy! My last landlords in West Hollywood called themselves the baron and the marquis, and they gave black tie receptions in their condo drawing room with more ancestor portraits in ermine than His Serene Highness Prince d'Arenberg.

The Marquis and I were great pals; he wore more jewels than the Baroda and stumbled about the compound in Louis XIV heels. He was seventy, looked fifty, and gave me his beauty secrets. His afternoon receptions were something else and almost gave me another breakdown. When I would enter his candlelit drawing room with three hundred Louis-the-Terrible chairs, he'd take my arm and introduce me: "May I present the Duchess of Marlborough . . . Lady Somerset . . . Prince Thurn und Taxis . . . Baron von Steuben . . ."—and even—"Count Maestriossi. . . ." And one lad was called Anthony Van Dyke IV (known as the Bull). I asked him if he was related to the great painter, and he looked blank. "Huh?" The Marquis's guest list was sometimes more stimulating than the AA parties with their desperate Hollywood hopefuls. "I'm going to be the new Bette Davis!" I heard a thousand times. "Man, I'm going to be the new Marlon Brando!"

Despite Lithium, I felt my sanity slipping in Hollywood, so after a time I came back to old Manhattan—the Bronx and Staten Island, too.

"Where you belong, sweetie," says Joan Maule, looking very much like Iris March with her long spindly legs and black picture hat over haunted eyes.

My outings with Joan never last more than two hours. Both of us have low tolerance levels, and our energy fades after 3:00 P.M.

"We're fragile, Philip," she says.

At Gino's and at Mulholland Drive there's a Venetian baron who always cuts me. He's my age, soft and pasty, with rubber lips and an arrogant manner. When I sit down, he moves to another table far from me. And he does an elaborate turn when he sees me on the street. This pasty-faced baron was never *in* the Maestriossi world; in fact, he was one of the people in Venice *off* Maestro's list. Maestro called his family "insignificant." So why is he judging me?

My father telephoned me just before he died last year; it was a shattering experience. I couldn't believe my ears when his weary voice said, "Phil, I love you very much and always have." I was speechless, and he added, "When are you coming up to see your old father?"

"Father?" I said, angrily. "You weren't my father!"

"I certainly was, Phil."

"My father was Frederick Lewisohn," I said coldly.

"What do you mean, Phil?" CAVR, Jr., said, the defeat ringing in his voice.

"The man who pays, who is responsible, is the father," I replied. "And, Mr. Lewisohn paid for everything, and was responsible for me. Mr. Lewisohn was my father."

There was a sound like a sob, then CAVR, Jr., said, "That's a terrible thing to say, Phil. I guess people who live alone don't really know how to love."

He had the last word. He hung up and that was the last I heard of him. He cut me out of his will, leaving two valuable seventeenth-century Van Rensselaer portraits to Rensselaer Polytechnic. My brother and I certainly could have used the money in the 1990s; Van Rensselaer portraits bring a million dollars at auction these days.

I return to my walk-up studio with a heavy sense of failure, of defeat. I think of ways to sabotage myself. To escape these defeatist thoughts, I lie down and reread *Cousin Bette, Anna K, Gatsby*, all the greats. When the words begin to blur, I put down my glasses and turn on the television.

Last summer, in the midst of a heat wave, in Calcutta humidity, I saw *DOA* twenty times, at least. I couldn't understand why I kept watching it. Edmund O'Brien, a vigorous and attractive fellow, is the star of *DOA*. The scene that riveted me most was that with Ed sitting at a crowded bar where someone will soon slip some poison into his martini glass. Watching Ed about to swallow the lethal dose I cry out, "Oh, Ed, please don't take that drink!" But of course he does, and his fate is sealed. As my fate was sealed when I called the Gritti and ordered the taxi to come to Rosalia.

Fierce regrets and recriminations shoot through my head. *Turn back the clock! Time must be stopped! If only I hadn't returned to Venice . . . If only . . . If only . . .*

I was also riveted by the scene when the doctor tells Ed that he's been poisoned, there's nothing he can do, the X rays show that he will die in a few days. Ed goes berserk and runs out into the street. He stands there and watches some young lovers embrace and some children playing, knowing that all these things are over for him. Watching him, I feel a sharp stab of recognition.

Suddenly the movie ends. I sink into despair. It's too bad I hadn't been poisoned *before* that infamous day in 1973, which I have relived again and again.

I fall onto my bed, curl myself into a fetal position, and escape into a deep sleep, as Fred Beckman used to do in that isolated Arizona house. I remember Mother gasping on that hospital bed, a skeleton hanging on to my hand. "Please make something of your life. Wherever I am I'll be thinking of you."

Later I wake up, stand in front of a tall mirror, and stare searchingly at my face. Why not call it a day? Everything is finished.

Still later, I am drinking some fragrant Lapsang souchong tea. I raise my head and look out the window. The flower stall of the Koreans is radiant with lilies, carnations, tulips, iris, peonies. Life is a precious thing, and I must respect it. The devil possessed me for a long time, but I have conquered him. I will not allow him to win out.

I rush out the door, not even locking the bolt, and stumble down the steep flight of dusty, grimy linoleum-covered the stairs. The acrid stench of burning hair comes from the second-floor hairdressing salon, and Franco himself rushes out and gives me a friendly, "Hello there!"

The stink of glue comes from the Oriental nail shop, and an Oriental beauty smiles, "Hi there!"

"Hello, Philippe," says the French chef who lives above me. I shake his hand and give him a warm smile. I admire him tremendously because he's so full of love. After a lifetime spent with narcissists, I'm appreciative of human beings who care for other people more than themselves! This thirty-five-year-old chef is always taking his little four-year-old boy to school, or for a walk, and he's always quiet and patient with the child. The boy is blond and as pretty as his mother, with big blue eyes and silky hair falling over them. He looks rather like me when I was that age in Mallorca, when Fred Beckman took me swimming on his shoulders far beyond the turquoise shore and out to sea. . . .

I almost collide with an eighty-year-old woman bent over with arthritis. On very hot days she allows me to carry her shopping bags up the stairs, but today she tells me she needs the exercise, thank you very much.

As I'm rushing out the door, I think of something Carole had written me. "If I'd known I was going to live so long, I would have taken better care of myself and my finances! Philippo, can you believe the peacocks are in their sixties?"

I run out into the street like Edmund O'Brien. The overly crowded streets are a shock; they confuse me. I avoid eye contact, looking up at the sky. It's as rosy as a Venetian twilight long ago. People invariably ask me if the high point of my life was living in the Maestriossis' palace, and I invariably reply that the high point of my life is this very moment!

I certainly feel that way now. The streets are colorful, with people of all nationalities, just like the Piazza San Marco when I was the golden boy of Venice. Koreans, Chinese, Africans, Indians, Greeks, Puerto Ricans, Israelis, French, Egyptians, Italians—New York has become an international city, like Paris, Tokyo, Bombay, Mexico City. How lucky I am to enjoy it! God has given me an extra nineteen years of life. After all, I should have died back in December 1971. Dick Evans told me I was pronounced "DOA" at the Greek madhouse. The knowledge of my extra time, of all the glorious days since then, fill me with enormous gratitude.

I run blindly into the tall, graceful outline of Joan Maule walking her poodle.

"Sweetheart, you must look where you're going. And where *are* you going, prince?"

"Kabul? Samarkand?" I smile.

"Backgammon?"

"How about tea at the Lowell first?" I say.

"All right!" We link arms and start toward Park Avenue. We run into the O'Connor twins, Consuelo Crespi, and Gloria Schiff. It's always a treat to see beautiful things. Across the street is the Georgian red brick pile of the Colony Club and coming out of the entrance are ladies as fine-featured and impeccably dressed as Aunt Bessie. Nothing really changes.

"What's the secret of your cheeriness, Philip?" Joan asks me.

"I no longer feel special, and I don't ever feel arrogant anymore." Then I go on and tell her about an old asylum friend who makes an extra thousand or so getting "impossible" people into the Social Register and Knickerbocker Club. Recently she called me and said she could reinstate me in the blue book and get me a membership into the Knick—for a few thousand. I declined, saying that those kinds of things made me feel superior and I never wanted to feel superior again.

314

In the old days when Mother lived at the Pierre and later at the Waldorf Towers, I'd felt special, superior, when the fleet of elevator men and doormen, the waiters from room service, bowed before me as if I were someone important. At the Maestriossis' palace, being bowed through all those towering doors by an army of white-coated footmen with white gloves brought out all the arrogance. I cannot afford to ever feel that way again. To be a loving human being is what matters.

As we step into the lobby of the Lowell, the doorman and concierge smile warmly at us. Up in the richly subdued Park Room on the second floor, Joan asks me what I'm going to drink.

"Prune juice," I reply. "Prune juice and soda water."

Joan giggles.

"That's just what Freddy Lewisohn ordered at the Sherry Netherlands and El Morocco."

"So, let's toast him."

"Sweetheart," says Joan Maule, gazing at me affectionately, "do you miss Carole Morton very much?"

I nod emphatically, then turn a mournful face toward her. "Carole and I were too messed up ever to be happy together. Plus, any man she lives with becomes an enemy. In 1980 we shared a Hudson River country house, but of course we turned on each other, as we'd turned on everyone who loved us."

"That's why you turned on the Maestriossis?"

"Yes," I reply, feeling the old sadness coming over me.

Joan gives me a bright smile. "Whom do you think you'd be happy with for your twilight days?"

I reflect for a moment. "Angela Lansbury, that goes without saying. And perhaps Barbara Bush, she's so natural, so pretty. I'd have to bump off George. Now that would be a *real* scandal, wouldn't it?"

"Oh, Philip, you're still fantasizing and laughing!"

"Listen, Joan, I suppose you'd like one of the Toms for *your* twilight?"

"What Toms?" she asks, mystified.

"Cruise and Hanks, idiot, but I might introduce you to Berenger if you're awfully sweet to me."

"What would they want with me?" she asks.

"Joan," I scold. "Joan, you have to adopt my philosophy: Anything is possible, at any age."

"I'm ready," she says, eagerly.

"And I'm ready for anything the future holds. It's the unexpected things that always happen which make my days so interesting."

As if on cue, my cousin Anne Van Rensselaer appears. Anne is a love goddess, and another dear friend. Cousin Anne embraces me and says, "Philip dear, you look the spitting image of Roger Moore, so elegantly turned out. Turnbull?"

"Turnbull, via a thrift shop," I chuckle, and the girls scream with hilarity. "Thrift? You?"

"Heavenly days, my treasures, Turnbull shirts cost two hundred dollars almost, and chalk stripe suits like this one cost thirteen hundred at Bergdorf. Wouldn't you much rather take a trip to Mont St. Michel, or to Cairo?"

Anne Van Rensselaer smiles and has another spasm of laughter when she sees us drinking prune juice and soda water.

Unexpectedly Cousin Anne invites us to a fireworks-display dinner this evening at her daughter's apartment at the River House, once the home of friends and saviors, Isabel and Freddy Eberstadt. And a home for me, too, after the Maestriossi scandal, until I stood on the terrace to jump, and Clarence, the butler, saw me poised there on the parapet and had a heart attack.

Clarence lived to tell the tale, but that's another story.

Index

Index

Index